AF574176

'FARMER' GEORGE'S BLACK SHEEP

To Doris Tanner

‘FARMER’ GEORGE’S BLACK SHEEP

The Lives and Loves of George III’s Brothers and Sister

CHARLES NEILSON GATTEY

British Library Cataloguing in Publication Data

Gattey, Charles Neilson
'Farmer' George's black sheep: the lives and loves of George III's brothers and sister.
1. Royal houses—Great Britain 2. Great Britain—Kings and rulers—Biography
I. Title
929.7'2 DA506.A1

ISBN 0-946041-23-7

Published by The Kensal Press
Kensal House, Abbotsbrook, Bourne End, Buckinghamshire

Printed and bound in Great Britain by
Butler & Tanner Ltd, Frome and London

Contents

		PAGE
LIST OF ILLUSTRATIONS		vi
PROLOGUE	The Lightfoot Legend	vii
CHAPTER I	Edward Augustus, Duke of York	1
II	William Henry, Duke of Gloucester	8
III	Henry Frederick, Duke of Cumberland	11
IV	The Grosvenors	20
V	A Letter from 'Jack Sprat'	26
VI	Love in Easy Stages	40
VII	'The Adventure at St Albans'	48
VIII	The Trial	54
IX	No Divorce for Lord Grosvenor	64
X	Mrs Bailey	74
XI	Anne of the Amorous Eyes	84
XII	Queen Caroline Matilda	102
XIII	The Royal Marriage Act	110
XIV	The Wandering Royals	124
XV	The Cumberland Fleet	136
XVI	Temporary Reconciliation	144
XVII	The Cumberlands Discover 'Brighthelmstone'	154
XVIII	The Importunate Widow	170
XIX	'Olive, Princess of Cumberland'	185
XX	'A Claim to the Throne'	196
SOURCES		203
BIBLIOGRAPHY		209
GENEALOGICAL TABLE		211
INDEX		213

List of Illustrations

Between pages 118 and 119

Lady Grosvenor and Henry Frederick, Duke of Cumberland surprised by the Countess of D'Onhoff, 1771. *British Museum*

William Henry, Duke of Gloucester, by Francis Cotes.

Maria, Duchess of Gloucester, engraving by H. Bryer. *British Museum*

Henry Frederick, Duke of Cumberland from a portrait by Gainsborough, photograph by John R. Freeman. *British Library*

Anne Horton, later Duchess of Cumberland, by Gainsborough 1766. *National Gallery of Ireland*

Henrietta, Countess Grosvenor, by Gainsborough 1767.

Edward Augustus, Duke of York, engraving after J. Macardell.

The Duke and Duchess of Cumberland strolling in the grounds of Cumberland Lodge, Windsor Great Park. *By kind permission of H.M. The Queen.*

PROLOGUE

The Lightfoot Legend

At ten o'clock in the evening of March 20, 1751, Frederick, Prince of Wales, died at Leicester House in London. He was the unloved heir to King George II, and the Prince's mother, Queen Caroline, when lying on her death-bed some thirteen years earlier, had said of him: 'At least I shall have one comfort in having my eyes eternally closed—I shall never see that monster again.'[1] If Lord Hervey is to be believed, on an earlier occasion, she had denounced her first-born as 'the greatest ass and the greatest liar, and the greatest canaille, and the greatest beast, in the whole world, and I most heartily wish he was out of it'.[2] And the King himself declared that he had always hated the 'false, lying, cowardly, nauseous puppy'.[3]

Despite his faults and his womanising, 'Poor Fred', as this Prince of Wales was dubbed, had adored his wife, Augusta, and she had been equally fond of him. When widowed, she was expecting her ninth child, and, in the following July, a daughter, Caroline Matilda, destined to become the tragic Queen of Denmark, was born. The thirty-one-year old Princess Dowager had always loyally left all family decisions to her husband and she was faced with the onerous responsibility of bringing up a large family. Alarmed lest association with a dissolute aristocracy should corrupt the children, she determined to keep them isolated from such a society as long as possible. Her third son, the Duke of Gloucester, later commented: 'No boys were brought up in greater ignorance of evil things than the King and myself. At 14 we retained all our native innocence.'[4]

The brothers entered the schoolroom at eight a.m. and remained with tutors until eight p.m. except for short breaks. Then, following supper, they had to read on their own and later were thoroughly questioned to ensure that there was no idling. Only one hour was allowed for recreation and that on alternate days. On Sundays, they dutifully attended grandfather George II's court and were given religious instruction. At least, they were not reared on asses' milk like their father, 'Poor Fred'.[5]

The Princess Dowager certainly succeeded in preventing her eldest son, the future King George III, from turning into a salacious sovereign, but her other children's behaviour, once released from her control, grieved her and proved that they were indeed true descendants of the first two Georges. Charles II had at least shown taste in his choice of mistresses. The early Hanoverians had none. George I shared the vicious Countess von Platen with his father, the Elector of Hanover, before falling for her twice-married graceless sister, Leonore de Maysebourg-Züschen. In England, George I's seraglio was headed by scraggy Ermengarde Melusine von Schulenbourg, Duchess of Kendal, nicknamed the 'Maypole', and the bulky Charlotte Sophia von Kielmansegge, known as the 'Elephant', daughter of the Countess von Platen and supposed to have been his half-sister. According to Sir Philip Francis, these two charmers were created peeresses 'to reward their merits in their respective departments and to encourage the surrender of prudery in younger and handsomer subjects'.

George II's first mistress was Henrietta Howard, wife of the third son of the Earl of Suffolk, and the King's grandmother, the Electress Sophia, on being told this, exclaimed: 'Oh, good—it will improve his English.' Mrs Howard was succeeded by Madame Walmoden, whom he created Countess of Yarmouth, and who was a member of the Platen family so popular with both his grandfather and his father and just as ugly as her predecessors. When away in Hanover, the King wrote practically every day to his wife, Queen Caroline, about the pleasure his new beloved gave him, and she broadmindedly replied that it made her glad to know he was happy.

It is not surprising in view of such promiscuity in her husband's family that the Princess Dowager should have taken immediate steps to ensure that her eldest son made a suitable marriage on ascending the throne in 1760. She persuaded Lord Bute to send a secret envoy to the German courts and let him have a considered report on the characters of all unmarried princesses, which, when received and studied, led to a rather plain outsider being chosen as George's bride. This was Princess Sophia Charlotte of the insignificant duchy of Mecklenburg-Strelitz—disdainfully dubbed by those who had visited it, Muckleberg Strawlitter. Her main merit in Bute's eyes was that she gave all her winnings at lotto to the poor. She proved a worthy and fruitful consort sharing with her husband a horror of taking any form of life.

Whenever a death warrant was passed to him for signing, he did so with a shaking reluctant hand; and if when walking in the gardens at Kew, he saw a worm in his path he would step over it saying: 'Thou hast a right to live as well as I, my brother worm.'

Such a trait in George III's nature led to his admiration of the Quakers. He told Bishop Hurd that they were 'a body of Christians for whom I have a high regard. I love their peaceful tenets and their benevolence one to another, and but for the obligation of birth, I would like to be a Quaker.' Benjamin West, the painter, who was one, also states that the monarch once confided: 'I was born to fill the station of King and head both the Church and State. I remain in the line of my duty. But had I been left to my own choice, I should have been a Quaker myself.'

Robert Huish wrote that King George III's approval of Quakers and his friendship with them amused the cynical and worldly members of the court, and Sir Nathaniel Wraxall says that when George came of age at eighteen years, he was offered his own establishment but declined it, preferring to continue living with his mother at Leicester House until his accession. Sir Nathaniel goes on that, despite this, later: 'Stories were generally circulated on his attachment to a young woman, a Quaker.' But the diplomat adds that those who knew the King best did not believe that he passed the 'limits of innocent gallantry or occasional familiarity'.

Nevertheless, a fanciful legend has been woven round the figure of Hannah Lightfoot. Born in Wapping, she lost her father at the age of twelve and was adopted by her maternal uncle, a linen draper, whose shop was in St James's Market. Here the fifteen-year old Prince George is supposed to have noticed her when he passed in a sedan-chair to and from the Palace, visiting his grandfather, George II, and to have fallen in love with her. When the Princess Dowager discovered this, she is said to have made the girl marry one Isaac Axford on December 11, 1753, at the Mayfair Chapel in Curzon Street. The registers which form part of those for St George's, Hanover Square, record this. Following the ceremony, Hannah disappeared and one can only speculate as to what happened to her from the few clues available.

In 1756 Hannah was expelled in her absence from the Society of Friends on the charge of having been married by a priest 'to some person unknown or not of this faith', then three years later Isaac Axford remarried which suggests that he had certain knowledge of her death—followed on May 16, 1770, by that of her mother. Some sixteen years later there appeared in *The Citizen* for February 1776, an advertisement promising the early publication of 'The History and Adventure of Mrs Lightfoot the Fair Quaker; wherein will be faithfully portrayed some striking pictures of female constancy and princely gratitude, which terminated in the untimely death of her disconsolate mother.' The present author did not succeed in finding a copy of this, and it may not after all have been published.

A more important piece of evidence in the Lightfoot mystery is a portrait in the picture gallery at Knole, which is shown in the catalogue there as one of Mrs Axford by Sir Joshua Reynolds and which was bought by the third Duke of Dorset (1745–99) from Earl de la Warr. It is believed to have been painted about 1759 and this has given rise to the theory that Hannah after leaving Isaac went to live under the protection of someone of means and position and that he was Prince George. The myth-makers further allege that he kept her in a house at Peckham where she bore him children.

Over a hundred years later, in 1866, in a sensational law-suit, a Mrs Ryves, was to claim that her mother, Mrs Olive Serres, was the daughter of George III's brother, Henry Frederick, Duke of Cumberland, and Olive Wilmot and that they had been secretly married by the latter's father, who eight years earlier in 1759 had also married George III, then Prince of Wales to Hannah Lightfoot. The whole bizarre story will be told later in this book.

Our concern is first with the lives and loves of the Farmer King's black sheep brothers and sister.

CHAPTER ONE

Edward Augustus, Duke of York

One day King George III, then Prince of Wales and aged eighteen, was walking in Kensington Gardens with his eleven-year-old brother, Prince Henry Frederick, later Duke of Cumberland, when the notorious courtesan, Kitty Fisher, strolled by. 'She's a Miss that sells oranges,' the small boy whispered—and George, surprised, asked: 'Is there any harm in selling oranges?' To which the other replied: 'Oh, but they are not such oranges as *you* buy. I believe they are a sort that our brother Edward buys.'[1]

Edward, one year younger than George, had been their parents' favourite son,[2] a feeling which they had never tried to disguise, and it had much distressed his widowed mother when his precocious flirting with women led to his seducing them. Soon after his father had died and when he was only twelve, he happened to be playing with George and remarked: 'Brother, when you and I are grown men, you shall be married and I shall keep a mistress.'

George told him to be quiet lest his nonsense anger their mother and added: 'There must be no mistresses at all.' But the Princess Dowager had overheard Edward's words and cried in her broken English: 'What you say? You more need learn your pronouns, as the preceptor bid you do. Can you tell what is a pronoun?'

'Yes, very well,' replied Prince Edward, 'a pronoun is to a noun what a mistress is to a wife—a substitute and a representative.[3]

It was some relief to his worried mother when Edward at the age of nineteen wearied of London society's frivolities and decided on a naval career. So, in May 1758, he joined the 64-gun third-rate *Essex* as a midshipman under Howe, thus becoming the first British royal to adopt the Senior Service as his profession in the strict sense of the word.

Howe had been sent instructions that the recruit who came without any kit, was to receive no special treatment on account of his rank. 'I was not told how to provide for his Royal Highness,' he complained later, 'and all the answer I could obtain from ministerial authority ... was to act respecting him just as if I had not any such person on board the ship. He came not only without bed and linen of almost every kind, but I paid for his uniform clothes, which I provided for him with all other necessaries at Portsmouth. I made no inquiries how I was to be indemnified for every requisite attention to the then presumptive heir to the crown.'[4]

Prince Edward, no doubt due to shyness, did not take off his hat when the Captains from other ships in Portsmouth harbour came on board. A seaman remarked to a companion: 'The young gentleman ain't over civil—look if 'e don't keep 'is 'at on before 'em.' To which his mate retorted: 'Why, you stupid lubber, where should 'e learn manners, seeing' as 'ow 'e never was at sea before.'[5]

Although very good-tempered and affable, the new midshipman was insignificant in appearance, being rather undersized, knock-kneed, pale faced, with colourless eyelashes and brows, and very fair hair. He was also courageous. Britain was at war with France and that September when Howe gave naval protection to the military force sent against St Malo the Prince volunteered to join the invading spearhead. Although the harbour installations were destroyed as planned, casualties were high and he not only narrowly escaped being shot but was nearly made prisoner. Later, he served on the *Ramillies* in the squadron commanded by Rodney which sailed to Le Havre to destroy the barges assembled to attempt the invasion of England.

For those of royal rank promotion came rapidly and in 1759 Prince Edward gained command of the 44-gun *Phoenix* and was given the task of blockading with other vessels the coast of France. In the autumn his ship suffered damage from the gales and limped back to Portsmouth for a lengthy refit. Then on April 1, 1760, he was created Duke of York and displaying naval ability rose to become Vice-Admiral of the Blue. When the war ended in late 1762, Edward was appointed Commander-in-chief in the Mediterranean and paid 'show-the-flag' visits to the principal ports there of the defeated enemies. On returning to London, he resigned and devoted himself to dalliance.

During his brief life, Edward had many mistresses, the most notorious being Kitty Fisher, the leading *poule de luxe* of her day, who charged as much as 100 guineas a night for her favours. When he gave her only 50 guineas, she chased him out of her bedroom, then contemptuously baked the note in a pie and ate it for her breakfast. Among those of his own class with whose affections the Duke toyed were the Duchess of Richmond, the Countesses of Essex and Tyrconnel, Lady Anne Stanhope and Lady Mary Coke, daughter of John Duke of Argyll. Lady Mary was married for her dowry and against her will to the Scottish gambler, Viscount Coke, who, according to Horace Walpole, had been rejected as a possible husband by 'all the great lumps of gold in the city'. On learning her fate she cried 'her red eyes to scarlet'.[6] Eventually the couple were separated and when the Viscount died in 1753 there was talk of her being matched with Walpole.[7]

Lady Mary was in her thirties still a remarkably beautiful woman, who in many ways looked well suited to the rôle of a Queen, having a stately figure, a noble neck, fine teeth and a pleasing smile—but her blonde hair and eyebrows, extremely white skin and bright feline eyes caused her to be called the 'White Cat'. One of her sisters, Anne, married Lord Strafford, brother of Lady Harriot Vernon, who was Lady of the Bedchamber to Princess Amelia, the Duke of York's aunt, and through this connection Lady Mary met him. She had for long regarded herself as superior to most people and became convinced that it was her destiny to be, if not Queen of England, at least the power behind the throne, so she was delighted when the Duke appeared to fall in love with her, although twelve years younger.

Lady Louisa Stuart, in a memoir, printed in *The Letters and Journals of Lady Mary Coke*, wrote that the widow having 'a reverend care of her reputation, kept upon high ground, admitted his Royal Highness's visits but sparingly, and wholly avoided any suspicious familiarity. In consequence, his letters abound with complaints of the prudish strictness that holds him so far aloof, and inspires him with such awe that he hardly dared hazard the most innocent expressions for fear of being misunderstood, and giving her nicety a causeless alarm.'[8]

One letter from Edward tells Lady Mary he has been studying the history of Scotland and is wonderfully struck with the resemblance of character between herself and Queen Elizabeth. This pleased her immensely. Lady Louisa says that the Duke daily diverted his sister, Princess Augusta, with accounts of Lady Mary's pomposity and 'of the awful reserve maintained and the distant encouragement held out by turns, and, more than all, of her evident intention to become the wife of his bosom'. In fact, she was so sure that he would one day propose marriage that she used to amuse herself signing pieces of paper as though she were already his Duchess.

Lady Louisa disapproved of the Duke, saying that he had 'a certain tremulous motion of the eye that was far from adding to the beauty' of his pale face.[9] She also wrote: 'He was silly, frivolous, and heartless, void alike of steadiness and principles, a libertine in his practice, and in society one of those incessant chatterers who must by necessity utter a great deal of nonsense.... He was the first of his race who began the good work of demolishing it, by running about giddily to all sorts of places with all sorts of people—of course, principally the worst sort—until his frolics won the public attention, and the Duke of York's crew, a phrase used, as the lawyers say, in common parlance. The friendship—or call it league—he formed with the Delavals, a family renowned for their wild profligacy, spread his fame through the northern counties where he more than once visited Sir Francis and his sister, Lady Mexborough, at their country seats; and Yorkshire rang long and loudly of the orgies therein celebrated.[10]

The most innocent of such pastimes were practical jokes. Samuel Foote, the actor, was a friend of Sir Francis and a very poor rider, so it was thought great fun to mount him upon a most vicious horse which was described as gentle enough to carry any lady. The animal threw him as expected and the surgeons were only able to save his life by instantly cutting off a leg which was horribly fractured. However, the accident made his fortune, since the Duke, feeling some compunction on this occasion, persuaded the King to give the actor playwright the patent of the little theatre in the Haymarket, which became the source of all his future affluence.

The King often urged Edward to settle down with a good wife. Once he wrote back: 'I am highly indebted to you for your advice ... but, if you will allow me to say it, I am not wholly ignorant of the precepts of a book which you are always extolling, and one which I am determined to keep, which is—"They who marry do well, but they who keep single, do better."'

George showed his disapproval of Edward's way of life by not nominating him to become Bishop of Osnabruck when that ecclesiastical state with its annual revenues of £20,000 became vacant in 1761. Under the terms of the Treaty of Westphalia the Elector of neighbouring Hanover and the Roman Catholic chapter shared the rights of appointment to it. Thus Catholic and Protestant held this rich see alternately, and there was no need for the occupant to take holy orders. It was now Hanover's turn and George as its ruler could make the choice. Had past precedent been followed, Edward as his eldest brother would have gained the bishopric, but the King gave him

£16,000 to have a house built in Pall Mall instead and waited till his own second son, Prince Frederick, was born two years later and then arranged for the baby to fill the vacancy. This disappointment was followed by an affront when in 1765 George attempted to exclude Edward from the Council of Regency. As a result he began to side with the parliamentary opposition and two years later the rift between the two brothers widened when he voted against the Government in the Lords.

In the spring of 1767, the Duke visited the Dutch and French courts, then travelled to the south of France. Like his brother, Henry, he enjoyed most of all dancing and after attending a ball near Marseilles one evening in August, he caught a severe chill. Horace Walpole wrote later: 'His immoderate pursuit of pleasure and unremitted fatigues in travelling ... succeeded without interruption by balls and entertainments, had thrown his blood, naturally distempered and full of humours, into a state that brought on a putrid and irresistible fever.'[11]

When Edward realized that he was dying, he wrote to his brother, the Duke of Gloucester, asking him to pay 'my last weak duties to the King, and if at any time I should have incurred his displeasure, I hope the generosity of his temper will at least make him forgive my unheeded past conduct which is all at present I have it in my power to offer'.[12] Eight days later, on September 17, he died in the Prince of Monaco's palace and his embalmed body was then brought back to England on the frigate, *Montreal*, and interred in the Henry VII Chapel of Westminster Abbey. Sir William Musgrave in a letter to Lord Carlisle, dated October 16 that year, states that the King was 'most seriously grieved for the loss of his brother, and literally almost cried his eyes out'.[13]

Even more upset than the King was Lady Mary Coke who behaved as though she were the deceased's widow—so much so that Horace Walpole started calling her in his letters 'the posthumous Duchess of York'. She attended the funeral at Westminster Abbey wearing full mourning, and went down afterwards into the vault, attended by Colonel Morrison, the Duke's Groom of the Bedchamber, to kneel and weep beside the coffin. He was a tall, lank man with a rueful, ugly face. On hearing this, that cynical wit, George Selwyn, commented: 'If her ladyship wished to enact the Ephesian matron, I wonder she did not choose a better-looking soldier.'[14]

For some years Lady Mary constantly repeated these visits to the

Duke's last resting-place, whenever the opening of the royal vault on the demise of a Prince or Princess gave her an opportunity. All her acquaintances were expected to know that the hallowed building containing his remains must never be mentioned in her presence, states Lady Louisa Stuart. Once when Lady Emily Macleod as a girl pointed out to Lady Mary a view of the Abbey from Greenwich, she shrieked: 'Child, what do you mean? Have you a mind to make me faint away? Didn't I forbid you to say anything about the Abbey?'[15]

It particularly annoyed Lady Mary that Edward had not mentioned her in his will. On October 5, 1767, three weeks after he died, she wrote: 'The poor Duke has left his House & everything in it to the Duke of Gloucester and his Diamond George to the Duke of Cumberland. They have neither of them his Understanding or his Manners. He was a Gentleman, but they were not; he never was guilty of incivility, but the others don't give themselves the trouble of pulling off their Hats.'[16]

Lady Mary never married again and died at the age of eighty-five murmuring Edward's name. To the end she refused to believe that he had been promiscuous and had sired bastards.

At the time of his death, the Duke was living with another woman who claimed to be a daughter of Prince Charles Edward Stuart and whom he may have secretly married. She was pregnant and, according to the claims later made by the Rev. William Groves, Curate of St Margaret's, Westminster, came back to England where she died in giving birth to him on 15 March, 1768, at the Castle of Haverford West, when he was then committed to the care of King George III's bricklayer and was later sent to Eton where the King regularly visited him. Later he went to Oriel College, Oxford, took Holy Orders, and was for a time Chaplain to Queen Victoria's father, the Duke of Kent. He died in 1851 at Bexley, Kent, leaving a manuscript in which he recorded his claims to royal descent and which was published by a Kent antiquarian.[17]

The Duke of York, it would seem, also had an illegitimate daughter by another woman. Nearly two years after his death, the *Town and Country Magazine* published a report from Portsmouth, dated July 29, 1769: 'A singular circumstance happened here yesterday morning which has occasioned a good deal of conversation. When His Royal Highness the Duke of Cumberland was reviewing the marines, a woman decently dressed, with a beautiful girl in her arms, made several attempts to speak to His Highness. The woman declared that the child was nearly related to His Highness, being the daughter of a great naval officer.... The story was corroborated ... upon which His Royal Highness with great affability, after kissing the child, put a twenty-pound banknote into her hand and assured the mother, if she convinced him of the truth, she should be provided for.'

The report in the *Town and Country* is also to be found in other newspapers of the time. The *Annual Register* adds that the woman in question was 'an upper servant in a certain nobleman's house, where the Duke of York resided some years ago when he was going out on an expedition' and that 'soon after she was brought to bed she married a person employed about the dockyard from whom she concealed her having the child; but as her husband had left her, she thought it her duty to publish the circumstances'. Her story was corroborated 'by several persons who knew the woman, and further strengthened by the great similarity between the girl and the declared father'.

Anne Sheldon, later Mrs Archer, was a well-known courtesan and procuress of the period, described on the frontispieces of her four volumes of reminiscences as: 'A lady who figured during several years in the highest line of public life.' In her final chapter she describes how in the 1780s a woman stayed in her fashionable bagnio who left behind a manuscript in which she claimed to be 'the natural daughter of the late Duke of York, the brother of his present Majesty'.[18] As the then Prince of Wales, later George IV, occasionally patronized this establishment he may possibly and unwittingly have come to close quarters with his cousin.

CHAPTER TWO

William Henry, the Duke of Gloucester

Prince William Henry, the third son of Frederick, Prince of Wales, was born at Leicester House on November 25, 1743. In boyhood serious and reserved, he was regarded by his mother as the least intelligent of her children and, according to Horace Walpole, she used to upset him by deriding his dullness before the others. Once she bid them: 'Laugh at the fool!' The highly-strung lad paled and hung down his head. Whereupon she told him not to sulk. 'I'm not sulking,' he muttered, 'only thinking.' 'And, pray, what are you thinking of?' she asked scornfully. 'I was thinking,' came the reply, 'what I should feel if I had a son as unhappy as you make me.'

In appearance, the Prince resembled his eldest brother, George, who loved him dearly. Sir Nathaniel Wraxall in his *Memoirs*, described him as having 'a decent and sober deportment, and possessing a plain understanding though no brilliance'. When, on the verge of middle age in 1769, he visited Copenhagen to see his sister, Caroline Matilda, wife of the Danish King, Christian VII, the latter was told by his favourite, Count von Holtke, that the Englishman reminded him of an ox.

Five years earlier, in November 1764, the new King, George III, had created William Duke of Gloucester and Edinburgh, and Earl of Connaught. Two years later, deciding to make the army his career, the Prince was commissioned colonel of the 13th Regiment of Foot, and was then given the ranks of major-general, general, and field marshal in 1770, 1772, and 1793, respectively. Sir Horace Mann, the British Envoy in Florence, once said that he was 'a brave soldier without military talent, and a good man without any ostentation of goodness'. However, as far as his relations with the King were concerned they were eventually almost wrecked by his secret marriage in 1766 to the widow of George III's former governor, Earl Waldegrave.

The Dowager Countess was seven years older than the Duke of Gloucester and had three children by her first husband who was twice her age. She was extremely beautiful and the second of the four illegitimate daughters of Sir Edward Walpole, Horace's elder brother, by a mistress he had 'fairly beckoned in from the top of a cinder cart', a Mrs Maria Clemens of Durham, whose ambition when a child was to become 'a lady'. Her father, who sold brooms upon the Yorkshire moors, told her that was impossible 'for she was a beggar'—and to this she retorted: 'Then I will be a lady beggar.'

Prince William had first fallen in love with Maria Waldegrave a year before she was widowed, in 1762, when he was nineteen. Then, in December 1764, we find Giddy Williams writing to George Selwyn: 'The Duke of Gloucester has professed a passion for the Dowager Waldegrave. He is never from her elbow. This flatters Harry Walpole not a little, though he pretends to dislike it.'[1]

In March, 1766, Lady Sarah Bunbury, wrote: 'The report of the week is that the King has forbidden the Duke of Gloucester to speak to his pretty widow. He has given her five pearl bracelets that cost £500—that's not for nothing surely?'[2] Then on October 6 Lady Mary Coke recorded in her journal some intriguing information she had received from Lady Pomfret. It was about how the Dowager Waldegrave had ordered a rocket to be let off in Windsor Park's Great Walk at nights as soon as the Castle clock had struck twelve. 'This it seems was a signal—for soon after a Royal Chaise came down, and out of it a certain Duke who usually pass'd the remaining part of the night in her Lodgings. The rocket at last became such a ridicule at Windsor that She was obliged to leave it off, but the Chaise with the Duke arrived at the same hour and Lady Pomfret added that his being there five nights in the week was known to all Windsor.'[3]

Later that month, on the 23rd, Lady Mary wrote: 'A lady has just been with me whom I knew formerly that confirms the rocket story, but adds everybody here says she [the Dowager] was married—time, I suppose, will discover the truth.'[4]

When Lady Mary discussed the matter with Lady Charlotte Finch, governess of George III's children, she revealed that such tales had reached the King but he regarded them as false after being assured by his favourite brother that he would never marry.

The truth, however, was that a month before Lady Mary Coke first heard the rocket story, on September 6, the couple had been made husband and wife by Maria's chaplain in a rite solemnized at her Pall Mall house and without witnesses so as to guard against disclosure.

The Gloucesters were careful to keep their real relationship a secret, but on one occasion they were somewhat indiscreet. At a grand Masquerade held at Mrs Cornelys' in Soho Square on February 26, 1770, the Duke appeared disguised as King Edward IV 'in the old English habit with a star on the cloak' and the Duchess was dressed as Elizabeth Woodville, the widow to whom that monarch had been privately married and later declared his Queen. 'Methinks,' commented Horace Walpole, Maria's uncle, 'it was not very difficult to make out the meaning of the masks.'[5]

Then, two years later, whilst the Duke and Duchess were in Italy, his youngest brother, the Duke of Cumberland, also married a widow but kept it no secret from the King arousing in him such anger that the Royal Marriage Act was forced through Parliament in 1772. Gloucester's affairs thereafter became so closely linked with those of Cumberland's that we must now relate the events in the latter's early life before returning to the former.

CHAPTER THREE

Henry Frederick, Duke of Cumberland

In November, 1745, owing to Bonnie Prince Charlie's early success, it looked as if he would succeed in his adventure to try and regain the crown for his father, the Old Pretender. That he might soon find himself without a kingdom to inherit left Frederick, Prince of Wales, unruffled like the feathers in his crest. The pursuit of arms did not appeal to him and he preferred to play the 'cello and leave the fighting to his brother, William Augustus, Duke of Cumberland. He was much more interested in his fourth son, born on the seventh day of that month, and destined to become the first member of the royal family to be sued for adultery.

When 'Poor Fred' heard that Carlisle was under attack from the Jacobites, his reaction was to instruct his pastry cooks and confectioners to make a huge cake covered with icing-sugar and shaped to resemble the besieged citadel. Then, at the supper held at Cliveden to celebrate the christening of Henry Frederick, he ordered the servants to carry the cake into the dining-room and place it in the centre of the table. Next, dishes piled with sugar plums were set before the company as ammunition with which they bombarded the model fortress.

After this mock battle the proud parents led the revellers into the drawing-room where under a canopy lay the infant prince in a magnificent cradle guarded by his governess, Mrs Herbert. Old Sir William Stanhope peered shortsightedly at the tiny form. 'In wax, I suppose?' he enquired, then with a start exclaimed: 'Lord, it sees!'[1]

The Prince of Wales told his friends that on becoming King he would create his new son Duke of Virginia, but, owing to his own death, this never occurred, and Henry Frederick was later made Duke of Cumberland by his eldest brother, following the decease without legitimate issue of their uncle, the already mentioned William Augustus, better known as 'Billy the Butcher' on account of his ruthless suppression of the '45 Rebellion.

The Cumberland title was first conferred by Charles I on his nephew, Prince Rupert. Other bearers of it were Prince George of Denmark, Queen Anne's husband, and Ernest, fifth son of King George III, popularly regarded as Queen Victoria's wicked uncle, who also became King of Hanover.

It was Henry Frederick who gave the Princess Dowager most concern and of whom John Heneage Jesse wrote: 'Kept in close and irksome seclusion till he reached the years of manhood and accustomed to no other society but that of sycophants and dependants, it is perhaps not much to be wondered at that a young Prince of warm passions and weak character should on obtaining his freedom have rushed from the schoolroom to the stews and night cellars.' He adds that 'a handsome countenance made some amends for the shortness of his stature and the meanness of his abilities'.[2]

Horace Walpole, prejudiced for personal reasons, dismisses this Duke of Cumberland from the pages of his Reign of George III as 'a weak debauched boy',[3] and Lady Louisa Stuart gives a similar appraisal. But in the diaries of contemporaries with no cause for animosity against him are several references to his charm and affability. These favourable comments came, however, in the latter part of his life when he had settled down.

The Duke followed the example of his brother, Edward, not only in embarking early on amorous escapades, but also at his own express wish, in entering the Royal Navy. Soon after York's decease, Henry joined the frigate *Venus* as a midshipman—but with a difference for he had nine attendants. At 23 he was well over the usual age of entry. Gaining swift promotion, on October 28, 1768, he was appointed Captain of his ship and on March 10 of the following year Rear-Admiral of the Blue Squadron of the Fleet.

An anonymous contributor to the *Town and Country Magazine* for September, 1769, gives us in the tongue-in-cheek style of the gossip-writer a description of the Duke's person as 'comely, his manners graceful and engaging, his conversation sprightly and polite', adding that 'trained from his youth to a marine life' he had already risen 'by his merit only' to a command in the Navy and had sailed twice on 'hazardous voyages' to the Mediterranean. During these he had taken part in 'several battles that have been purposely fought to give him a proper idea of a naval engagement, and from which he has reaped the intended benefit, without the least injury to his health, having very judiciously provided in his own ship a cold bath, which his physicians recommended him to use every morning, as a proper precaution against the disorders incident to that element, and to strengthen his nerves against the horrors of a real engagement'.

In 1765 on the death of his uncle, 'Butcher' Cumberland, Prince Henry had been given by King George III the Rangership of Windsor Great Park which carried with it the tenancy of Cumberland Lodge, the most attractive of the secluded dwellings belonging to the Crown to be found there. It had once been the love nest where Charles II had kept Lady Castlemaine. The new owner grew very attached to the Lodge with the opportunities it gave him for riding and hunting and secret meetings with his mistresses.

Not far away was Fort Belvedere, the Folly built by the 'Butcher' and destined to become the retreat, when Prince of Wales and later as King, of the Duke of Windsor, who was Henry's nephew in the fifth generation. Both were fair, short and slight, loved riding and were prone to accidents. The *Annual Register* for June, 1765, records that at Ascot Races Prince Henry's horse rode so violently that it threw him over its head, which fall left him with a slight facial scar that was to betray his identity despite disguise in his affair later with Lady Grosvenor.

The following year he was created Duke of Cumberland and Strathearn and Earl of Dublin, then in 1767 a Privy Councillor. The *Annual Register* next mentions him in March of that year when 'the Lord Mayor, several aldermen, the committees of common council and of the skinners' company, went from the Mansion House in a cavalcade of about thirty coaches to present the freedom of the City of London on the Duke of Cumberland.' But the freedom which the twenty-one-year-old Duke now most enjoyed was to indulge in all forms of sensual pleasure in the English capital.

London was becoming one of the liveliest cities in Europe. Fashionable society flocked to the balls at the Assembly known as Almack's in King-street, St James's, to Mrs Cornelys's enticing establishment at Carlisle House in Soho Square for concerts and masquerades, to the rival emporium of sophistication, the Pantheon, in the Oxford-road, and to the long-established pleasure grounds at Ranelagh and at Vauxhall. The latter's riverside gardens, some twelve acres in extent, were the more inviting with their attractive approach by water. They were originally the most popular evening resort, but lost some of their appeal as more and more pimps and prostitutes took over the Lovers' Walk.

'It is said that voluptuousness, evil and debauchery have never been so rampant in London as they are at present,' wrote a foreign visitor, Lichtenberg, in 1772.[4] Chastity was certainly out of fashion with the aristocracy and considered unhealthy. Lord Carlisle told a friend: 'I was afraid I was going to have the gout the other day. I believe I live too chaste—it is not a common fault with me.'

The King himself regretted that he lived in what he regarded as 'the most profligate age'. Even one of his Prime Ministers gave him cause for such condemnation. In that position from 1767 to 1770 was Henry Fitzroy, third Duke of Grafton, great-grandson of Charles II by Barbara Villiers whom that Merry Monarch created Countess of Castlemaine and Duchess of Cleveland. Grafton once cancelled a Cabinet meeting so as to attend the races at Newmarket and he was the first of his office to flaunt in public and with pride his mistress, Nancy Parsons, who called herself Mrs Hoghton.

On April 16, 1768, a distinguished audience, including Queen Charlotte herself, filled the King's Theatre in the Haymarket for the première of Piccini's opera, *La Schiava*. As the rise of the curtain was awaited, all eyes were fixed not on the Queen but on a lower box where sat the Prime Minister with his paramour. Though he was separated from his faithless Duchess, those present thought he was establishing a dangerous precedent. True the First Lord, the Earl of Sandwich, known as 'Jeremy Twitcher' kept his Martha Ray at hand in the Admiralty during the day so as to obtain occasional relief from the tedium of official business—but that was out of sight of the public.

This was the London where the young Duke of Cumberland with, as Jesse put it, 'his warm passions and weak character' rushed on escaping from 'the close and irksome seclusion' in which his mother had kept him. He was a dashing and deft dancer, and most of the women in his life first entered it as partners at some ball. Elizabeth Ingram, third daughter of the 9th Viscount Irwin, wrote in a letter, dated March 23, 1767, that the Duke of Cumberland attended a magnificent Indian ball to which she went in London and that he danced 'with all his heart and soul' labouring 'more to put people in a right strain for dancing than a downright dancing master'.

Looking through the *Annual Register* once more, we find it mentioning that on December 21, 1767, at a meeting of the corporation of Windsor it was 'unanimously agreed to present the Dukes of Gloucester and Cumberland with the freedom of that ancient borough'.

To glean information about the Duke of Cumberland's amorous

adventures, however, one must turn again to the pages of the *Town and Country Magazine*, which are the main source for scandal of the late 1760s and the early 1770s, provided by anonymous contributors who mixed in well-informed circles. Most months this *Universal Repository of Knowledge, Instruction and Entertainment* published what it called *A History of the Tête-à-Tête, or Memoirs of* some noble lord and his current mistress, alluding to them either by using only the first and last, and sometimes middle, letters of their names or by employing sobriquets, such as *Nauticus* in the case of the Duke of Cumberland. We are told that whilst training for a naval career, he occasionally relaxed in the arms of a kind mistress and that his first was Signorina Anna Zamperini from Venice, also born in 1745, a star of the London opera, esteemed for both her singing and her dancing. Then *Scotius* (Lord March, later the Duke of Queensberry, and better known as 'Old Q') made overtures to her.

Zamperini was for some time doubtful whether she should yield to her new suitor, when the Duke discovered a love letter to her from him. He accused her of being unfaithful, and she insisted that she had rejected all his rival's proposals as she much preferred the Duke. However, a short time after, a diamond solitaire which *Scotius* opportunely threw into the balance poised the scale of Zamperini's love in his favour.

According to the *Town and Country*, the Signorina was succeeded by Anne Elliott, the actress, a sexton's daughter, on whom he doted for two years, giving her such presents that at her death she was able to bequeath nearly ten thousand pounds to her indigent relations. 'Her capital stroke was persuading him to mortgage a certain house to enable him to raise six thousand pounds, with which he actually presented her. This sum she had prudence enough to invest in the funds, where it was found untouched after her death—an event brought on by an inflammatory disorder that seized her soon after the desertion of her lover.'

Lady Mary Coke sorrowing sourly over the Duke of York's death the previous September wrote in her *Journal* for Monday, April 19, 1768, that the Duchess of Norfolk had confided having met the Duke of Cumberland in the park with Miss Elliott in an equipage and that he bowed as she passed. 'The Duchess was shocked at the indecency and indeed, I believe that he is the first of the Royal Family that carried their mistress in the Royal Equipage.'[5]

The Duke's aunt, Princess Amelia, was also beginning to disapprove of him, for a month later Lady Mary mentions that when dining with the Princess at Gunnersbury: 'She told me the Duke of Cumberland had been with her, but described his behaviour not much to his advantage. She said she never saw such want of breeding, that indeed it was very bad. I really felt sorry. I once had a very good opinion of the Duke of Cumberland & thought he would have turned out extremely well, but I fear the low Company that he keeps has been of great disservice to his manner, which certainly was once very pretty.'[6]

The *Town and Country Magazine* says that various reasons had been given for the Duke's breaking with Anne Elliott. One was that after mortgaging the house already alluded to, he was ordered by the King to end the affair. Others asserted that the breach came when he surprised her in bed with a barrister, after which event he went on a sea voyage to try and forget her.

Apparently the Duke did not entirely succeed in doing this, for when Anne died in her lodgings in Greek-street, Soho, a year after they had parted, Lady Mary Coke wrote on June 4, 1769, that he did not attend the Duke of Bolton's Masquerade at Hackwood because ''tis said he is greatly affected with the death of Miss Elliott and 'tis believed his lowness of spirits on that occasion prevented his going: 'tis reported She wrote to him when She was dying'.[7]

Feeling no doubt that, having given the actress so much, he was entitled to the furniture and other effects, the Duke sent his representative to demand their return. Her executor replied that they were in his custody for the purposes of her will and the Duke could not recover them but by due course of law. We learn this from the letter dated August 20 published in the *Town and Country* and written to its printer by Polly Jones, Anne's successor, who had by that time quarrelled with Cumberland and left him. She alleged that after his failure 'all his vengeance was wreaked upon me, an innocent, blameless victim. He immediately sent the proper officers to dispossess me of my household furniture, which had been provided at his expence, and left me destitute, friendless and almost pennyless, after he had professed the greatest regard, esteem, and even love for me; without the least provocation on my side, or even the shadow of a pretence for such conduct, except the refusal he met from Miss Elliott's executor....

'You are at liberty, Sir, to make what use you please of this letter, as it may be a means of encouraging every female who has pretensions to beauty to lead a virtuous life, since constancy or generosity is not to be expected even in lovers of the most exalted rank.'

The Duke's action was due to his being short of funds at the time. He was in the midst of his affair with Lady Grosvenor.

A glimpse into Polly Jones's life with Cumberland and her past is to be found in the brazen reminiscences of Mrs Archer who first encountered the Duke when she was being kept by a wealthy admirer in a farm outside Wokingham, Berkshire. She writes: 'In one of our walks we met the Duke of Cumberland and Miss Jones, who then lived with His Royal Highness. The Prince did us the honour to take great notice of us; the consequence of which was an intimacy between myself and that lady, and a pressing invitation to visit her at Sunninghill ... I made frequent visits to Miss Jones, and used to accompany her and the Duke in their evening walks which seemed to be chiefly taken in order to amuse His Royal Highness with her tumbling in the grass. Nothing could be more indecent and unbecoming than this exercise, but it suited the Prince's taste, and while she was tumbling heels over head, and throwing herself into the most indecent postures, he used to laugh with a degree of violence that I never beheld either before or since. But all the charms and even tumbling could not keep the heart of her Royal lover, for it now began to wander towards myself, and His Highness took an opportunity of informing me, that Miss Jones's vulgarity had quite disgusted him, and accompanied the declaration with a proposal to succeed her in his affections and protection.

'An offer of this nature was calculated in every instance to flatter my vanity, but though my innocence was no more, my heart was not yet corrupt, and I was determined not only to refuse the proposition, but to inform my friend of the royal infidelity. I therefore took an opportunity of asking Miss Jones concerning her lover to whom she declared she had no objection but one, which was, that there was somebody in town whom she liked better; this favoured person was one of the Kennedy's famous for the murder of the watchman on Westminster bridge ...

'In the course of her conversation, she gave me the following sketch of her history. Her father and mother were hawking pedlars who sold wooden ware and cabbage-nets about the street, while Polly attended them with her moving shop of water-cresses and common herbage. In this situation she happened to attract the notice of Mrs Mitchel, a well-known inhabitant of King's Place. That good lady, hackneyed in the arts of seduction, attacked at the same moment, the vanity of the girl, and the wants of her parents.

'In short Mrs Mitchel wanted a servant—exactly such a servant as Polly—and, perhaps, she did not deviate from truth when she told the pedlar that she would take the same care of this child, as if it were her own. So the poor girl was taken to Mrs Mitchel's house, stripped naked, put into a large tub of water, when after having been cleansed from the dirt and defilement of her late situation, she was handsomely cloathed, and at night consigned to a defilement of another and more fatal species, in the arms of a gentleman, who gladdened Mrs Mitchel's heart with the sum which he gave her for the prize she had so luckily procured him.

'Here she remained for some time, when being at Vauxhall Gardens, she happened to captivate the Duke of Cumberland, who arranged the matter with Mrs Mitchel by paying her about seventy pounds which the said Miss Jones owed her. The young lady was then taken home by his Royal Highness where she declared, she had every reason to be contented, except her distance from the particular object of her affections.

'Having heard her history, I immediately informed her of the proposals which the Duke had made me. At first she rather hesitated in believing me, but on my reiterating the truth of my relation she declared she would be even with him; and while they were at supper, that very night, she told his Royal Highness that she would go to town the next day to meet a person she was very fond of, and on his remonstrating against such ungrateful conduct, she told him, without any ceremony, that he might turn about and mend it. So she ordered the servant to get her a chaise immediately, and away she went.'[8]

But Mrs Archer did not long succeed Polly in the Duke's affections, for she states in her *Memoirs* that he was next attracted by the Countess D'Onhoff or Dunhoff, born Lady Camilla Elizabeth Bennet, daughter of Charles, third Earl of Tankerville. According to *Burke's Peerage*, she married on September 5, 1764, Count Dunhoff of Poland, who died on the 25th of the same month, leaving her a widow.

The *Town and Country Magazine* paints a more exotic portrait of Camilla. We are told that she was sent to Paris to finish her education and there she made the acquaintance of a former lover of Catherine the Great, Stanislaus Poniatowski, the handsome young King of Poland, who fell in love with her. Camilla went to Warsaw with him and 'remained there nearly two years, being created Countess of D—ff, living in the utmost splendour ... as the mistress of a great and youthful monarch.' Then, apparently, she was foolish enough to flirt with a certain noble and the jealous King discovering this banished her which, commented the *Town and Country*, shows 'that Caesar's mistress should not only be virtuous but unsuspected'.

According to the same source, upon her return to England Camilla judiciously gave out she was the widow of the King of Poland's brother and was 'courted and adulated by the first nobility—the men offered their hearts; the ladies tendered their purses; and she so condescending as not to want much pressing to accept of both'. She resided first in St James's Place, then at Number Twenty Cavendish Square where she had frequent drums and routs patronized by the *haut ton* and 'among the rest *Nauticus* [Cumberland] never fails to be present'. It was certain that he professed the greatest affection for her. She in return had 'such sympathetic feelings' that she had been prevailed upon by his 'irresistible rhetoric to retire into the country to a snug retreat near his hunting seat'.

It was not long before Camilla in her turn lost the affections of the Duke to Henrietta, Lady Grosvenor, and embarked on an affair that was to make him not only notorious but cause the Royal Marriage Act to be passed. In fact, according to the evidence provided by Lady Mary Coke, he had already been attracted by Henrietta in 1766 when he was living with his first mistress, Signorina Zamperini.

CHAPTER FOUR

The Grosvenors

Lady Grosvenor's husband, Richard, was of Norman descent. The family had grown in importance as landowners following a Grosvenor's marriage with the heiress of Eaton, in Cheshire, in the fifteenth century. In 1622, an earlier Richard Grosvenor had been created a baronet and, half a century later, his grandson, Sir Thomas, whilst on a visit to London met and married Mary Davies, the only child of a cowman who owned some 70 acres south of Oxford Street, between Marble Arch and Bond Street, and also another 360 acres between Knightsbridge and the river. This was marshland and those who lived there suffered from ague and rheumatism, and from the footpads infesting it. Later, however, it was to become fashionable Belgravia, thanks to Cubitt's architecture and scientific drainage.

Richard Grosvenor was Sir Thomas's great-great-grandson. Born in 1731 and educated at Oxford, he was elected MP for Chester when twenty-three and in 1761 was raised to the peerage as Baron Grosvenor of Eaton, thanks to his parliamentary services to Pitt the Elder. But his chief interest lay in the turf and he gained a great reputation as the leading breeder of racehorses of his time, won the Derby thrice in five years, and is usually regarded as the father of English racing. A discerning collector of paintings, he was the patron of Stubbs and Benjamin West and Sir Joshua Reynolds' friend.

Lord Grosvenor would appear, too, to have been a nature lover, for the *Annual Register* for 1768 contains some verses, *The Hamadryads*, in praise of his public spirited act in preventing some rows of beautiful trees from being cut down near a place of entertainment. There was, however, another side to his character. Charles Pigott, author of *The Jockey Club, or a Sketch of the Manners of the Age*, a collection of scandalous and scathing pen portraits of prominent persons of the times, published in 1792, when Grosvenor was sixty-two, writes: 'In tracing the lineaments of his Lordship's countenance we behold the faithful index of a sordid vicious mind, with no moral beauty to counterbalance the blemishes of physical deformity.... Perhaps this noble peer laboured so heavily under the impression that he should one day be hanged that he was desirous of saving Jack Catch the trouble of his office when he was found hanging and unfortunately cut down by a Stable Boy at York.... At present he appears recruited in spirits and he pursues with unabated perseverance, the same plan of filthy debauchery that he followed in his younger days, with this only difference that as his powers decay, his vices, if possible, are more loathsome and degenerate.'

Mrs Archer claimed in her *Memoirs* that after having had over fifty English and French peers as her lovers, including the future Philippe-Égalité, she became a procuress for Lord Grosvenor, whose family motto was ironically 'Virtue Not Ancestry'. At their first meeting he told her that he had 'a very great partiality for lasses with golden locks. I offered to recommend him one of that description, whom I had every reason to believe would meet with his approbation. He readily accepted my proposal and appointed to meet her at Mrs Townshend's, a very miserable place indeed, near Argyle-buildings. His Lordship was very well satisfied with my recommendation and behaved very generously to me in the occasion.' This led to his suggesting that she, too, should lay with him, but that honour was declined as she was then connected 'with a gentleman who deserved every mark of regard and attention from me'. Lord Grosvenor, it seems, approved of such loyalty.

But though Mrs Archer did not become the peer's mistress, we learn later that he engaged her 'in the number of those who procured novelties for his seraglio', and at his request took a house in Lambeth Marsh 'where a hundred thousand lords and commoners might have come daily and nightly without notice or observation', and it was not long before this place was 'as well stocked, both for number and variety, as even his lordship could wish for'. However, contrary to her expectations, he soon tired of these lights o' love and she was sent hither and thither trying to procure for him beauties the sight of whom had taken his fancy.

His lordship, Mrs Archer complains, never rewarded her financially as he had promised and eventually to avoid doing so ceased visiting her. She wrote that she realised a former lover of hers, Lord Bateman, had been right when he had warned her not to have anything to do with Lord Grosvenor, saying: 'Nobody will tempt you with such fine promises, and no one will be so backward in performing them. He will bid you to hire a house, and it shall be furnished at his expense without delay, but no sooner is the house got than he will refuse to put a scraper at the door—to give you a rush-bottom chair to sit on—or even to purchase a penny-worth of sand to strew in your passage.'

Mrs Archer recorded this when Lord Grosvenor was in his late fifties. According to the period's scandal, he had begun patronizing prostitutes in his teens and by the age of twenty-three had so undermined his health that the physicians he consulted all stressed that he could recover only if he changed his way of life, either by keeping to the same mistress or marrying. So he went in search of a wife and chose Henrietta, daughter of Henry Vernon of Hilton Park, Staffordshire, MP for Bedfordshire, and Lady Harriot Vernon, sister of the 4th Earl of Strafford and Lady of the Bedchamber to Princess Amelia, the Duke of Cumberland's aunt.

Horace Walpole describes Henrietta in his *Memoirs* as having 'a good person, moderate beauty, no understanding and excessive vanity'. His comments concerning her hair once caused a breach between him and her mother. It had become the fashion for women to have the head *moutoné*. About six months after her marriage she attended a social gathering at Northumberland House with 'such a display of friz, that it literally spread beyond her shoulder', so claims one of his letters dated February 12, 1765. He observed to a guest that 'it looked as if her parents had stinted her in hair before marriage and that she was determined to indulge her fancy now'.[1] Unfortunately this sally went on being repeated until it reached Lady Harriot.

The author of a pamphlet printed at the time of the law-suit of 1770 gives a more favourable description of Henrietta's person. He says: 'She was formed by nature to captivate the hearts of all who saw her, being one of the handsomest women of the age. In her earliest years she discovered an irresistible passion for intrigue, which was not a little heightened by her frequenting all public places as soon as she had attained the age proper for making a figure there. Through the coquettish airs she assumed, the pride she took in outshining in dress the young ladies of her own age, she was sought after as a wife by many till she accepted Richard Grosvenor.'[2]

Kensington Gardens originally occupied only twenty-six acres. Queen Anne doubled their extent, then George II's wife, Queen Caroline, added nearly three hundred acres out of Hyde Park, had them fenced round and attractively laid out by Charles Bridgeman, the Royal Gardener. By the time George III came to the throne only well-dressed people were admitted to the Gardens, and on week-days they were considered the close preserves of the upper classes. A visitor to London then wrote: 'For the better regulating the company servants are placed at the different entrances to prevent persons meanly clad from going into the gardens.' Here ladies who would be guarded by male relatives or retainers while walking in the robber-ridden London streets, might go alone as it was assumed that they would encounter no one but other persons of their own standing.

According to the same pamphleteer, when strolling one spring day in the Gardens, Richard Grosvenor saw Miss Vernon and another young woman sitting in an arbour. A heavy shower compelled him to ask if he could take shelter where they were. They consented, and to pass the time indulged in chit-chat. When the rain ceased, the ladies signified their intention of returning home and Lord Grosvenor asked if they had a carriage, and on their replying that they hadn't he offered transport in his, which they accepted.

'On their way, Miss Vernon observed that it was the most comfortable carriage she had ever ridden in. To which Lord Grosvenor replied that she could use it when she so wished. He had already fallen in love with her and within a month of the meeting they were married.' The ceremony took place on July 19, 1764, at St George's, Hanover Square.

It has already been mentioned that Lady Harriot Vernon, Lady Grosvenor's mother, was Lady of the Bedchamber to Princess Amelia. The latter, whose engagement to Frederick the Great was broken off, had never married. A compulsive card-player who took snuff and dressed in male attire, she divided her time between her country home, Gunnersbury Park, where she revelled in showing off her knowledge of equine diseases, and her Palladian mansion on the corner of Harley Street and Cavendish Square, where she would often sit at her window contemplating sadly the clumsy gilded equestrian statue of her brother, 'Butcher' Cumberland, which in those days stood in the centre of the Square with a few sheep grazing round it. She had been very fond of him, although he had habitually borrowed money from her and then forgotten to repay it.

The first Lord Holland described Princess Amelia 'as a lively, mischief-making and mischief-meaning woman'. Although caustic in her condemnation of the prevalent permissiveness, her own virtue when young was not thought immaculate. Greville, the diarist, mentions that after the death of her father, George II, someone asked if she was to have Guards, and George Selwyn then remarked: 'One every now and then!'[3]

A friend of this formidable eccentric was Lady Mary Coke, who corresponded regularly with her sister, Lady Strafford. The latter having married Lady Harriot Vernon's brother was Lady Grosvenor's aunt. Lady Mary's journals and letters provide not only colourful insight into the Court life of the period but also into some aspects of the Grosvenor–Cumberland affair.

Already in August, 1766, Prince Henry (two months before being created Duke of Cumberland) was attracted by Lady Grosvenor. Lady Mary in her *Journal* for Sunday, August 23, describes a visit to the Royal Drawing Room: 'Lady Grosvenor was in the most joyous spirits I ever saw. She twice burst into such violent fits of laughter that she was obliged to hide her face behind her fan ... It was something, Prince Henry said to her that made her so merry.'[4]

Next at the Opera on November 11 Lady Mary notices Henrietta 'as gay as ever' enjoying 'lively' conversation with the Duke for 'some time'.[5] Though expecting a third child, yet two days later at Almack's, she was 'dancing away to the great surprise of Lady Catherine Beauclerk, who I believe is as far gone with child as her and did not think herself in a condition for dancing'.[6]

In mid January, the following year, Lady Mary records having heard of a quarrel between Lord Strafford and Lady Harriot because he thought his niece was becoming too intimate with Cumberland, whilst his doting sister refused to countenance criticism of her daughter.[7] Shortly after this our practised observer spies Henrietta at the Opera placing herself 'close to fops' alley that she might not be overlook'd'.[8] Then that summer on June 7 in a letter to Lady Strafford describing a rout at Lady Barrington's place in Stable Yard, St James's, Lady Mary mischievously sowed seeds of suspicion by mentioning: 'Your husband's niece, Lady Grosvenor, came in at ten o'clock from walking in the Park in a hat, a night gown and white apron, yet she did not seem the least ashamed of her dress.'[9] Three weeks later, Lady Mary hastens to inform her sister, Lady Strafford, that whilst she was at another rout of Lady Harrington's (whom the *Town and Country* called the Stable-yard Messalina) Henrietta again caused raised eyebrows by arriving after ten o'clock from walking in the Park.[10] Edward Bennet, a footman, was later to testify in the divorce proceedings that the Duke of Cumberland accompanied her at these routs and handed her afterwards to her coach or chair.

As time passed, Lord Strafford's disgust with his sister's motherly refusal to believe ill of Henrietta grew to such an extent that he became violent. On February 27, 1768, Lady Mary writes that she had been told by Princess Amelia that he had given Lady Harriot such a blow with his shoulder at the Opera that the ladies accompanying her were shocked.[11]

From the way in which Lady Mary hastened to send Lady Strafford every item of news she could collect about the latter's sister-in-law and nieces by marriage, it would seem as though, following Lord Strafford's attack, they rarely communicated with these relatives, if at all. In a long letter dated September 20, later that year, our correspondent states: 'I now come to a piece of news which, if you have not already heard, will surprise you.' This was that Lady Harriot's third daughter, Caroline, had been appointed Maid of Honour in place of one who had left to marry.[12]

Caroline Vernon, known among her intimates as 'Carry', was to play an important part in her eldest sister's affair with the Duke of Cumberland. Lady Mary approved of her and informed Lady Strafford on November 2, 1768: 'I've seen the new Maid of Honour, Miss Vernon, twice since she was appointed, & I must do her the justice to say that her behaviour is remarkably modest.'[13]

But if Caroline received general approval, opinion concerning Henrietta was in complete contrast. Lord Grosvenor was probably aware of his wife's behaviour. No doubt it suited him, for marriage had not really cured him of his itch to change his sleeping partner almost as often he changed his shirt. Apart from this, his time was fully taken up with his other passion, horse racing.

Ever since the spring of 1768, the Duke of Cumberland and Lady Grosvenor arranged to be together whenever possible. The theatres, the opera house, Almack's, Ranelagh, Vauxhall and Mrs Cornelys's were all judged safe meeting-places, because they could easily step aside from the busy crowd and entertain each other without risk of being discovered or interrupted. But as time passed the lovers grew less discreet. At the much publicized grand Masquerade held at Mrs Cornelys's on Monday evening, February 27, 1769, both were present—he audaciously arrayed after his namesake as Henry VIII and she as the Goddess of Night dressed in flowing black silk scintillating with silver stars and wearing a crescent moon in her hair. It was remarked that the couple were together for nearly every dance.

CHAPTER FIVE

A Letter from 'Jack Sprat'

In her sworn statement made on April 27, 1771,[1] Camilla, Countess D'Onhoff, who then gave her age as twenty-three, was to record that for nearly four years she had been friendly with the Grosvenors and had gone with them frequently to Ranelagh, Almack's and other public places of entertainment where they were joined by the Duke of Cumberland, who spoke to them and handed Henrietta to her coach or sedan-chair. In March, 1769, the latter called at Camilla's house—20 Cavendish Square—on several occasions and the Duke arrived soon after.

'The first time he came I was much surprised, as I did not expect to see His Highness. Lady Grosvenor pretended to me that she wanted to talk to him about her brother, William Vernon, who was in the Navy, in order to interest His Highness in her brother's career. I asked Lady Grosvenor how she came to arrange to meet the Duke at my house, when she had one of her own where she could see what company she pleased. She replied that the reason why the Duke did not come to her house was because His Highness and Lord Grosvenor had had a little dispute together.

'I remember in particular one evening in April, 1769, I cannot recollect the exact date. Lady Grosvenor and the Duke were in my dining room. She asked me to leave the room for awhile. She gave the excuse that she wanted to speak to him about her brother, so I retired into a back room, where I stayed for about half an hour. Tiring of remaining alone I rejoined them. As I opened the door, I saw Lady Grosvenor reclining on a couch with her petticoats up. The Duke's breeches were unbuttoned and he was lying upon her and his body was in motion. His Highness cursed and swore at me, and I returned to the room I had left. They remained together in the dining-room for about two hours, and then they went away, the Duke going first, and Lady Grosvenor after him.'

The Countess claimed that Henrietta later promised not to

misbehave in such a fashion again, and on this understanding the couple were allowed to continue meeting in her house. Then, some weeks later, when it became clear from the conversation that Lady Grosvenor wished to confide to the Duke something concerning her husband, Camilla declared that she tactfully withdrew once more into the other room and that, after a quarter of an hour on going back to fetch a workbag from a table, she was 'as much surprised as she was before' for Henrietta had broken her word and Camilla now witnessed a repeat performance of the earlier scene.

A fortnight after this, went on the Countess, just as she was about to retire to bed, Henrietta called saying she had come to enquire after her health. Shortly afterwards, the Duke arrived also making the same pretext, but both left after an hour when all hints failed to persuade their hostess to leave them on their own.

If we are to believe the Duke's former charmer, Lady Grosvenor shamelessly continued to try and make use of her ... Next she called and said she was on her way to visit her sister, Caroline Vernon, the Maid of Honour to the Queen. She asked Camilla to accompany her, which the latter did, but when they reached the royal apartments, she whispered: 'Don't go in—I must speak to the Duke of Cumberland. We'll enter by the back door.'

The Countess allowed herself to be hurriedly led through a passage leading from St James's to the park, where they found the Duke and his equerry, Captain Foulkes, waiting. All four then entered Cumberland House by the rear entrance. Henrietta and her admirer then slipped away whilst the other woman was talking to the Captain, who soon after went off to Ranelagh. After a while, complained Camilla, she wearied of being by herself and, deciding to ask for a book to read, invaded the apartment where the pair were closeted, and surprised them in more love-making.

D'Onhoff still did not let such episodes break her apparent friendship, for she reveals in her deposition that twice following this Lady Grosvenor met her royal lover at the Countess's but the latter insisted that on neither occasion did she leave them alone, so they ceased visiting her.

Similar allegations were made by Mrs Elizabeth Sutton engaged in May, 1769, by the Countess to look after her house whilst she was in the country. According to this witness, during the first week of employment, the Countess was visited on several occasions by Lady Grosvenor, who at six-thirty on the very next evening after the servant had been left on her own called and asked to see her mistress. The housekeeper replied that she was away, but the visitor insisted she knew the Countess was due back by nine o'clock so would await her in the dining-room. Once seated there, Lady Grosvenor said her own brother would also be shortly arriving, and about half an hour later 'a gentleman, muffled up so that his face could hardly be seen, arrived in a hackney chair, the curtains of which were drawn very close'. He told Mrs Sutton he was Lady Grosvenor's brother and asked if she were there.

'I said she was and he ran upstairs as hard as he could. When it was dark, I carried up candles to the drawing-room. Lady Grosvenor and the gentleman were then sitting upon the couch with a round table near them. I went to put the candles upon it, but the gentleman hastily pointed at the furthermost card table and told me to put the candles there, which I did.'

The couple stayed together for about three hours, then at ten o'clock Lady Grosvenor went away first in her coach. Her 'brother', to Mrs Sutton's surprise, did not accompany her, 'I waited to light the gentleman out, and as he was coming downstairs, I met him with the candles, and he asked me if I was alone in the house. I said, "No, Sir, I have my husband and family," and he said, "Oh!" and I had a good look and saw he was a fair-looking man, and had a scar on one side of his face. He then put his coat about his neck; but I met him full face with the candles in my hand, and took another look so to recognise him if I saw him again. Then he went away on foot.

'About seven o'clock the next evening, Lady Grosvenor came again, and inquired for the Countess D'Onhoff. Soon afterwards the same gentleman came again in a chair, with his great coat on, and I carried them candles when it was dark. They did not ring, or call for candles, but I thought it a shame for them to be in the dark.

'When the gentleman went away, I was busy so I asked my husband, who was with me to go and open the door for him, which he did, and when Mr Sutton came downstairs, he said, "Do you know who the gentleman is?" I answered, "Why, Lady Grosvenor's brother, is it not?" And my husband said, "No, it was the Duke of Cumberland." I said, "Are you sure of that?" and my husband said, "What, you fool, don't you think I know him?" My husband, you see, had been a soldier.

'Lady Grosvenor and the gentleman, whom I now know to have been his Royal Highness the Duke of Cumberland, came in like manner once or twice more to the Countess D'Onhoff's house. They generally came about seven o'clock, and stayed till ten. They were once there till about eleven o'clock, and were always alone together in the drawing-room, and constantly sat upon the couch, which appeared to be tumbled by their sitting on it, but in no other manner than what might be done by sitting on it.'

In all the couple paid four visits to the house. 'Sometimes he came first ... at other times she did ... always they inquired for each other as brother and sister.' The Countess was away some time, and Mrs Sutton stated that she soon realized the excuse given by Lady Grosvenor when she first called was a false one and that her mistress had never told her ladyship she was returning.

From April, 1769, till the October of that year the couple were aided in their intrigue by a widowed milliner in her forties, Mary Vemberght, who was known as Mrs Reda as she was living with a fencing master of that name whose wife would not divorce him. This widow had first met Lord and Lady Grosvenor at Tunbridge Wells five years earlier, and as a result her ladyship had become a customer of hers. Lord Grosvenor in his law-suit claimed that the milliner allowed the Duke to meet his wife in an upstairs room of her house, leading into another conveniently furnished with a large bed. Here they would remain for two or three hourly sessions. He also alleged that she permitted them to use a back room behind the shop for shorter sessions and for writing notes to each other, which the widow would then deliver.

In the spring of the year mentioned, Mrs Reda admitted, she was approached by Captain Foulkes, who enquired if she rented the whole of the first floor in Pall Mall where she lived, as he was seeking apartments for his master. Occupying only the ground floor at the time, she prevailed upon two of her men friends to rent the upper part of the house for her. A few days later the Duke called to inspect these rooms and seemed very pleased with them, especially as there were two doors, one leading down into the Mall and the other into a little used side street.

In a sworn statement made on November 1, 1770, before Lord Grosvenor's lawyers, Mrs Reda gave her version of what ensued. 'I told his highness that although I was poor, yet I would not for any money have any thing *bad* done in my house, and that I would *have no girls* there; and his highness assured me that the apartments were for no such use, that he had some particular business with Lady Grosvenor, but nothing criminal; and that she would come there now and then.'

From that time the Duke came to her house for an hour or two almost daily, and either wrote in a room behind her shop or brought a letter, already written, which at his request she either personally took to Lady Grosvenor's house and handed to her or left concealed in a parcel of millinery.

In May, 1769, the Duke told the milliner that Lady Grosvenor wanted to inspect some foreign silks at the opera house, where Mr Reda rented rooms to teach fencing. She told the Duke she would bring the silks there, when her friend was away in the city. 'Accordingly one morning his Royal Highness called upon me at my house in Pall Mall, and we went to the opera house in the Haymarket, and I let his Royal Highness into Mr Reda's apartments.

'No sooner had I returned to my shop than Lady Grosvenor called and I told her that his Highness and the silks were at the opera house. She asked me to take her there, which I did. When I showed her in, the Duke kissed her and I opened the silks for her ladyship to see. The Duke then sent me out of the room for something, and thereupon he, or Lady Grosvenor, immediately locked the door behind me. I went into the kitchen, and, whilst there, heard them laughing and playing together. The bell to the opera house door being rung, I went below stairs, and was there about a quarter of an hour or more, and then went up again. As I was going through a passage which adjoins a bedchamber, belonging to Mr Reda's apartments, I heard a great noise coming from the direction of the bed. I was extremely surprised and frightened.

'In the passage where I was, there is a door, which is nailed up, and which door made part of the wall adjoining to the bed-chamber, and the bed was close to the door, and being so very near, I very plainly heard the bed crack, and his Highness and Lady Grosvenor pushing very much, and I heard him cry: "He, he!" in a gruff manner as if he was doing hard work, and Lady Grosvenor in a softer manner, in a kind of laughing manner, and like sighing.'

This, Mrs Reda stated, convinced her that the couple were having sexual intercourse. Later, she heard them laughing and playing in the dining-room. She knocked and, on being admitted, told Lady Grosvenor it was time she left in case her husband should pass by and, seeing her coach outside, catch her with the Duke. Following this warning, Lady Grosvenor went out, attended by the milliner, who carried a piece of silk prominently under her arm to still the suspicions of anybody who might be watching. The Duke departed ten minutes later.

Mrs Reda continued that, fearing Mr Reda's bed might need attention, she went into the chamber and noticed the marks of two hands and arms upon the couch as well as those of some one's knees. Recollecting that Lady Grosvenor was then 'very big with child', she believed that such 'pressures' were made by her when 'in the act of carnal copulation with his Royal Highness'. What made her more certain was when she then noticed 'upon the carpet, near the bed-side, three or four drops, which appeared to me to come from man. ... I wiped the same up to prevent anything being known afterwards.'

Next morning Cumberland called and asked Mrs Reda to deliver a letter to his *inamorata*, which at first the woman claimed she declined to do, but that after he had begged her 'on his knees' she took it hidden among some millinery to her ladyship. From then onwards, she received letters almost daily from him which she passed on in various ways. He or his gentleman porter, Robert Giddings, would call to collect Lady Grosvenor's replies.

In June that year, the Duke was appointed Commander-in-Chief of the Channel Squadron of the Fleet and his first task would soon be to take his ships on a training cruise as far as Gibraltar and back, still carrying his flag on the frigate *Venus* to which he had become much attached. This, however, could not have come at a more inopportune time in view of the fact that Henrietta was with child. Now she had to stay at home and it was difficult for them to meet. Cumberland on social calls to the Countess D'Onhoff asked her postillion, John Bourne, to take two letters to Lady Grosvenor as if they came from his own mistress and gave him half-a-guinea for his trouble.

In the first letter to his 'dearest love', the Duke wrote: 'I wish I dare lye all the while by your bed and nurse you—for you will have nobody near you that loves you as I do, thou dearest Angel of my soul. O that I could but bear your pain for you I should be happy.' What grieved him was that her husband did not appreciate 'what an inestimable Prize and Treasure' he had in her. How glad he was that her time should come when Mr Croper (their name for Lord Grosvenor) was away, like that she could be quiet for a few days. 'I am sure my Angel is not in greater pain than what my heart feels for my adorable Angel.' The Countess was away, so if Henrietta sent her reply to Cavendish Square, Bourne had orders to bring it to him without his mistress's knowledge. 'God bless you and I hope before Morning your dear little one.'[2]

One wonders if the Duke of Cumberland could have been the

father of this child. As Lord David Cecil wrote in *The Young Melbourne*: 'The historian grows quite giddy as he tries to disentangle the implications of heredity consequent on the free and easy habits of the aristocracy at this period. The Harley family, children of the Countess of Oxford, were known as the Harleian Miscellany on account of the variety of fathers alleged to be responsible for their existence.' Lord David comments that for all their dissipation there was nothing decadent about the 18th century aristocrat. 'Their excesses came from too much life, not too little.'

On June 7, Henrietta gave birth to a son christened Richard. It proved a weakly infant and died within a year. Next evening, according to the *London Evening Post*, after the Duke had set out from town for his Lodge at Windsor 'an express was sent to inform him that his Majesty desired his attendance at the Queen's Palace, whither he came and had a long conference with his Majesty'. There are no references to this interview in the Royal Archives so one can only conjecture about it.

A few days later, under pretence of calling to receive an order for millinery, Mrs Reda arrived at 39 Grosvenor Square and was shown up into her ladyship's bedroom. Shortly afterwards, Lord Grosvenor came in unexpectedly and his wife had barely time to hide under her pillow the letter from the Duke which the milliner had handed her in exchange for one for him. Slipping this surreptitiously into her pocket, Mrs Reda withdrew, telling Lady Grosvenor to deceive her husband that she would send her the things ordered as soon as possible.

The following week, when Caroline Vernon and Lord Grosvenor were with his wife in her bedroom, Hannah Birch, her personal maid, came in and said that Mrs Reda had sent the patterns. Henrietta asked her sister to bring them to her. When she brought back the package, Richard demanded to see the contents, but his wife refused to show them to him. He, however, tried to snatch the parcel, but Caroline pulled him away. Meanwhile, Henrietta, under cover of the bedclothes, started tearing up a letter she had taken out. Once he had disengaged himself, Richard hurried over to her and seized the pieces of paper, which he discovered to be a love letter addressed to 'my little Angel', written by the Duke from on board the *Venus* and dated June 15.

For some days, Lord Grosvenor avoided his wife, then, stealing into her bedroom, he surprised her folding some sheets of paper. After a struggle, he seized not only the letter she had just finished but also two from the Duke written before he left London and a further two delivered that day by her sister Caroline (whose pet name of 'Carry' was from now on to become particularly apt in the circumstances). Henrietta begged Richard not to read them, but he ignored her and went downstairs with the correspondence.

The first of the two letters Lady Grosvenor had just received was dated June 16, the day following the Duke's previous letter. He began by describing life aboard his flagship. He dined at two and then spent the afternoon listening to music played by his servant and 'a couple of hands from London'. He went to supper about nine, but did not eat anything and retired to bed at ten.

'I then prayed for you, *my dearest* love, *kissed your dearest little Hair* and laye down and dreamt of you, *had you on the dear little couch ten thousand times in my arms*, kissing you and telling you how much I loved and adored you and you seemed pleased, but alas when I woke I found it all delusion. Nobody by me but myself at Sea.' (The jury at the time of the subsequent trial were to have their attention repeatedly drawn to the implications of the words in italics by counsel for the plaintiff.)

The Duke continued that after rising at half-past five and walking on deck with a friend for about an hour, he breakfasted at eight, and by nine began exercising the ships under his command. This lasted till midday. It was now one and when he had finished writing to her he would dress and go to dinner at two o'clock. He mentioned all this so as to keep his promise 'always to let you know my motions and my thoughts'. This he would continue to do 'untill the very last letter you shall have from me, which will be when between 5 and 6 weeks hence I send the Admiralty word that I am arrived at Spithead ...' Then he could return to her.

The wind had been contrary that day so he had ordered the ships of his squadron to anchor for the night in Portland Roads, two miles off Weymouth. But the weather was not so adverse that he could not have sailed on had he wished. He had made the excuse to his second-in-command that he had important despatches to send to London. 'Indeed, my dear Angel, I need not tell you, I know you read the reason too well that made me do so. It was to write to you. For God knows I have wrote to none else but to the King. God bless you, most amiable and dearest little creature living—*aimons, toujours, mon adorable petite amour, je vous adore plus que la vie meme.*'

He had been reading that morning verses by Matthew Prior and had come across some lines applicable to themselves.

'Now oft had *Henry* changed his sly Disguise,
Unmarked by all but beauteous Harriet's eyes;
Oft had found means alone to see the Dame,
And at her feet to breathe his am'rous flame:
And oft the pangs of absence to remove
By letters soft interpreters of Love
Till Time & Industry (the mighty two
That bring our wishes nearer to our view),
Made him perceive that the inclining fair
Received his vows with no reluctant ear;
That *Venus* had confirmed her equal Reign
And dealt to Harriet's heart a share of *Henry's* pain.'

Such was his amusement 'to read those sort of things that puts me in mind of our mutual feelings and situations'.

Dated Saturday, June 17, the second letter from the Duke began that as the wind was not fair 'I shall laye here in Portland Road till it is and take this precious moment in sending this other Note to you.' He hoped she was not afraid of going out of Town before he returned to 'thou loveliest dearest Soul'. Since his letter of the day before he had been reading more of Prior and had found many sentiments to coincide with his own, such as:

Hear solemn Jove; and conscious Venus hear;
And thou bright Maid, believe me, whilst I swear,
No Time, no Change, no Future Flame shall move
The well-placed Basis of my lasting Love.'

Writing constantly to her was his only entertainment and hearing from her would be, apart from his duty on board, 'the only thought or employment I shall have or ever wish'.

He had just received a message from shore at Weymouth, which was two miles away, to go 'to the rooms there this Morning'. But he had excused himself 'being much quieter on Board and happier in writing to you'. She was not at Weymouth 'or else the Boat that should carry me would go too slow ... I send you ten thousand kisses, pray when you receive this, return them to me for I want them sadly'. He ended in indifferent French: '*Addieu je vous aime adorable petite Creature je vous adore ma chere petite bejoux l'amant de mon coeur.*'

It would seem from these letters that the Duke was genuinely in love with Lady Grosvenor. He certainly kept faithful to her. The Countess Cowper, writing from Mount Edgecumbe on July 11 that year to her friend, Miss Dewes, states: 'The Duke of Cumberland is expected here tomorrow from on board his frigate, but His Royal Highness returns on board at night by way of example to the sea officers.'

The letter seized by Lord Grosvenor which Henrietta had been folding was dated Sunday, June 18, at the beginning and addressed to her 'Dearest Friend.' In it she said her husband appeared in better temper, so she was 'in great hopes' that he had not taken from her enough of the torn pieces of the Duke's previous letter 'to make out much'.

In future Henrietta thought it would be safest if she used the services of her sisters, both to forward letters to Henry and deliver his to her. Carry was going away for a few days, so in the meantime she would send her letters through her elder sister, Mrs Hill, who visited her every day and thought it was some business she had with Mrs Reda about millinery concerning which she did not wish her husband to know. So if this sister ever should receive correspondence for her, she knew she must not take it out of her pocket till they were alone. The letter ended abruptly with the words: 'He is coming upstairs I find, so I shall conclude till tomorrow.'

Then, after the date 'Monday the 19th'—'I resume my pen to tell you today how sincerely I esteem you. He is still rather more come about again today. Yesterday he shook hands with me, and this morning he came and kissed me and said he was going out of Town to Walthamstow to dine with his Brother. Perhaps he is gone to ask his advice, but I don't care. He may take what measures he pleases with me, if you will but love me.'

Henrietta hoped to be in London when the Duke returned. She fancied her husband 'had not a mind to part' with her. 'Let him have seen what he wou'd in the Letter, for he asked me Yesterday when I shou'd be able to go into Cheshire. I told him I co'd not give the least guess as it depended entirely upon how I was, and I think I've lay'd a good scheme for I've already complained I've got a pain in my side & I intend to say it's much worse at the end of the month & that I can't bear the motion of a carriage. It will I really believe be a very good plan, for if I said, I had a Feaver or any thing of that kind a physician wou'd know by my pulse I had not & might discover me to him, & besides this will be a more lasting complaint, so at the end of five or six weeks, I'll grow very ill and send for Fordyce the Apothecary and make him send me a quantity of nasty draughts which I'll throw out of the window. Only think how wicked I am, for in reality I'm already as strong and as well as ever I was in my life.'

Henrietta had heard nothing from 'D——' (Camilla D'Onhoff) and supposed she was afraid of writing or visiting her whilst Richard Grosvenor was in Town. 'My month is out by the week the 5th of July, but by the month not till the 7th so I'll take it at the longest and not be well at the end of it, so that we maint lye together.' Her husband would be going to Newmarket on the 8th or 9th for the Races and planned to stay there some days. When he returned, he would find her worse with the pain in her side. The Duke's six weeks at sea were due to end on the 26th and she hoped to see him again shortly after that. 'I'm quite in sperrits with the thoughts ... Adieu till tomorrow when I shall add more. Continue to love me, pray.'

Resuming her letter next evening, Henrietta began that she was going 'to teize my dear little Friend with more of my stupid Letter'. She had not seen 'Mr Croper' since the previous morning. He had returned very late the night before from calling on his brother, went early that morning to sit for the portrait Benjamin West was painting of him, just came home to dress, and hurried out to dine. She supposed that this meant his brother had advised him to avoid having anything to do with her.

At this stage, Henrietta suddenly announces that she has just received two letters from the Duke and goes on to express ravishment with their contents. 'How sweet those verses are you sent me! They are heavenly sweet because they are marked by you. I always liked Prior, but I shall adore him because you like him ... How happy will that day be to me that brings you back. ...' This letter, penned over the course of three days, was enclosed in an envelope addressed to 'His R.H. the Duke of Cumberland'.

Subsequent to Lord Grosvenor's seizing this correspondence, he had no further marital relations with Henrietta and slept in the separate bedroom he had occupied since his son's birth in June, and, except when they had company, never ate at the same table. But, apart from cold-shouldering her in this way, he took no other action. Possibly, he hoped the shock of discovery and the knowledge that he possessed the incriminating letters would frighten her into breaking with her royal lover. Meanwhile, Richard enjoyed life with his whores and horses.

During the divorce proceedings, Grosvenor was to claim that, whenever he asked Henrietta to travel to his seat in Cheshire, she answered at first that she could not undertake the journey before fully recovering her strength, and later, taking advantage of her sister Mrs Hill's being with child, she would say she must remain in London till the birth. He contended that his wife made such excuses so as to be in town for Cumberland's return which took place on July 29.

Before the Duke went on his cruise and after it, Lady Grosvenor visited him at his house in Pall Mall, making as if she were calling on her sister, Caroline, who, thanks to her position as a Maid of Honour, had apartments in St James's Palace. Henrietta would go in her coach to the Palace gate and there, after giving the servants orders to fetch her later, she would slip through the court-yard into St James's Park and make for the Duke's back door, where he would be awaiting her. Then shortly before the appointed time, she would leave him and hasten to her sister's quarters so as to be there when her coach arrived.

The Grosvenors' first coachman, in his sworn statement, told how he often used to take his mistress to Mr Scarborrow, the Duke's perfumer, immediately opposite Cumberland House. 'Whenever I did this, I usually noticed His Royal Highness standing at his window, obviously awaiting her arrival.' If he were not to be seen, she would order the coachman to proceed to some shop and to return by way of Pall Mall. Sometimes, he had to do this up to eight times a day until the Duke appeared. Also, whenever the man conveyed her from Grosvenor Square to Tavistock Street, she would tell him to go down St James's Street and along Pall Mall, whereas the quickest route was through Piccadilly. Again, when he had driven her to a haberdasher's in Coventry Street, she had insisted on his taking her there via Pall Mall, and they usually stopped at Scarborrow's twice a day so that she could collect some message from the Duke. One morning the perfumer forgot to pass on a note and ran after the coach and handed it to her.

> At the end of July and during August and September, 1769, the coachman had often driven Lady Grosvenor, accompanied by Miss Caroline Vernon, to the King's Palace at Kensington. He used to pull up at the gate in the yard which led into the gardens, and the ladies would enter the place that way. Occasionally, the Duke arrived shortly afterwards in a hackney-coach and followed them. When later Lady Grosvenor returned, she would always be 'very much disordered in her dress, her hair loose behind, ruffles and

apron very much tumbled'. Once the latter was torn. Every time, she seemed to have less powder in her hair when she came back from the palace than when she went in.

Thomas Dennison, one of Lady Grosvenor's footmen, testified that one evening in February, 1769, when she visited Almack's, her coach failed to arrive to take her away, so she ordered Dennison to call a hackney-chair. He did this and the Duke handed her into it. Her Ladyship then gave directions for the chairman to proceed to the Countess D'Onhoff's house. On the way the footman had caught sight of a chair following them till they reached the square, when it took another turning.

On arriving at the house, Dennison noticed that the Duke had reached it ahead of them by urging his chairmen to hurry and take a short cut, for the front door was open and he glimpsed His Highness hastening upstairs. Lady Grosvenor followed him in and they did not emerge again till about one o'clock in the morning. To his knowledge, the Duke had on many occasions met her Ladyship there.

Other people beside the Grosvenors' servants had learned of these meetings with the Duke. From her home in Notting Hill Lady Mary Coke wrote to Lady Strafford on Friday, September 18, that 'strange things' were being said of the latter's niece. 'I was told She came every day to Kensington Gardens for a very bad purpose.'[3]

Lord Grosvenor himself was fully aware that the affair with his wife had been resumed by the Duke on return from naval duties, but he took no steps to prevent it. There was one person, however, who was not content to allow things to remain as they were. This was the Duke's former mistress, whom Lady Grosvenor had supplanted, the Countess D'Onhoff. Hoping that the Duke might one day return to her, she pretended to stay friendly with the lovers, but secretly resented the use they had made of her and determined to have her revenge.

In early September, Lord Grosvenor received the following anonymous letter:

> If you have a mind to see your Wife go off with her gallant place yourself at the King's garden door at a little before Eight and you will see her and her little Sister go with him to his own back door a little way off and so return the same way at half an hour after nine. If you are fool enough to discover this information or not be thankful for it, you shall have no more. That's all at present from your humble Servant
>
> Jack Sprat

After studying this, the recipient felt obliged to take some action. So, at the suggested time, he arrived at Kensington Palace's garden gate, but he must have been seen, for he failed to catch Henrietta and Carry.

For a while, the lovers were more discreet, but they soon became foolhardy again. In October, Lord Grosvenor was sent another letter which read:

> I know you did as I instructed you to do some time ago concerning the Garden Gate, but they were alarmed and made their escape some other way to their married sister's. The little Devil is in all the schemes and goes into the garden with them over against your Windows continually playing fine pranks under your nose. I dare say they will meet there tomorrow Evening—Kensington Palace in the morning (where no servant is allowed to follow) is the constant practice. As you did not discover my first intelligence I shall give it to you, till you do, from your unknown friend
>
> Jack Sprat

The allusion to the garden 'over against your Windows' refers to the pleasure ground in the centre of Grosvenor Square. Matthew Stevens, Lord Grosvenor's butler, in his sworn evidence was to state that during October, 1769, he heard talk that Lady Grosvenor was being unfaithful to her husband, and became suspicious when she and her sister went walking in the Square garden after dusk and even stayed out in the rain. One evening, about October 9, when the ladies were there he noticed two gentlemen leaving by another gate. He recognized them as the Duke of Cumberland and his equerry, Captain Foulkes.

This letter as well as the earlier one was produced later in Westminster Hall when Lord Grosvenor claimed damages for criminal conversation from the Duke. The latter's affair with Henrietta had lasted longer than any other and showed no signs of ending. Indeed, it looked as if it would soon become the talk of the town. So, once Mrs Hill's child was born, Grosvenor refused to listen to any more of his wife's excuses for not going to Eaton. It was over a hundred and eighty miles from London and a long stay there, he hoped, might lead to the Duke, left on his own in London, finding consolation in some other woman's arms. Unfortunately, Richard made the mistake of not accompanying Henrietta, for he would rather be parted from his wife than from his racing at Newmarket.

CHAPTER SIX

Love in Easy Stages

On October 23, Lady Grosvenor and her two young sons, attended by Matthew Stevens, the butler, and other servants, left London at two o'clock in the afternoon on their way to Eaton. They broke their journey at the *White Hart*, St Albans. Usually, when travelling alone, because she feared attack from thieves in public inns, Henrietta saw that her personal maid slept in the next room so as to guard her. But here, contrary to custom, her ladyship selected accommodation for Hannah Birch and the boys at some distance away and banished them there, saying that they, like her, must be travel-weary and should go to bed early. She was to repeat these orders wherever she stayed on the road to Cheshire.

Meanwhile, the Duke of Cumberland had also left London, and arriving at the *White Hart* later the same afternoon, chose a bedroom next to the one occupied by Lady Grosvenor and which communicated with it through a door that was bolted on her side. After Hannah had laid out her mistress's night clothes and was out of the way, the Duke joined Henrietta.

Next morning, the happy lover left early for the *Saracen's Head* at Towcester in Northamptonshire, which he reached at two o'clock in the afternoon. He was accompanied by Robert Giddings, his gentleman porter, and his groom, John Swann. All three were in disguise and each had a pair of saddle bags upon his mount. The Duke was wrapped in a common drab-coloured coat, which he kept pulled up round his face, whilst a black scratch wig hid his own long fair hair. At the *Saracen's Head*, the pair pretended to be farmers, saying that the Duke's name was 'Jones' and Giddings's 'Tush', and they asked to be put up for the night. Later, Cumberland, unaware that a suspicious servant was spying on him, marked his door with chalk, and after a meal the two men retired.

In the evening, Lady Grosvenor arrived and chose a room for herself next to the one chalk-marked. Once children and servants were out of the way, the lovers were thus reunited. This ruse was repeated at the *Bull*, Coventry, the *Four Crosses*, Wolverhampton (where Giddings told the innkeeper that his companion's name was 'Squire Morgan', who was 'a little disordered in his senses', and that he was paid £200 a year for looking after him), and at the *Red Lion*, Whitchurch (where Giddings this time gave his own name as 'Trusty' and the young squire's as 'Griffiths' who was 'a little foolish, but a very good-natured man'.)

Jane Richardson, a maid servant at the *Red Lion* noticed that Mr Griffiths had white eyebrows and a scar on the right side of his face, caused she thought by a burn 'which might have happened from his being silly'. Trusty informed her that he had travelled 2,030 miles with his master who had to be constantly cared for. Jane noticed, as she put it later in her sworn statement, that the Duke had made 'the devil of a tumbled bed' and that she found the pillow at the very foot between the sheets. In view of their condition, she threw them 'with foul clothes' instead of keeping them for the next visitor 'upon their having been used but once'.

On Saturday morning, October 28, Lady Grosvenor and her party reached the country home at Eaton. The heavy-roofed Hall built by Vanbrugh in the William III style was three miles from Chester. She had spent five days on a journey which previously with her own horses had taken only four. This time she had travelled post, changing horses at every stage, and inventing some excuse at the inns to detain her so that she could spend the night with the Duke. He for the most part was obliged to travel on horseback so as to best conceal his real identity, and therefore could not travel so fast as she did in her carriage with post-horses.

The Duke and Giddings accompanied by John Swann, were now staying as Squire Griffiths and Mr Trusty at the *Falcon*, Chester. On that Saturday morning, they rode disguised to the public house kept by one Barbara Jones at Eccleston, a village within a mile of Eaton. Here, Giddings asked the way to 'the great gentleman's house'. She replied that if he meant my Lord Grosvenor's, they must keep to a certain road. After being shown it, they left their horses in Swann's care and set off on foot.

Towards four o'clock in the afternoon, Lady Grosvenor went out and met the Duke in the fields. Then at seven, when it was already dark, she went home, and the two men walked back to Eccleston, collected their mounts and rode off.

The same evening, Lady Grosvenor wrote to the blacksmith and ordered him to make duplicates of all the keys of the garden doors, gates to the park and meadow, and the door to the playhouse, a building about one hundred and fifty yards from the house. On receiving a message next morning that the work would take two or three days, she sent a footman, Edward Bennet, to borrow the housekeeper's keys, though she herself had a set. Then she ordered fires to be prepared in the saloon next to the garden and also in a closet situated in an isolated part of the house. For a number of nights following this, the outer door of the saloon was left open on her instructions, and a light placed on a stand by it.

The Duke and Robert Giddings retained their rooms at the *Falcon* until November 1. Those serving them at meals noticed that they spoke to each other in French when they did not wish to be understood. They would ride away in the morning, return in the afternoon for dinner, set out again immediately after the meal, coming back at ten for supper. On most of these excursions, they would leave their horses at the public house in Eccleston, where they pretended to be farmers from Staffordshire, speaking in such an unconvincing dialect that the locals thought them really highwaymen or horse-stealers. From here they would walk to Eaton.

During their stay the two men rode about the countryside in various disguises. They made a special visit to the Grosvenor seat at Halkin in Flintshire, where they asked to see and were shown his lordship's stud. Giddings told William Griffiths, the groom, that he was a servant of the French King and had a commission to buy two hundred horses, and offered to purchase some of Lord Grosvenor's. He spoke in broken English and in French, and the Duke acted as interpreter. On leaving, they told Griffiths they would return in three or four days' time, but did not. In his deposition later, Giddings claimed all this was done in fun.

At about three o'clock in the afternoon of Sunday, October 29, the day after her arrival, Lady Grosvenor was with the Duke in a field, when Thomas Dennison came in search of her to deliver a message from a curious neighbour who had called 'to enquire after her health and the children's'. The young footman was to state in his deposition: 'I saw her with a man, sitting down or lying down, I could not tell which. On seeing me, she suddenly got up and ran towards me.' The man, whom he believed to be the Duke of Cumberland, jumped up and 'skulked behind a tree'.

After Dennison had delivered the message, Lady Grosvenor gave him a reply for the caller, adding that she would not return home just yet but would take a little walk and then rest herself. Once the footman had departed, she rejoined the Duke and remained with him for over an hour, so alleged another servant who was spying on her.

That very evening, too, Henrietta went out at five and did not reappear until after seven. According to the lodgekeeper's wife, she continued doing this every day till the following Thursday: 'I did wonder at her going so much in the dirt and being out after dark. ... Once a red riding-dress that she had on was torn when she returned.'

Giddings in his sworn statement countered such innuendoes by claiming that, complying with the Duke's 'absolute orders', he always stayed near him when Lady Grosvenor was in the fields and was 'never out of their sight and hearing'. They might have sat on the grass 'when His Highness read a play or book to Lady Grosvenor'.

On Tuesday, October 31, an unfortunate incident occurred when Cumberland and his companion were on their way to Eaton. They were riding royal horses that had shoes marked with crowns and the letters 'G.R.' A loose shoe on the Duke's mount forced them to stop in a village where it was fastened by a man who had been an under farrier in the King's Mews and he recognized the marks. Suspecting that they had stolen some of the King's horses, he therefore had them apprehended, obliging the Duke to reveal his identity before they were allowed to continue on their journey.[1]

As a result of this it was thought wise to change inns, so next day the three men all moved five miles from Chester to the less frequented *Toll House* at Marford Hill, wearing new disguises and claiming to be farmers 'come into the country to buy fat cattle'. Then, after a meal, they went to a farmhouse on the road to Eaton and here the Duke and Giddings left John Swann to look after their horses whilst they walked as usual to the Grosvenor estate.

By now the 'Young Squire' must have tired of walking, for the following morning he and 'his guardian Farmer Tush' rode all the way from the *Toll House* to Eaton, where some of the watchful servants detected him and Lady Grosvenor lying behind some bushes in the park for four hours, while faithful Giddings stood at a discreet distance from them holding the two mounts.

Then came the unexpected news that Lord Grosvenor had sent John Anderton, his travelling groom, to Eaton with orders that his horses should meet him that Friday, November 3, at Whitchurch to bring him home. On learning this, his wife at once told the Duke and it was agreed that, in order to avoid discovery, he should set off that afternoon for London. So on returning to the *Toll House*, 'Guardian Tush' took the innkeeper aside and confided that the 'Young Squire' had received an urgent message that 'his father lay a-dying'. They feared he would be dead before they could get to him, but they liked the place vastly and would come again when his affairs were settled.

After the lodgers had left, the innkeeper's wife told her husband that, like the locals, she was sure they were highwaymen in disguise, for the three men had brought five hats, one of which was laced, and four different riding coats with them, and had changed clothes with one another every time they went out.

The reason for Lord Grosvenor's visit to Eaton was that he had received another letter from 'Jack Sprat' on returning to Grosvenor Square from Newmarket on Monday, October 30.

> Once more and no more if I have not often enough pointed out ways for you to be convinced of the Truth, I am not your Friend but if you have not a mind you will take no Notice perhaps of a certain person that is gone in disguise and ly's at every Inn where She does. Examine your servants and they will be more able to tell you of his constant attendance. He is now about your house and Gardens in the Country.
>
> Jack Sprat

A friend of his lordship's, Edward Toms, happened to be dining with him that evening. Toms, one of the office of trumpets of the King's household, was interested in horses, and had attended York races with Grosvenor that summer. Over the meal, Richard showed him the anonymous letter and asked for assistance in catching his wife's gallant. Toms agreed to help, and next day at noon, together with Richard's brother, Thomas Grosvenor, they set off for Eaton, which the trio reached the following Friday evening, November 3. Thomas lived at 13 Cavendish Square near Camilla D'Onhoff.

Following his arrival, Lord Grosvenor, without Henrietta's knowledge, questioned the servants and others, and they told him how she had gone out in all weathers and often after dusk, and had been seen alone with a man and sometimes two men. Hannah Birch, her personal maid, informed him that after these outings her ladyship's stockings and petticoats 'both upper and under' were remarkably dirty as high as her knees with field dirt or clay, which they never used to be before.

On their reunion, as he later told his lawyer, Richard Grosvenor found his wife 'in visible confusion' and observed she was 'continually going out of one room into another'. He summoned the butler, Matthew Stephens, who had accompanied her from London to Eaton, and showed him in private the anonymous letter.

'Stephens told me he was afraid such information was true and then recounted to me the behaviour and conduct of my wife. He mentioned the reports about the men in disguise having been seen about my house, garden, park and fields. I ordered him to send for his brother, Mr John Stephens, who was the adjutant of the Cheshire militia, and when the latter arrived I acquainted him with the whole matter.' Grosvenor then asked the adjutant to trace all those who had met or seen the men and to question them closely. This he proceeded to do with speed and success, and reported the results to Grosvenor, who now gave instructions that letters sent by his wife for posting should be intercepted.

On November 17 the butler was handed a letter addressed to 'The Honble Miss Vernon at St James's Palace, London'. Matthew Stephens immediately sent a servant with it to Lord Grosvenor, who had gone with Edward Toms to show him his horses at Halkin. The two men were actually on the road returning to Eaton in a post-chaise when the messenger met them.

On reaching the village of Harwarden, they paused for refreshment and Lord Grosvenor asked Toms to open the envelope and hand him the contents. These proved to be as expected, a letter to Caroline Vernon and another for the Duke, which Grosvenor read, then asked Toms to copy.

In the first, to her 'dear little sweet Carry', Henrietta wrote that her husband was away and had left her with his brother, Thomas Grosvenor. 'They are all pestering me to come to supper. God, curse them. I wish them at Jerricoe. First one peeping their head in, then the other, and Mr Grosvenor shut up taking snuff in my dressing room; I'm stole into my Bedchamber *coute se qui coute* I'll finish my stupid Letter. I promise you a much longer soon. I hope you amuse yourself well in London. Poor little Carry I do love you dearly ... will you, my love, be so kind to let me trouble you to send the enclosed?'

The letter 'to her dearest Soul' said that it seemed ages since she had heard from him 'but Minutes count for years with those that love'. She was upset to hear that he still had 'a little cough'. He did not take enough care of himself. 'I wish I could take care of you indeed.' She had been entertained by 'a very odd discourse' about her husband with his brother who had complained about his giving up 'his whole time, attention and fortune to horses' and was 'worse and worse infatuated than ever about them and could never talk upon any other subject . . . and would lose all his acquaintance but Jockeys'.

She could not help but laugh at Thomas Grosvenor's description of Richard's behaviour when at home, as it was so true. 'For, says he, he will sit for half an hour with his eyes fixed on a Table or Chair and then apply to Toms or anybody that is by, "Do you know what Mare such a Filly was out of?" or "Can you tell what Horse such a Colt was got by?" or "By God, I have got the best stud in England. Nobody will have any horses to run but me very soon!"' If anybody then tried to change the conversation he would become 'as cross as any thing for half an hour, and then fall fast asleep'.

This was so exact a picture of her husband that she was resolved the Duke should have it. One can imagine that reading such disparaging references to himself must have proved galling to Lord Grosvenor. He then went home, where on November 20, Matthew Stephens handed him another envelope addressed to Caroline, which her sister had asked the butler to post. This, too, contained a further letter for the Duke in which she told him how her personal maid had confided that some of the servants had said it was widely known that he had visited Eaton. 'I denyed it and said I would acquaint my Lord and make everybody prove what they had said. Upon which she turned pale ... and said it was from one person she had heard it, begged it might not be mentioned unless she heard more. This makes me hope she made the most of it, but yet I fear it has been talked much of by her naming so many particular facts.'

She went on that her 'dear Friend' was to act as he thought best regarding his suggestion that he should pay her a brief return visit. They would in any case see each other before long, for her husband had told his brother in her presence that they would all be in London in about a month. Nothing would make her so unhappy as not to see him, but at the same time they had better not do anything imprudent. She left the decision to him. 'Pray let me have a few lines in Lemon Juice by Carry to tell me. I wish I could find a method for you to write in ink. I'll consider about it night and day, but I fear I can't. But really I make out the Lemon Juice very well.' She ended: 'What Joy will it be to me when I can see my Dear Soul! *Bon Soir.*'

Lord Grosvenor had copies of this correspondence made by Edward Toms, then compared with the originals by him and Matthew Stephens, who both signed the transcripts acknowledging they had done this. The letters were posted to Caroline.

At about eight a.m. on Saturday, December 2, the Duke and his equerry, Captain Foulkes, both disguised, reached Chester from London in a post-chaise and took another to the *Toll House* at Marford Hill where Robert Giddings and John Swann, who had arrived there two days earlier, were awaiting them with the news that Lord Grosvenor was away again visiting his stud so Cumberland could safely meet Henrietta in the fields where she would be looking out for him. So, after a quick breakfast, the eager lover and Giddings set out for Eaton and did not return until dusk.

Nathaniel Abraham, a farm labourer, later made a sworn statement that whilst he was mending a fence he saw Lady Grosvenor walk along the side of a field, descend into a ditch, climb over the hedge and join a man under a tree, where they sat closely linked for a very long time.

Early next morning the Duke made once more for Eaton and stayed until four in the afternoon with Henrietta. Then came news that Lord Grosvenor had returned sooner than anticipated from Halkin, so after dining at the *Toll House* the Duke and his party started on the way back to London.

CHAPTER SEVEN

'The Adventure at St Albans'

Three days later, Lady Grosvenor gave a cover addressed to Caroline Vernon to Matthew Stephens for posting. This contained the usual *billet-doux* for the Duke, and was dealt with as before. The note to Carry, dated Tuesday, December 5, began by saying that a letter just arrived from her had made Henrietta 'very uneasy'. The report mentioned in it that she and her husband had parted was false gossip spread by some spiteful person, and it was ridiculous of their mother, Lady Harriot, to have paid any attention to such tittle-tattle.

Henrietta assured her sister that she intended behaving in a manner 'as will be quite proper and clever' on returning to London. Her 'poor Friend' had seen her only twice, and very prudently had then told her that he and his companions would not come back again 'for fear of danger'.

Apparently, Caroline must have complained that her servants had become suspicious about leaving letters for the Duke at Scarborrow's, his perfumer, and collecting his for forwarding to Lady Grosvenor. 'I would not have you run a risk for me for the world.' She thought that 'as it was only now and then it would not be suspected'. But in view of Carry's misgivings, she assured her she would not be seeking her services in this way much longer. 'I'd lay anything some of the Grosvenors have been at Mama canting, the Devil take such deceit, and told about your going out with me. Never mind she can't prove anything. Don't be frighted for that's impossible. Let her suspicions be what they will, for she is very credulous ...'

In the letter she enclosed for the Duke, Henrietta wrote how the trouble he had taken to travel such a distance thoroughly convinced her of his love. It worried her to think of his making the 'cold dreadful' journey 'in those post chaises—how starving it must be—I'm so in fear it should hurt your breast'. (All his life the Duke had trouble with his right lung.) The best thing they could do about her husband was to make him believe all was over between them. 'We have really blinded him. For some time at least he had no proof about us, and I hope to God that by degrees his suspicions will be lulled and then we may form some plans for our meeting. . . .'

Inside the flap of the envelope Henrietta wrote, referring to Foulkes the Duke's equerry's own love affair, 'to advise him not to mind the old people' and 'to persuade her to run away with him. It will be delightful. I wish to goodness they would'.

Once more, on December 9, Lady Grosvenor handed a letter for her sister to the butler for posting. This contained another for Cumberland—and the contents of both were copied. In the note to Carry, she informed her that Richard would be leaving for London on the coming Wednesday as he had to visit Newmarket on racing business. She would follow with the children 'about Monday or Tuesday'.

To her royal lover, Henrietta also gave 'the delightful news' of her return a few days after her husband's departure. 'He said he desir'd I stay till then as he would only stay one day in Town & then go to Newmarket ... Only think he said Yesterday he had so many Horses & so much to do at Newmarket he believ'd he should go there every fortnight.' This would give them many opportunities for meeting during his absence.

Lord Grosvenor delayed setting out on his journey for a day. Before doing so, accompanied by Edward Toms, he secretly instructed Matthew Stephens and others due to attend his wife on the way south to keep a close watch on her. John Anderton, a groom, who went early each morning to the post office at Chester for letters, was to take any addressed to her to Mr Vigars, the steward, who lived at Eaton Green, a quarter of a mile away.

Meanwhile, Robert Giddings had been sent by Cumberland to Chester with orders to learn from Lady Grosvenor personally the exact time of her departure. Immediately on arrival on Friday the 15th, he posted a letter to her, signed 'Trusty', in which he wrote that he would be at his 'Old Lodgings every Day about twelve and one o'clock' to receive any message from her.

At eight o'clock next morning, Anderton collected this letter and took it, as arranged, to Vigars, who opened it in Stephens's presence, copied the contents, then delivered it to Lady Grosvenor. Anderton was told by Vigars to keep a look-out for 'Trusty'. At midday, he noticed a man waiting by the lodge gates. It was Giddings. Soon after one o'clock Henrietta came out for a stroll with some friends.

Catching sight of him, she made the excuse she wanted to feed the cattle and, leaving them, crossed a hedge, a stile and a ploughed field until she reached a shed—the 'old lodgings' mentioned in Giddings's note. He was already there to hand her a letter from the Duke and to receive one in exchange. Then she rejoined her companions, and 'Trusty' went back to Chester and from thence to London.

On the previous day, December 15, Carry had written at length and in near-panic from St James's to Henrietta. She had not received her sister's last letter till the 13th and wondered if someone could have intercepted and read it. 'I am in affliction not to be described.' A story was widespread that she had helped Henrietta to have assignations with the Duke. 'I find the Queen & the Princess of Wales [George III's mother] have heard me censured in this curs'd Affair and speak with anger about me. ... But what is worse I have enclosed a paragraph that was in the News Papers to Day from which you will learn how scandalously you are talked of. It frights me to death. ... I am watched every time I stir. I *frankly* tell you absolutely let me never hear anything more concerning your Friend, as to my being your Bearer any longer I will not. I wish very much for your coming to Town as that is the only thing to appease the wicked world—the seeing you and your Lord living amicably together.'

But this jeremiad came too late to Chester for the addressee to receive it, as she had already begun her journey.

Meanwhile, 'Trusty' had delivered Henrietta's note to the Duke in London. Though we do not know its contents, she must have suggested that they spend the night together at St Albans. As a result, early on Thursday, December 21, he left the capital, attended only by Giddings, and arrived in a hackney post-chaise at the *White Hart*. St Albans, towards eleven in the morning. His greatcoat had its cape drawn up round the lower part of his face, whilst the heavy fringe of a new black wig half hid his eyes.

After breakfast in the parlour, the Duke said he felt unwell and must lie down. He asked for the bedroom he had slept in on his previous visit, but, on being told it was occupied, chose instead one directly opposite that where Lady Grosvenor had rested on the journey to Eaton.

On receiving from his steward the copy of Giddings's letter, Lord Grosvenor had concluded the Duke would endeavour to meet Henrietta somewhere on the road to London, and was strengthened in this belief when on enquiry he learned Cumberland had left town that very morning. The peer told John Stephens, who was with him, what he suspected and arranged for the man to join his brother and assist him in obtaining evidence for a divorce.

Stephens alighted at the *White Hart* at about half-past five, soon after Lady Grosvenor and her party reached it, and, taking Matthew aside, explained why he had come. The butler then told John that his mistress had demanded and been given her former bedroom. They decided it was likely the Duke was already hiding in the inn. On enquiry, they learned two gentlemen had recently arrived, one of whom had behaved oddly over the location of his bedroom, and whom the innkeeper thought 'out of his mind' and probably there to consult a 'a famous mad doctor' in St Albans.

Confident now that here was their chance to catch the philandering couple, the butler took the opportunity that evening, whilst Lady Grosvenor was having supper, to bore two holes in her door and then carefully stop them with paper.

Immediately after the meal, Henrietta retired upstairs, where she found the bed being warmed by Sarah Gilby, a maid, who was astonished when her ladyship looked under it and into the closet to make sure nobody was hidden there. Downstairs, Matthew had made her a negus, as was his custom. When he carried it into the parlour and found her gone, he went up with it. She barely opened the door, took the drink, then locked herself in.

Returning towards half-past ten, the butler removed the paper from the holes and listened. He heard two voices very plainly, one of which was hers and the other the Duke's—and both came from the direction of the bed, suggesting that the pair were lying on it. He roused his brother John, the under-butler, Robert Belton, and the footmen, Thomas Dennison and Edward Bennet, all of whom also listened.

Whilst they were debating what to do, John Anderton, Lord Grosvenor's groom, came up and whispered that he had just been informed the Duke had ordered a chaise to be ready to take him away at two o'clock in the morning.

It was then about eleven o'clock. Determined to lose no time, Matthew Stephens procured an iron poker and he and Bennet attacked the door, which gave way at the hinges. 'Who's there? What's the matter?' the couple kept calling from within. The room was in darkness except for the firelight, which revealed the Duke, with his waistcoat loose, sitting on the bedside next to Lady Grosvenor, who had her dress unfastened, exposing her bare breasts. She jumped to her feet and ran in dismay towards the door communicating with the next room. In doing so, she fell down and the butler went to her assistance. She said reproachfully: 'I suppose you think you have done a very clever thing.' He replied: 'My lady, I am sincerely sorry,' to which she returned: 'I am sure you are.'

The Duke hastily buttoned his waistcoat and, rising, stood for a moment undecided what to do. According to the evidence later given by Dennison in court, he looked 'very much confused, like a statue, and could not speak'. But when he did, he said: 'Gentlemen, I hope you will not hurt me.' Then, suddenly managing to evade them, he ran off into his own room from the threshold of which he announced: 'Take notice I am not in my Lady Grosvenor's room,' to which the butler answered: 'No, you are not now, but you were a minute ago.' The Duke retorted: 'I'll take my Bible's oath that I was not in there.'

Matthew Stephens asked him who he was, but he made no answer, so the butler called in the rest of the servants, who all declared they knew the man to be the Duke of Cumberland. When lighted candles had been brought in by the inn's waiters, Stephens examined the bed and later claimed to have found the sheets very tumbled and dents in the pillows as if made by two heads.

After the scene in the bedchamber, the Duke and Robert Giddings left the inn and hastened to the *Woolpack*, where they hired a chaise and went back to London.

Next day, Lady Grosvenor's two children (the youngest of whom was only six months old), as well as seven out of her eight servants and the coach were taken from her, so attended only by her personal maid she departed in a post-chaise for London towards four in the afternoon. A crowd gathered outside the inn to try and catch a glimpse of her, but Henrietta disappointed their curiosity by wearing a black velvet mask, and once seated within the vehicle drew down the blinds and kept them lowered until she arrived at her town house. Lord Grosvenor, however, refused to allow her to continue living there, and by his orders lodgings were taken for her in Bond Street, where she moved without the children.

News of the scandal spread fast. Lady Mary Coke, who was abroad in Aix, recorded in her *Journal* for Thursday, January 11, 1770, that she had received a letter from Lady Greenwich with a full account of 'the Adventure at St Albans'. She comments: 'So Ly Grosvenor is at last catched! I'm sorry Ld Strafford has so unworthy a Niece, and very sincerely pity her Mother, whose affection had blinded her to all her faults. I wish it may not be a disadvantage to her unmarried Sisters. As to herself, I think I am generous when I say I don't rejoice at her present distress, for tho' I am persuaded a Person who is gone [the Duke of York] never consider'd her but in the light of a Woman of the Town, yet it gave her an opportunity of behaving with great impertinence to me, which however I kept to myself. Ld Grosvenor has had great patience, for I believe no one can doubt, that if he had taken proper precautions he might have had a divorce much sooner.'[1]

Four days later, Lady Mary notes, having heard from London that Lady Harriot Vernon had seen her daughter, Lady Grosvenor, and adds: 'I cannot imagine why, for if the accounts are true that She stands at the window with a pocket glass to place her hair in order, I don't think there is much reason to believe She has any sense of her crime or stands in need of consolation.'[2]

The King on the contrary was certainly in need of consolation. He regarded his youngest living brother's behaviour as inexcusable and as damaging not only to the royal image but also to the whole of society. When, in January 1770, His Majesty opened Parliament, he began: 'My Lords and Gentlemen, it is with much concern that I find myself obliged to open this session with acquainting you that distemper among the horned cattle has lately broken out in this kingdom.'

'Farmer' George was, of course, referring to livestock, and Edmund Burke later complained that he was treating Parliament 'like an assembly of cow doctors'. Lord Grosvenor and the Prime Minister, the Duke of Grafton, who the previous March had divorced his wife for adultery, however, were it is said taken aback by this unexpected beginning and bowed to each other as if to say he must mean us.

CHAPTER EIGHT

The Trial

Lord Grosvenor, having played the part of the complaisant husband for so long, was now swift to take action, both against the Duke claiming substantial damages for 'criminal conversation' with his wife, and against her for a divorce.

On February 3, 1770, Cumberland was seen at the Registry of the Bishop of London, examining the letters in his handwriting which were being exhibited as evidence in the divorce proceedings.[1] Then on March 1 when these opened at Doctors' Commons, Lady Grosvenor's counsel asked for a postponement to which the plaintiffs unsuccessfully objected. Both, however, joined in a request, granted by the Judge, that he order 'letters, written messages, and other informations relative to the affairs of Lord and Lady Grosvenor should on no account be communicated by copies or otherwise to any person except the immediate agents, previous to the determination of the cause in litigation'.[2] But, despite this prohibition, copies of all the correspondence between Henrietta and her lover somehow came into the possession of the *Middlesex Journal* and were published in its columns. Then pamphleteers reproduced them, some even adding spurious letters to add colour to their exaggerated accounts of the affair.

During the anxious period of waiting, Henrietta's mother continued to support her daughter. Lady Mary Coke wrote from Notting Hill on June 15 to Lady Strafford that Lady Harriot 'still affirms She believes her Daughter innocent: 'twill be happy if She can persuade others to be of that opinion'.[3] Next day, Lady Mary mentions that when she dined with the Duchess of Norfolk her hostess 'shew'd her in the *Middlesex Journal* a long letter of the Duke of Cumberland's: it seems all H.R.H. correspondence with Ly Grosvenor is to be printed in that paper: one of her Ladyship's follow'd in the next & though I never had any great idea of her delicacy, I own the indecency of her style quite shocked me'.[4]

Some eleven days later, on June 27, Lady Mary records that Lady Harriot looked well and appeared in good spirits, which surprised her 'at this time, when her Daughter's unhappy conduct is publishing every week in the *Middlesex Journal*'. She wonders whether Lady Grosvenor's maternal uncle, Lord Strafford, has seen them 'for tho' I believe his opinion of Ly Grosvenor was not much better than mine, yet I think they will amaze him'.[5]

On Thursday morning, July 5, at eight o'clock, being the first sitting after term, there came before Lord Mansfield in the Court of King's Bench 'the long depending and much celebrated cause,' as the *London Evening Post* phrased it, between Lord Grosvenor and his Royal Highness the Duke of Cumberland for *crim. con.* with Lady Grosvenor; the damages being laid at one hundred thousand pounds, the equivalent of several millions in today's values. The trial was held in Westminster Hall.

Apart from the huge sum claimed, and that the defendant was the King's own brother, the fact that the love letters seized by Lord Grosvenor or copied at his behest were still being published in the *Middlesex Journal* had thoroughly roused the prurient interest of many. Others were outraged, such as that close friend of the King and Queen, Mrs Delany, who, corresponding with a Miss Dewes on July 22, declared: 'I have been shocked with reading Lady Grosvenor and the Duke of Cumberland's letters. Such folly and wickedness and withal so *vulgar*; and as to the sister at St James's she makes a sad and pitiable figure, and if she is not an idiot I think she must have as little virtue as her wretched sister. But leave this sad company to their own remorses . . .'[6]

A Scot named Murray before being raised to the peerage, Lord Mansfield has been described by John Brooke in his life of George III as 'one of the greatest judges of modern times'. His decisions were regarded as wise ones, his wit was devoid of malice and his voice was pleasant and unaffected. Of probing look, he had the gift of detecting legal trickery, of not being sidetracked by misleading arguments. He would not allow justice to be strangled by red tape, and was tireless in search of the truth. Thanks to his remarkable memory, he took few notes and rarely consulted them.

He also had a sense of humour. A bishop founded an almshouse at his own expense for twenty-five poor women, and young Mr Murray was invited to suggest what inscription should be placed over the portal of the place. He wrote down the following:

Under this roof
The Lord Bishop of—
keeps
no less than 25 women.

Mansfield was an excellent psychologist. Once when Bishop Trevor of Durham, a friend of his, was ill he called to see him. While he was with Trevor's secretary, the physician, looking alarmingly pale and too feeble to stand, arrived in a sedan chair carried by two able-bodied chairmen who wanted to convey him upstairs in it to his patient. The Bishop's secretary, fearing that his master would be depressed by such a sight, begged Lord Mansfield to intervene and go up first. 'By no means, let him go, you know nothing of human nature,' the Judge retorted. 'The Bishop will be put in good spirits on seeing any one in a worse condition than himself.'

Mansfield was right. The doctor had no sooner left with his chairmen than the Bishop, sitting up in bed, said with a smile: 'I fear the crows will soon have my excellent physician.' But he was mistaken. The Bishop died a few weeks later. The doctor lived on for many years.

Another example of Mansfield's insight into human nature occurred when controversy raged over whether or not Wilkes should be prosecuted. He commented to some friends: 'I am decidedly against the prosecution. His consequence will die away if you will let him alone; but, by public notice of him, you will increase his importance; the very thing he covets, and has in full view.' Had this very sensible advice been followed, the King would have saved himself a great deal of trouble and not lost popularity as he did.

This was the Judge called upon to decide a case which closely concerned the Sovereign and public respect for the monarchical system.

Leading counsel for Lord Grosvenor was Alexander Wedderburn, a brilliant Scottish advocate, who as an M.P. changed his party from Tory to Whig and back again for the sake of his own advancement, eventually attaining his lifelong ambition in 1793 when he became Lord Chancellor. George III disapproved of such tergiversation and wrote on his death that he had 'left no great rogue behind him'.

The Duke of Cumberland was defended by John Dunning, who was M.P. for Calne and had been until the beginning of that year Solicitor-General, and who was regarded as one of the most powerful orators of the day, though he was ungainly, had a husky voice and a Devonian accent. It was he, who in April, 1780, was to propose the famous motion, carried by the Commons, that the influence of the Crown 'has increased, is increasing, and ought to be diminished'.

Wedderburn, opening for the plaintiff, argued that the damage done was all the greater on account of the defendant's rank. He referred to two other cases in support of his contention, and then described how the Duke on visits to Towcester, Coventry, Marford Hill, Whitchurch, Chester and St Albans, in order to meet Lady Grosvenor, assumed, at different times, various aliases. Witnesses would testify that Lady Grosvenor was carried on several occasions near the back door of the Duke's house in Pall Mall, where she went in and stayed for a considerable while. They would also testify regarding a certain event at St Albans.

Counsel went on that, before calling witnesses, he felt he should read to the court some letters written by Lady Grosvenor to the Duke of Cumberland, and from him to her. These were such as could pass only between persons who had laid aside all reserve. He would like particular attention to be paid to the passage where the Duke mentioned the incident of 'the dear little couch'. The obvious interpretation of this would be supported by such evidence that left little doubt of Lord Grosvenor's dishonour being complete.

Sarcastically Wedderburn observed: 'The seeming simplicity of the style in which these letters are written is also convincing evidence of the couple's guilt. One cannot suppose that a Prince so eminently distinguished as His Royal Highness is for his great abilities and very liberal education would condescend to write in a manner so simple and so void of meaning, if it were not to answer the purpose of intrigue.'

Counsel told the court how Lord Grosvenor had discovered the letters, then he read them aloud, deliberately drawing attention to the misspellings and faulty grammar in the Duke's so as to ridicule him, which, as the *London Evening Post* put it, 'occasioned great entertainment to the whole Court, as they may truly be said to add to the novelty of epistolary writing'.

After Wedderburn had spent nearly an hour doing this he told the Jury that it would be given them in evidence that His Royal Highness had assumed the fictitious name of Morgan, a young country Squire not very sound in his understanding, that he had taken down with him to St Albans a servant, who went by the name of Trusty, for the purpose of 'facilitating this amour'.

Plaintiff's counsel contained caustically: 'What agony of mind it must have caused His Royal Highness for one of his elevated station to associate himself not for one or two but several days with a mere servant, to pass under a fictitious name and forego all those honours and distinctions usually paid to his rank. Surely he could have only endured all this because he was obsessed with the pursuit of a dishonourable scheme.'

Wedderburn pointed out to the Jury that there were two considerations they must have constantly in their minds. 'The first is the very great quality of the defendant and the second the irreparable injury sustained by the plaintiff. As to the former, no given sum could be punishment sufficient, for the elevated rank and situation of life the Duke sustains should the more deter him from setting a bad example to the more subordinate classes of society.'

Counsel stressed that though the damages might be thought to be laid high, yet, as it was all the punishment the law could inflict, none of it ought to. be remitted, as they had it now in their power to convince His Royal Highness in particular, and men of rank in general 'that the laws of England in the hands of a British Jury are always superior to situation and connections'. He likewise hoped that this would in future direct His Royal Highness to nobler pursuits than the seduction of the wife of a Peer.

'And now, Gentlemen, I shall leave you in possession of these sentiments, and only direct one thing more to your consideration.' This was that on their verdict depended the chastity and honour of the fair sex, the sanctity of marriage and the custody of British morals.

Wedderburn then called his witnesses. The first, the Rev. Mr Taylor, Lord Grosvenor's chaplain, said he had solemnized the marriage of Miss Henrietta Vernon with his patron in 1764 and that they had lived 'happily and well together from that time until the present affair'. He was followed by the housekeeper to the Countess D'Onhoff, Mrs Elizabeth Sutton, her husband, Samuel, and the Countess's postillion, John Bourne. The Countess herself refused to appear as a witness for the plaintiff, neither would Mrs Reda, the milliner. Next, Lady Grosvenor's two footmen, Thomas Dennison and Edward Bennet, and Robert Giddings, who, whilst admitting that he had accompanied the Duke on his journey to Eaton, insisted that he had observed nothing to suggest that his master was having criminal conversation with Lady Grosvenor.

Other witnesses were John Burton, a waiter at the *Saracen's Head*,

Towcester, Jane Richardson of the *Red Lion*, Whitchurch (who now mentioned what she had not stated in her earlier deposition that the Duke's bed was not only 'most exceedingly tumbled' but that 'there were she did not know how many pins in the bed'), Mary Spencer, mistress of the same inn, John Jones, who kept the *Toll House* on Marford Hill, Matthew Stephens and his brother John, and several others who all corroborated the discovery at St Albans of which as evidence of *crim. con.*, Wedderburn made the most. When the butler testified, someone called out: 'It was a pity to disturb them when they were going to prince-making.'

Opening the defence, John Dunning said: 'That Lady Grosvenor and His Royal Highness the Duke of Cumberland formed an imprudent and, if you please, a violent attachment to each other, or a violent passion for each other: all this may be true, and yet criminal intercourse may never have passed between them, as the action supposes.' The evidence produced by Wedderburn, far from giving positive proof of *crim. con.*, did not even qualify as circumstantial evidence, and if admitted upon this occasion would open a door 'for many artifices that might be practised upon the unwary by artful women in combination with their husbands'. His learned friend based his conclusions on the extravagant professions of love to be found in the correspondence between the Duke and Lady Grosvenor. He thought the reverse was true. 'The language of lovers after enjoyment is generally very languid and spiritless. These letters are too ardent and too passionate to have been written by lovers whose passions had been previously gratified. I will allow the Duke of Cumberland and Lady Grosvenor have been imprudent, blamable, inexcusable, and censurable. I can suppose every thing to have passed between them but the criminal act upon which this action is founded.'

Dunning then called exculpatory witnesses. Mrs Langford, mistress of the *White Hart* at St Albans, said that when she entered Lady Grosvenor's room, the bed looked to her as if it had been sat upon by somebody, expecially on that side next to the fire, but not at all as if lain upon. Similar evidence was given by her chamber-maid, Sarah Gilby, and a waiter, Thomas Robinson. Mrs Langford added that Lady Grosvenor appeared 'much in the same dress as when she came in, and her head dress in no way disordered'.

Needless to say, counsel for the plaintiff, Alexander Wedderburn, did his best to discredit these three witnesses with veiled suggestions that they had been bribed by Lady Grosvenor's brother.

Mr Skinner, John Dunning's junior, spoke next. Even allowing for argument's sake that her ladyship might have been guilty, he said he had several witnesses to prove that Lord Grosvenor was the first violator of the rights of marriage. By Lord Mansfield's direction, leading questions only were put to them.

Mrs Boisgermain said she had known Lord Grosvenor ever since May, 1768. 'I first saw him in Jermyn-street, at a staymaker's, where lodgings were taken for me by a Mrs Mullman in order for me to see Lord Grosvenor in them. I had particular connections with him as man and wife ... I lay in in April, 1769. The child was his. It died within a month. He sent me a twenty pound note.'

When cross-examined, Mrs Boisgermain acknowledged that she knew Mr Giddings, the Duke's porter, very well. He had come to her lodgings to bring her the subpoena. 'I told him the whole story some time ago, and have come here merely to serve Lady Grosvenor and to support the cause of the whole of my sex. I am married to a Captain of a French ship and have expectations from a brother of my husband.'

Mrs Boisgermain was followed by four other women of the town, Mary How, Mrs Waters, Mrs Tremilly and Mary Smith. The last, when asked the usual question as to what acquaintance she had had with Lord Grosvenor, replied: 'A very intimate one.'

'Did you eat together?'

'Yes.'

'Did you lie together?'

'Yes.'

'Any further connection?'

'Yes, in every respect like man and wife.'

When these witnesses had been examined, Alexander Wedderburn replied in a speech that lasted a full hour. There was an outburst of laughter when he observed: 'However aggravating the circumstances are otherwise, one cannot charge His Royal Highness with intriguing merely for the sake of intrigue, as the incoherency of his letters, plainly prove him to be really a lover.'

At about half-past six Lord Mansfield began his summing up. 'Gentlemen of the Jury, this action is brought against the defendant for what is called criminal conversation with the plaintiff's wife.' Unless they were satisfied that the precise act of carnal copulation had occurred, they must find a verdict for the former. If on the other hand, they found for the plaintiff, then in assessing damages they must ignore the rank of either party 'for an injury done to the bed of any commoner of England is as much an injury to him and to his domestic peace, as to a peer of the realm ... and, therefore, the situation of the parties is not the measure by which damages are to be governed; but they are to be governed by the nature of the cause, upon the evidence'.

Lord Mansfield went on to tell the Jury that there was no difference between adultery of the husband and wife in point of law. 'A woman may have a divorce for adultery from a husband in the ecclesiastical court, as well as the husband a divorce from the wife; but if one sues for a divorce and the other recriminates, by the rule of the ecclesiastical law, no divorce can be given. They are both guilty, and the law does not interpose.'

This agreed with Mr Skinner's contention during his speech that though the charge might be proved against the defendant, the plaintiff could not be aggrieved 'because he had himself been guilty of the same crime he laid to the charge of the defendant'. Counsel had gone on to give 'this friendly piece of advice' that should the plaintiff make 'this trial a ground to institute a cause of divorce in Doctors' Commons, he had no probability of gaining it'.

The Judge's speech went on until a quarter to eight, when the Jury retired and he adjourned the court to his house in Bloomsbury Square. At ten o'clock, the Jury left Westminster Hall and proceeded in four coaches to the residence where they found the defendant guilty and awarded Lord Grosvenor £10,000 damages and costs, a tenth of the amount claimed. The crowd which had collected outside cheered when they learned the verdict.

The damages were much lower than the Duke had expected, but he did not have the money to pay them and made no attempt to do so. The fact that he had pretended to be simple in the head to try and disarm suspicion whilst clandestinely meeting Lady Grosvenor was a present to the newspapers, which named him the Royal Idiot. When Cumberland asked Samuel Foote what he thought about the love-letters read in court, the actor replied: 'Think, please, Your Highness, it is impossible to think about them, as you never once thought when you wrote them.'

Away from the Duke, Foote jested about the affair to his cronies and a witty comment of his was soon being circulated. 'The present King created Sir Richard Grosvenor a Lord and his brother created him a Cuckold; dignities somewhat similar according to these times, and the more as they had both tipt his head with gold, the first with his coronet, the last with his horns.'

Mauled by the press, ridiculed in cartoons, clubs and coffee houses, Cumberland never lost his equanimity. All Foote's barbed jests failed to affect his admiration for the actor's performance, even when he came into the Green Room at the Haymarket one night and pleasantly remarked: 'Well, Foote, here I am, ready as usual to swallow all your good things'—and was insulted instead of being thanked. The actor-playwright, known as the English Aristophanes, mercilessly retorted: 'Upon my soul, your Royal Highness must have a most excellent digestion, for I never hear that you bring any up again.'

According to the papers, when Lady Grosvenor heard the result of the case she exclaimed: 'Moderate damages, indeed! If my Lord does not sue for a divorce, I will, for I cannot be more exposed, and then I shall have my person as free as I will.'

'Civilian' argued that the damages should have been what the plaintiff had demanded. In *Free Thoughts on Seduction, Adultery and Divorce, with Reflection on the Gallantry of Princes* this anonymous pamphleteer accused Lord Mansfield of misdirecting the Jury and quoted a passage from Sir William Blackstone's *Commentaries on the Laws of England* where he declared that the quantum of damages in such cases 'should be proportioned to the rank and fortune, both of plaintiff and defendant' (Volume 3, page 139).

'Civilian' cynically suggested that in awarding low damages the Jury may have been influenced by the belief that the Duke would obtain whatever he had to pay from the Treasury, 'so that it would be impolitic and unjust to tax the already overburdened public to support the extravagant and lawless pleasures of a prince of the blood'. The writer also alleged it was 'confidently asserted' that Lord Grosvenor had been offered and had 'nobly refused' £50,000 from 'a certain quarter to stop the prosecution'; and he went on to paint a grim picture of the punishment that might have been meted out to the Duke had he lived in earlier times.

The old Saxons used to burn the adultress and hang the adulterer on a gibbet erected over her ashes. Canute banished the man and ordered the woman to have her nose and ears cut off. Adultery was once regarded as homicide even in England. In Spain they formerly punished the adulterer by cutting off his offending genitals, whilst in Poland they nailed them to a post in the open market and placing a razor within his reach left him at liberty to perish or castrate himself as he liked best. But, in the England of 1770, adultery had become so fashionable and divorces so frequent 'that it may admit of some debate in the polite world whether the first is criminal or the latter dishonourable'. The law, however, judiciously punished the one and stigmatized the other.

CHAPTER NINE

No Divorce for Lord Grosvenor

For a few days before the trial, Lady Harriot Vernon had leave of absence from her duties at Gunnersbury as lady-in-waiting to Princess Amelia. On July 7, Lady Mary Coke informed Lady Strafford that on return Lady Harriot seemed 'perfectly satisfied with everything that has passed in the Court of King's Bench ... but still says her daughter is innocent'.[1] 'Carry' Vernon, it was believed, would be resigning as a Maid of Honour to the Queen, who, however, forgave her and she remained in the royal service for many years and died a spinster. Caroline had hoped to marry Lord Carmarthen, but he did not propose on account of the law-suit. Frustrated in love, she appears to have found consolation in gambling. In 1791, she lost £200 at Henry Martindale's faro table and told him to 'mark it up'. He replied that he preferred a bankers' draft. She gave him one in a sealed envelope, and next morning he hurried to the bank, hoping to collect the cash, but the clerk returned the 'draft' for him to read. Caroline had written: 'Pay the bearer 200 blows well applied.' Such a punishment would have been well deserved for Martindale had become notorious for the running of crooked gambling tables.

Lady Mary next relates that five days after the trial, the Duke of Cumberland visited the King and Queen at St James's whilst she was there: 'He came into the Drawing room laughing, wink'd at Ld Mansfield, who pretended not to see him. He afterwards got into such fits of laughing that he held his handkerchief to his mouth. If these violent spirits were natural, one must say that 'tis extraordinary that the treatment he mett with from the Lawyers shou'd have occasion'd them. If they were put on, 'twas the worst judged conduct I ever heard of.'[2]

Ladies of quality 'of spotless reputation' near St James's, reported the papers, were no longer at home to Lady Grosvenor, who, when she now visited the theatre, went incognito in the pit. According to Lady Mary, the Duke did not drop her immediately the trial was over.

She mentions having heard from a Lady Greenwich that: 'Lady Grosvenor is come into her neighbourhood, & that the Duke of Cumberland has been seen with her, & is observed going towards Barnes Common every day. I heard that a very considerable Lawyer says there is very sufficient proof for a divorce, but that if She recriminates in Doctors' Commons, as She did in the Court of King's Bench, it puts an end to the proceeding, & 'tis believed She will.'[3]

The *Whitehall Evening Post* for July 18 quotes a report, that during the time 'the celebrated cause for Crim. Con. was trying, the two lovers went to Barnes in Surrey, and walked arm in arm up and down that village enquiring for lodgings; and at last engaged a house belonging to a Mr. Hunt, took possession thereof immediately, and have continued there ever since'.

When, by the end of October, the damages and costs totalling £13,000 were still unpaid, the Duke of Cumberland faced the prospect of the bailiffs moving into his Pall Mall house. He approached his brother, the Duke of Gloucester, and begged him to help. William could not lend any money, and said the only thing to do was to appeal to the King. He agreed to accompany Henry on the errand.

After the two men had left, George wrote to Grafton's successor as Prime Minister, Lord North: 'A subject of the most private and delicate kind obliges me to lose no time in acquainting you that my two brothers have this day applied to me on the difficulty that the folly of the younger has drawn him into; the affair is too public for you to doubt but that it regards the lawsuit; the time will expire this day seven-night, when he must pay the damages and other expenses attending it. He has taken no one step to raise the money, and now has applied to me as the only means by which he can obtain it, promising to repay it in a year and a half.

'I therefore promised to write to you, though I saw great difficulty in your finding so large a sum as thirteen thousand pounds; but their pointing out to me that the prosecutor would certainly force the house, which would at this licentious time occasion disagreeable reflections on the rest of the family as well as on him. I shall speak more fully to you on this subject on Wednesday, but the time is so short that I did not choose to delay opening this affair until then; besides, I am not fond of taking persons on delicate affairs unprepared; whatever can be done ought to be done; and I ought as little as possible to appear in so very improper a business.'[4]

The money was found by Lord North after some difficulty. The

King wrote: 'This takes a heavy load off my mind though I cannot express how much I feel at being in the least concerned in an affair that my way of thinking has ever taught me to behold as highly improper, but I flatter myself the truths I have thought it incumbent to utter may be of some use in his future conduct.'[5]

Meanwhile, undeterred by Lord Mansfield's warning at the trial, Lord Grosvenor had gone ahead with his divorce proceedings against Henrietta in the ecclesiastical court of the Bishop of London, and to improve his image in the Church's eyes became Church Warden at St George's, Hanover Square. His name in gold letters still glistens there in the roll of past Wardens on the side of the gallery.

Between March and the trial, and after, the various people involved made their sworn statements before Grosvenor's lawyers. Mrs Mary Reda Vemberght had refused to give evidence in the Court of King's Bench, but later that year Mr Reda, the fencing master, tiring of her charms, left her and her finances suffered in consequence. Grosvenor, when he learned of this, sent an emissary to call on her, who offered to help repair them if she would make a deposition, which she did then and there on October 25, and repeated it before the Grosvenor lawyers on November 1.

Camilla, Countess D'Onhoff, had left London in early 1770. Rumour at first had it that the Duke was keeping her in 'a snug retreat' in the country and had promised her a pension in the Irish establishment as the price for silence. None of this was true. She was probably staying at her father the Earl of Tankerville's northern home, Chillingham Castle, Alnwick, in Northumberland.

Then, the August issue of the *Town and Country Magazine* revealed that Camilla had written the 'Jack Sprat' letters to Lord Grosvenor. The following spring, she judged it safe to return to London and went to lodge in Quebec Street, off the Oxford Road (now Oxford Street). Lord Grosvenor's agents must have learned of this, and they persuaded her to make a sworn statement before his lawyers on April 22, 1771. *The Craftsman* for September 14 that year stated: 'The Countess of D—ff was not compelled, we are told, to make the affidavits ... but be that as it may, it is a known fact to all the people of fashion that Lord Grosvenor has presented the Countess with half of the damages, £5,000, which he received.' A fortnight later the same paper adds: 'There is not now a single lady of quality who will be seen in her company, or speak to her, on account of her behaviour. Her brother has forbidden her his house.' Some seven years later she married a

Robert Robinson 'of St George's, Middlesex' at St Martin's-in-the-Fields. Then, according to Sir Herbert Croft in *The Abbey of Kilkhampton*, published in 1788, she became Frederick William II's mistress in Potsdam. The *Gentleman's Magazine* records her death at Cottage-place, Chelmsford, on September 2, 1821.

Although these depositions of Mrs Reda and the Countess (already quoted from in Chapter Five) were far more conclusive proof of his wife's adultery than the evidence his lawyers submitted at the trial in July, 1770, it was impossible for Lord Grosvenor to justify the description of himself in the plea for a divorce made on March 1, 1770 that: 'The said Richard Lord Grosvenor from the time of his aforesaid marriage with the said Henrietta, now Lady Grosvenor ... was and is a person of sober, chaste and virtuous life and conversation, and one who would not be guilty of a breach of his marriage vow; and for and such a person he the said Richard Lord Grosvenor was and is generally accounted, reputed and esteemed to be, by and amongst his neighbours, friends and acquaintances and others.'

At the trial, Lord Grosvenor's claim to be a faithful husband had already been discredited by the women of the town who had given evidence to the contrary. During the months following, his wife's lawyers were diligently making researches into his amorous adventures, and a procession of prostitutes and brothel-keepers passed through their offices making depositions.

In December, 1770, Lady Grosvenor contested her husband's suit and made counter allegations at Doctors' Commons. She accused him of leading 'a vicious, lewd, and debauched life and conversation, by visiting, corresponding with, and carnally knowing, divers strange women of loose character ...' Then followed sworn statements. Elizabeth Roberts, describing herself as a spinster aged 21, in her deposition testified that one evening in June, 1769, when walking through Cranbourn-alley, near Leicester-fields, she overtook a gentleman whom she described as a tall, thin person, over forty, with a dark complexion, marked with the smallpox, and a longish nose. She enquired 'how he did?' To which he answered: 'Oh, how do you do, my little wicked? Will you go and drink with me?'

Elizabeth accepted the invitation and Grosvenor asked her to go on ahead to a house called the *Leicester Fields Hotel*, where he would meet her. They went into a room which had a green bed in it, and drank a bowl of arrack punch together.

'Then he said: "My dear little girl, are you well? Because if you are not, tell me, and I'll give you double the sum of money I shall give you if I roger you." To which I replied that I was very well, and he said that he would not be injured for all the world. He immediately asked me to lay down across the bed which I did. He rogered me and gave me a guinea.'

After ringing the bell and paying the waiter, Grosvenor said he liked Elizabeth very much, and she asked if she might speak to him when she saw him again, but he returned: 'No, not for the world, but if you see me and want me to recognise you, hold up your petticoats and show your legs. If I feel inclined to go with you, I shall follow you to some proper house.' He then left the Hotel. When she went downstairs, the waiter informed her that the gentleman she had been with was Lord Grosvenor.

About ten days following this, Elizabeth Roberts was again on her beat across Leicester Fields when she looked back and saw Lord Grosvenor near her, so she pulled up her petticoats. He noticed the signal and walked down the other side of the Fields to the Hotel. She followed him. Procedure and payment were as previously.

One Saturday evening, a month later, Roberts once more met Lord Grosvenor and gave him the same signal. When they entered the private room, he pointed at a picture of a naked woman and told her he felt sure she would look as well, and asked her to strip. At first, she demurred but he persuaded her. Finding when 'ready for action' that her thighs were hurt by his breeches, he pulled them off and his shoes before rogering her. She sat upon his lap for a quarter of an hour. Then, after rogering her again, he gave her a guinea and, having paid the house expenses to a certain 'French George', left.

Roberts went on: 'About a fortnight ago I happened to call upon Mr Stables, an attorney in Air-street, Piccadilly, on some business I had with him.' In the course of conversation, he had asked if she knew Lord Grosvenor. On learning about her dealings with him, Stables had enquired whether she would be willing to give evidence in court regarding these. 'I agreed and said I should be glad to do Lady Grosvenor any service in my power. Neither Mr Stables, or any other person has either given or promised to give me anything for consenting to give evidence.'

The next witness, Elizabeth Elmes described herself as the wife of a brazier who had left her, since when she had earned her living by 'seeing company' under the name of Elizabeth Newton. She had known Lord Grosvenor for about three years and he had nicknamed her 'Hornpipe'. In May, 1769, she went to Epsom races in a post-chaise accompanied by one Ann Wilmot, and saw Lord Grosvenor sitting in his phaeton with Sir Thomas Frederick. 'I ordered my chaise to drive up by the side of the phaeton when his lordship noticing me said to Sir Thomas, "There is Hornpipe!"' He spoke to her and asked his companion to change places with her and go to the other 'lady' in the chaise.

Lord Grosvenor then drove round the course with Elizabeth, but apparently was so intoxicated that he overturned his vehicle. 'This so frightened me,' she continued, 'that I said "I must go at once to the *King's Head* at Epsom to rest." He agreed and said that as soon as the race was over, he would come to me.' This he did and they supped together, and later retired to a private house opposite, where they went to bed together 'naked and alone' for over an hour. He then paid her five pounds and went away.

Nearly a year later, towards midnight in April, 1770, when she was in bed at her lodgings in King's Street, Soho, Elizabeth received a message from Lord Grosvenor, asking her to meet him in 'a house of ill fame' at the upper end of Bow Street, Covent Garden, kept by a certain Betty Johnson.

'I not being very well refused to go. His lordship sent three times during the night for me, and at last, about six o'clock in the morning, Betty Johnson came herself for me and made me go to her house where I found his lordship in bed in a back room.' 'Hornpipe' joined him and they made love till four o'clock in the afternoon, being brought breakfast and dinner by Betty. This time his lordship parted with an extra five shillings on leaving.

It is interesting to note that this episode took place just after Lord Grosvenor had applied for a divorce from his wife.

Another witness for Lady Grosvenor, Alice Tipping, was the wife of a soldier whom she had left, not wishing to accompany him and his regiment to foreign parts. So, assuming the name of Charlotte Gwynne, she joined Mrs Hayes's establishment in Duke Street, St James's. She claimed that Lord Grosvenor and a friend patronised the place one evening in September, 1765, and, after supping with her and Polly Jones [later the Duke of Cumberland's mistress], they all stripped naked and lay in the same bed. His lordship complained that he was cold, whereupon the bell was rung and a maid fetched extra blankets.

For the following five nights, Grosvenor returned to sleep with Charlotte till two a.m. At the end of that time he asked her to leave the bagnio, which she agreed to do. He said that he would arrange for his wife to advertise for a maidservant. Charlotte must then apply for the position, which he would see she was given. But the idea did not appeal to her. He next informed her that he had quarrelled with his wife, whom he had married the previous year and was now trying to manoeuvre into taking a lover so that he could divorce her. Once he was free, Charlotte should live with him, as he would rather 'kiss her lips at any time than lay with his wife'. In the meantime, he would maintain her in the country.

Grosvenor said that he was going to Newmarket and wished her to travel to Chester, where he would join her later. He gave her some money, and also paid Mrs Hayes to avoid any trouble over her losing one of her women. But Charlotte, who put up at the *Falcon* in Chester, did not remain there long. Lord Grosvenor sent Matthew Stephens, to bring her to him at the lodgings of the butler's sister-in-law, Mrs John Stephens, in Chester Castle. He said that as his wife was now staying at Eaton, he feared she might find out about their friendship and upset his plans for a divorce.

He therefore proposed that Charlotte should go back to London, handed her money and a letter of introduction to a Mrs Molesworth at Craven Hill, recommending the girl as an acquaintance of his seeking employment and requesting that she should be given everything she wanted at his expense. Mrs Molesworth had for many years been a mistress of Lord Grosvenor's, and acted as a procuress of young women with whom he had intercourse in her house. Knowing of her reputation, Charlotte did not go to stay with her but rejoined Mrs Hays's sisterhood in Duke Street instead.

Two months later, Lord Grosvenor came to town and when he discovered what Alice had done, expressed his displeasure at her conduct and demanded the return of several letters he had written her. She sought the advice of Mrs Hayes who, anxious to retain his custom, told Charlotte to surrender them, which she did—and then laid down with his lordship and earned herself another five guineas.

Having recovered his letters, Grosvenor dropped Alice, but, according to her, one day in October two years later, whilst visiting her mother in North Wales, she was riding along a country road when he went by in a coach and, recognizing her, jumped out, mounted one of his servants' horses and rode after Alice. He greeted her, enquired how she came to be in those parts, and where she was going. He professed that he still loved her and offered to set her up in a shop within easy reach of Eaton so that they might be together whenever convenient. It was not possible for him to stay any longer with her then, as he was going home to dinner and his wife's brother was in the coach.

A day or two after this encounter, Alice went to Chester and wrote to Lord Grosvenor asking him to meet her. He replied making an appointment for them to do so on the walls of Chester. There she told him that unable to find a place in the country where she would like to settle she was determined to return to livelier scenes in London. The peer again gave her money for the journey south, assuring her that if she could find 'a snug private place' there, he would keep her, but it would have to be secretly arranged.

Henry Vernon, Lady Grosvenor's twenty-two-year-old brother, in his deposition gave his version of this episode, stating that it occurred in November, not October, 1767, and that when his brother-in-law had returned to the coach, he had asked who the girl was. The other had replied that she was a milliner at Chester and an acquaintance of his, and would Vernon oblige him by not mentioning the meeting to his wife.

Vernon said he was certain that the girl in question was the same person as his fellow witness, known as Charlotte Gwynne, who had confided to him that Lord Grosvenor had tried to prevent her from giving evidence against him and had offered money in return as well as other inducements.

In reply to questions put by Lord Grosvenor's lawyers, Henry Vernon insisted that neither he nor, as far as he knew, his sister or her lawyers, had given or promised payment to Charlotte Gwynne for evidence against Grosvenor. Neither had Mrs Boisgermain been bribed for testifying against Grosvenor in the trial at Westminster Hall, nor to Vernon's knowledge had there been meetings between her and his sister's lawyer, Mr Buxton, to settle what Mrs Boisgermain should say in the present divorce proceedings. On the contrary, Vernon claimed having heard Grosvenor had somehow persuaded Mrs Boisgermain to go and stay in Flanders to stop her being further questioned.

Lord Grosvenor, according to the evidence accumulated by his wife's lawyers, certainly craved for constant change in his sexual relationships. Mary How, who had made a brief statement in the witness-box at the trial, gave further details in her deposition submitted at Doctors' Commons. She had been introduced to his lordship 'as a girl lately come out of the country' by Mrs Lisle, keeper of another brothel he patronized. After his first session with her she had received two guineas, and her employer five. Thereafter his payment varied from two to sometimes nothing, according to her performance, till Mrs Lisle, who was also suffering financially, switched him over to a buxom new recruit.

His lordship's lawyers here succeeded later in obtaining a contradictory statement from Mrs Lisle, made on March 1, 1771. She admitted having known him for some four or five years, as a result of a meeting at Newmarket races, but denied introducing him to Mary How, or that the latter had criminal conversation with him under her roof. She accused Lady Grosvenor's agents of having given her fifteen guineas and several parcels of clothes, as well as having maintained her from the beginning of December, 1770, till a fortnight previously, in order to try and induce her to give evidence against his lordship.

Mrs Lisle alleged that Lady Grosvenor's solicitor, Mr Buxton, had employed a Mr Gibbons and also a Mr Wallace to visit bawdy-houses in search of witnesses. Mr Wallace had confided that he had received two guineas and his wife twenty-seven shillings for their work, whilst Mr Gibbons was on weekly pay. They were authorised to offer any person they could find a handsome reward if he or she would attend to be examined on behalf of her ladyship.

The Consistory Court seems to have been reluctant to reach a decision, and the case kept being adjourned to allow for further enquiries to be made. Over sixty witnesses were examined. Then on May 25 Dr Bettesworth, chancellor of the diocese of London, having heard counsel on both sides, ordered Lord Grosvenor to pay his wife £1,600 per annum exclusive of the £400 he was already allowing her.

The Craftsman for June 1 commented: 'It is said that Lady Grosvenor has proved her recrimination ... The success of her ladyship's attack on his lordship will be very alarming to many men of fashion who neglect their ladies, for if the facts are proved, they will be in bar of any sentence of separation, although anything may happen to be proved against a lady; the law holding that persons of gallantry are the fittest to live together.'

It was not until the following year, on January 18, that proceedings were finally dropped between the Grosvenors. Richard settled £1,200 a year upon Henrietta and gave her as well £1,000 to cover legal expenses. Two arbitrators, Lord Camden for the husband, and Lord Apsley for the wife, proposed these terms. Although this meant a considerable reduction from the £2,000 a year she had been receiving,

Lady Grosvenor reluctantly accepted the offer, for her friends pointed out that if she went on with the suit, its outcome was uncertain and should her husband obtain a divorce she would be left without a shilling.

CHAPTER TEN

Mrs Bayley

Within a few weeks of his losing the law-suit, the Duke of Cumberland had embarked on a new affair. The *Freeholders' Magazine* for August, 1770, mentions that it had received a letter dated the 7th of that month from a correspondent living in Southampton, describing the arrival of the Duke there on horseback accompanied by one servant in livery. He had ridden up one street and down another, 'enquiring what fine women there were, and if there were any private balls: being answered in the affirmative, he then rode full gallop into the town: and remains there'.

One gathers from an account in the well-informed *Town and Country Magazine* for March, three years later, what had then happened. Apparently, after gaining admittance to a ball, the Duke found that the ladies all refused to dance with him, except a certain Mrs Bayley 'who taking compassion, generously lent him her hand'. The daughter of a rich tradesman in the City of London, she had been first seduced by a rising young barrister of the Temple who, after romps in his chambers, informed her that 'he would never think of making a woman a wife whom he had first made a whore'. This gave her such a shock that she accepted the very first offer of marriage she then received, which was from an impecunious timber merchant. The small fortune his wife brought Mr Bayley paid his debts and kept him solvent for a time. While he dissipated the rest of her money on the turf, she visited fashionable watering places and collected a string of rich admirers 'to which he raised no objection, being an easy compliant husband glad to see his wife when her purse was well filled and at other times just as well pleased with her absence'.

The Duke found Mrs Bayley a woman who could not only forget her husband but her former admirers. After staying a few days together in Southampton they toured the southern counties before returning to London, where their intimacy continued. Unfortunately, the Duke's finances were at this time very low and he was unable to supply his new dulcinea with the demand she made upon him. It was rumoured he had been obliged to borrow from his servants to silence her remonstrances.

The affair lasted for a year, then on July 25, 1771, the Duke was installed as a Knight of the Garter, in company with eight other new Knights, including his nephew George, Prince of Wales, in St George's Chapel, Windsor. Whilst there, he was fascinated by an unusually attractive widow, a certain Mrs Horton, whom he was destined to marry before the year was out.

Referring to the Duke as 'Squire Morgan', the name he had assumed when in amorous pursuit of Lady Grosvenor, and to Mrs Bayley as 'the lady of Hatton Garden', where she lived, the *St James's Chronicle* eight days later, on August 3, claimed that his 'violent attachment' to her as well as the husband's knowledge of it was 'beyond all manner of doubt'. They met at least four times a week at a 'Miss S——'s in B—w— Street'. The 'Lady' came openly in her husband's carriage, whilst the 'Squire' sometimes walked there both coming and going, and on other occasions arrived in a hackney chair. When he was feeling very ardent, he would be the first to arrive, but there were days when she would be so ahead of him that she would impatiently despatch a note to Pall Mall requesting him to hurry, with which request he would dutifully comply. Their tryst usually began at one in the afternoon and lasted until two or three o'clock, then she would leave first.

It was not true, stated the *Chronicle*, that the couple had been seen, as alleged in other papers, walking arm-in-arm in Windsor town. The 'Squire' had been with the 'Lady' before at their 'confidential and convenient' friend's, and had 'flown to her on Friday last on his return to town, but the Lady herself was not at Windsor'.

A week later, the *Chronicle* gave the news that Mr Bayley had lost his post in the City, his partner 'not having sense enough to conceive that royal visits to a merchant's wife are compatible with the situation of the husband, and that the oftener and more public they are repeated the greater was the honour conferred'. He had told all his friends both verbally and by letter that he was fully convinced of the innocence of the acquaintance between his wife and 'Squire Morgan'.

The day before this report appeared, the King's only other surviving brother, William Henry, Duke of Gloucester, had taken leave of him at St James's prior to setting out for Portsmouth to embark on the *Venus* for official visits to Lisbon, Gibraltar and Minorca, followed by a stay in Italy for the benefit of his health, which had been seriously impaired the previous year by a long and onerous tour of Germany and Austria. In Vienna he had met the son of the Empress Maria Theresa, the Grand Duke of Tuscany, who had invited him to visit his own court in Florence.

As Gloucester's marriage five years previously was still a secret, he was obliged to leave his wife behind. By now it was widely believed that she was his mistress, and we find *The Craftsman*[1] stating that the parting between him and 'Lady Waldegrave was extremely tender and affecting' and 'visible to the whole Court' and that she had also declared to 'a particular friend that she does not expect his Royal Highness to return alive'. The paper added that the Duke of Cumberland had begged in vain to be allowed to accompany his brother on the frigate he had once commanded.

It was said in the *Morning Chronicle* that Gloucester had seen the royal black sheep several times before sailing and had urged him to reform, 'enforcing these entreaties with tears' and repeating them in a farewell letter. The account also claimed that he reproached him for treating Lady Grosvenor badly, but this does not agree with what Lady Mary Coke wrote on the subject. Indeed, on the same day this was published, she sent Lady Strafford 'an anecdote of your worthy niece, Lady Grosvenor'. She continues: 'Not long ago she met Mr Hall, the riding master, and asked him if he had got her a Horse; to which he answer'd he could not recollect her Ladyship had given him her command to buy one. "No," said her Ladyship, "'tis true, but did not the Duke of Cumberland order you to get one?" "Yes, Madam," replied Mr Hall, "the Duke spoke to me about a Horse for a Lady." "That was for me," said she, "and I want to know if you had got it?" '[2]

The same paper also alleged that Mr Bayley, since being obliged to give up his partnership in the City, had intimated to his wife's royal friend that 'a Consulship, or some such mercantile-like post would be very agreeable to him as a compensation for his public loss of honour and rank in life. We are told that the young "Squire" has consented to solicit some such employment on the positive stipulation that Mrs. B— shall not accompany her husband abroad in consequence of her constitution being too delicate to support the fatigue of a sea voyage.'[3]

The Duke had in reality tired of Mrs Bayley since those meetings in Windsor with Mrs Anne Horton. It may well have been the widow with whom the inquisitive had glimpsed him walking hand in hand.

Several explanations were advanced at the time as to why he came to marry her, but probably the most feasible is that, unlike the other women he had until then pursued, she adopted the tactics so successfully employed by another Anne, Anne Boleyn, with another Henry, Henry VIII, and told him he must marry her or go without.

Rebuffed by Mrs Horton, Cumberland had no doubt hoped to try and forget her and at the same time escape from Mrs Bayley by joining his brother on his long sea tour. When this failed, he must have felt that he was inextricably caught in toils of his own making.

Then, in the *General Evening Post* for August 24, it was bruited that Mr Bayley one day 'when he had some particular friends at dinner chided his wife as tenderly as possible for a behaviour which subjected him to derision and both of them to dishonour; "Don't you like it?" said she. "Here then go and buy a rope—you can easily put it to a proper use" and at the same time chucked him half-a-crown across the table'.

Reading in the press such a story, whether true or apocryphal, must have cooled still further the Duke's ardour for Maria. He was finding it increasingly difficult to meet her monetary demands, and this led him into an uncharacteristic act of meanness which buzzed around London and was then published in the unfriendly *Morning Chronicle* in probably exaggerated form which hardly improved his popular image. It was said that after attending a race meeting, not wanting to return to London and Mrs Bayley, he proposed to several gentlemen of the town to have a dance and supper. They approved of the suggestion and gave him the names of the principal ladies of the place, to whom he wrote cards of invitation and most of whom accepted. The night was spent 'with great joy and festivity'. At two a.m. when the company prepared to dance after supper, the Duke thinking it time to retire, slipped unobserved downstairs with his aide-de-camp, called for the bill and, dividing by the number of persons present, found the cost per head amounted to seventeen shillings and sixpence. He ordered his aide to lay down thirty-five shillings, and then they whipped into his chaise and drove off.

When those left behind shortly afterwards missed Cumberland and learned what had happened, they were so annoyed that after settling the rest of the bill, they subscribed 'a handsome sum for the ringers to usher him out of town with as joyous a peal as if he had just arrived; which was accordingly done to the not inconsiderable diversion of a great crowd assembled on that occasion'.

Fortunately for the Duke, a way of at least temporary escape from Mrs Bayley now presented itself. Absence from London, too, he no doubt hoped would help him to forget the woman who, unlike the others, had demanded marriage before she would yield to his siege. The death had just taken place of Sir Francis Blake Delaval, whom Horace Walpole once described as the most fashionable man in England and who, according to his bosom friend, Samuel Foote, was so attached to the great star of the Order of the Bath, of which he was a Knight, that he even wore it when swimming in the Thames. The deceased's younger brother, Sir John Hussey Delaval, who was level-headed and industrious, had already taken over the family estates at Seaton in return for paying his debts and lived in the impressively baroque mansion built by Sir John Vanburgh in 1726, which still stands on a grassy hillock ten miles from Newcastle by the North Sea.

It so happened that Hussey Delaval was a close friend of the Duke's and had asked him to stay at Seaton, which invitation had been accepted just before Sir Francis's death. The latter's remains were conveyed with great pomp and expense north to rest finally in the Delaval mausoleum and Cumberland followed, always a discreet stage behind. So as to avoid attending the funeral, he spent a few days first with the *nouveau riche* Hugh Smithson, first Earl and then Duke of Northumberland and his wife at Alnwick Castle (not far from Chillingham Castle, the home of the Earl of Tankerville, Camilla D'Onhoff's father). This turned into a royal progress which did much to restore Cumberland's morale.

Dr Thomas Percy, the famous Editor of the *Reliques of Ancient English Poetry*, was chaplain to the Duke of Northumberland as well as having been one to the King since 1769, and he gives a detailed account of Cumberland's visit in unpublished letters, preserved in the British Library's Department of Manuscripts.

Writing on Friday, August 30, 1771, to 'my dearest Jewel', the antiquary divine tells his wife that the previous Sunday he preached at Alnwick Church before his Royal Highness who behaved 'remarkably attentive'. Dr Percy says that he hinted as gently as he could to the need for persons of the first rank to be circumspect in their conduct as no allowances would be made for their frailties. In fact, 'there was a Malignity in the World which was ever disposed to enlarge and exaggerate their failings' so they ought 'to endeavour by the exercise of every virtue and amiable Quality to make their enemies ashamed and weary of their Invectives'.

Cumberland had taken all this in very good part. 'He expressed himself very kindly to me: invited me to call on him often in London and spoke of me to others in a very obliging manner.'

After the service, continues Dr Percy, there was 'a great levée about the Prince and the Castle' when the Mayors and Corporations of Newcastle-upon-Tyne and Berwick-upon-Tweed together with their Members of Parliament and many country gentlemen presented to this controversial royal had 'the honour to kiss his hand'. Both cities were thirty miles away and their Corporations 'very tenacious of their privileges'. It resembled 'the attendance paid by the vassals and the old Earls of Northumberland in ancient times'.

Though Dr Percy does not mention this, it appears that Sir John Hussey Delaval, being M.P. for Berwick, had persuaded its Corporation to act in this way, and that of Newcastle, not to be outdistanced in the social stakes, had decided to attend as well—for after all the Duke of Cumberland was the King's brother and his love affairs a private matter.

In justification of such an attitude, there came news from London which read: 'The talk in the circle of the Court is that a Great Personage is not to be displeased with the conduct of the younger brother, relative to Mrs B—y as reported. The reason given for it is that the nature of the connection is not dangerous nor expensive; that an affair of the kind is what is to be expected from a younger unmarried Prince; and the attachment may prevent ... a marriage with an inferior.'[4]

'A grand dinner after the levée,' wrote Percy, 'consisted of 177 Dishes, exclusive of a very splendid Dessert' and that after the Duke of Cumberland's table and his own had broken up, 'the Prince laid hold of me and would make me go with him to the room where Lord Algernon was plying the Aldermen of Berwick with bumpers of claret and there his Royal Highness sat down with great good humour and began a round of Corporation toasts which though highly flattering to the Berwick gentlemen were highly alarming to so puny a Drinker as myself, which he perceiving very kindly gave me leave to withdraw and made the Rector of the Parish supply my place, and as for the body corporate they had all their full Doses.'

Two days later, they had set out for Berwick where the freedom of the city was to be bestowed upon the Duke, who travelled in a phaeton, his favourite vehicle, while Dr Percy went with Lady Delaval and her son in their coach-and-six. As this made 'the largest figure all the county people came crowding everywhere to our Coach-window, not taking any notice of the Duke of Cumberland, who rode before; which occasioned them no small disappointment'. They found that 'the lower sort of people thought it was the same Duke of Cumberland, who had beat the Rebels in 1745, a very natural mistake. People of a somewhat higher rank, who had from the London newspapers expected to see a lame deformed creature with half his face eat [*sic*] away with evil, were much surprised to see such a fine blooming young fellow and still more to see him dance in the evening, for he is one of the best dancers I ever saw and warmed with the exercise and glowing with pleasure he looked remarkably handsome'.

The procession including ten carriages, a large cavalcade of servants on horseback, followed by the county aristocracy, extended for half a mile when it arrived in Berwick, towards two in the afternoon and was greeted with a salute of 21 guns and cheering crowds. The Duke was then presented with the Freedom of the City, wrote Dr Percy, and later at a Dinner in the Mansion House attended by some 200 persons, behaved 'very properly and they were all much pleased with him: for to do him justice he has not the slightest pride'. However, Percy reveals, the new Freeman loved 'waggery in his heart, for I sate about the middle of the table at which he presided; and near me was a monstrous high pyramid of jellies that tottered exceedingly as the table moved: which his Royal Highness observing, he tried all he could, without being perceived, to shake the table and bring it down upon our heads, at the same time winking to me to take care of myself. Luckily he was too far off, or we should have had a woful [*sic*] crash and many a pompous periwig would have been all be-jellied'.

In the evening the whole of Berwick was illuminated and the Duke opened a Ball with the Countess of Home and afterwards danced with a 'fine, showy' Scottish girl, daughter of a small squire. 'The humours of the father and mother who were continually hovering over his Royal Highness were very diverting, for seeing the familiar way in which he talked to them, they were *quite hail-fellow-well-met* with him, and clung to him like Buns; which he with great humour encouraged.'

Although the Ball ended late, the Duke was up early for a review of the troops before returning to Alnwick Castle, then after dinner he travelled with Sir John Hussey Delaval to Seaton when the civic fathers of Newcastle heard of the magnificent reception at Berwick, they sent their Sheriff and Sword-bearer to wait upon Cumberland with an invitation to dine at their own Mansion House. Colonel Deaken, his Groom of the Bedchamber, according to a report in the *London Evening Post*, saw them and asked for the Duke to be given the freedom of their city as the price for a visit, to which they readily agreed. 'An attempt was likewise made by him to procure the freedom of Trinity House for the Duke as an Admiral, but some of that body had the insolence to mutter something about services and merits. A Scotch barber refused even to light a taper at Newcastle.'[5]

Another unfortunate incident occurred just as the Duke was entering the town towards two o'clock in the afternoon. Twenty-one swivel guns mounted upon Newgate began to fire a salute when one which was foul suddenly burst and killed a sailor on the spot and seriously injured two others. This nearly led to a riot as wild rumours swiftly spread among the crowds gathered to watch the pageantry and they were only pacified with difficulty.[6]

Dr Percy ends his letter to his wife with the news that the previous evening he had accompanied the Duke and Duchess of Northumberland and their family to meet Cumberland and attend the celebrations. 'But I must now conclude for I hear the guns firing which informs me his Royal Highness is come and we are all summoned to attend him.' Writing next on September 3, he proudly informs his 'dearest Jewel' that the parchment conferring the freedom of the city on the Duke was contained in 'a very handsome gold box of 50 guineas price, which I had in my hands next morning'. A grand Dinner in the Mansion House went off 'with great good humour and general satisfaction' and the Prince made himself 'extremely acceptable to everybody by the desire he showed to oblige them'. The two hundred guests had to be accommodated in different rooms and he went and sat in turn in each 'which pleased them much'. At a Ball in the evening which he opened with the Mayoress, the new Freeman further endeavoured to please everybody 'by taking different partners among the prettiest young ladies he could find'.

The next morning, when the Northumberland family and Dr Percy were having breakfast by the window of the Inn where they had slept, the Duke called and 'to oblige the people, who were assembled in the street, he sate an hour with us, with great good humour', before returning to Seaton Delaval.

On the Sunday evening the Duke left for London. When he arrived home on Wednesday, September 4, he found Mrs Bayley highly indignant at his having remained so long away from her, and he was obliged to buy her a gold watch chain, lavishly ornamented with diamonds and other precious stones, in order to placate her.[7]

Cumberland also came back to the bad news that on the previous day when his groom was exercising his horse, Sulphur, on the course at Hereford, a woman suddenly crossed before them and in endeavouring to avoid running over the woman the rider threw down the horse, and fell himself with such force as to fracture his skull. Though all possible care was taken of him and he was trepanned, he did not recover. The woman was only slightly hurt.[8]

The *London Evening Post* for September 14 reported that 'a separation between Mr and Mrs B—yl—y is actually in agitation' and jested: 'As bills of divorcement will soon be equal in number to statutes of bankruptcy, an act of relievancy, together with an act of insolvency, will be moved for next sessions to take place every seventh year, when the debtor and cuckold may be rid of his debts and encumbrances at one and the same time.'

The paper added that Lady Grosvenor was still living in a small house at Barnes, but was so upset over her former lover's affair with Mrs Bayley that it was said she had declared her intentions of going abroad, of residing there for life, and of secluding herself entirely from the world.

When, on the 26th of that month, the *Grafton* man-of-war was launched at Deptford by the King, the Duke was present and, according to *The Craftsman*,[9] after the dinner later 'a certain noble lord gave the toast, Mrs B—y, which was repeated by the Duke of Cumberland, who was present'. Elsewhere in the same paper, it claimed that he had apartments 'now fitting up at a house near St James's for his favourite Sultana'. Then, in its next issue, it alleged that the Duke had procured the post of Collector of Customs of Dominica for Mr Bayley, which would assure him an annual income of no less than £2,000.

The report about the apartments in St James's strengthened Mrs Bayley's growing suspicions that the Duke had taken a new mistress, for he had offered her no such accommodation, and no doubt if she questioned him about it he dismissed the report as unfounded gossip. She tried to revive his passion by making him jealous. The *General Evening Post* for October 26 contains this paragraph: 'The behaviour of Mrs B—y at Warwick Street Chapel suffering the Duke of Cumberland to wait for her at the door and coquetting with Sir Ed[ward] H[ales] in the chapel has occasioned the minister who officiated to forbid her the closet, on which account she does not go near to that place.'

Maria Bayley had discovered that the Duke was spending most nights at Mrs Horton's house in Hertford Street. Others, too, had learned of this. A month later *The Craftsman* quoted a correspondent as saying: 'The marriage of the Duke of Cumberland with Mrs Anne Horton lay long concealed, and probably would have remained so had it not been for the inquisitive zeal of some of his Royal Highness's late paramours, whose discoveries gave birth to intelligence in the public prints so highly injurious to the reputation of the lady as made his Royal Highness nobly resolve to avow the truth at any risk to himself.'

CHAPTER ELEVEN

Anne of the Amorous Eyes

Mrs Horton, born Anne Luttrell, was a member of a turbulent Irish family that could trace its ancestry back to the time of the Crusades. According to Horace Walpole, she had 'the most amorous eyes in the world and eyelashes a yard long. Coquette beyond measure, artful as Cleopatra, and completely mistress of her passions and projects—indeed eyelashes three-quarters of a yard shorter would have served to conquer such a head as she has turned'.[1]

There was a Lord Chancellor Lutterell in 1236 and a Sir Andrew Lutterelle in 1259. When James I planted Ireland with Englishmen in order to hold down the country, he gave a Luttrell a grant of land, four miles from Dublin, which became known as Luttrellstown. This immigrant married an Irish woman, and their grandson, Simon Luttrell, was appointed Governor of Dublin by James II, fought for him at the Battle of the Boyne and accompanied him into exile. Simon's treacherous brother, Henry, switched sides and thus obtained his estates. Murdered in 1717, he was succeeded by a son, Simon, who at the age of four had attended his parents' wedding when after living together for years they decided to marry. The couple led a stormy life at home and very soon after the ceremony the husband was killed, which crime, said the gossips, had been arranged by the widow.

Young Simon was sent to Eton, after which he led the life of a duelling rake in Dublin, where he became a leading light of its Hell-Fire Club that used to meet in a hunting lodge on the bald top of Mount Pelier south-west of the city. There is a story that the Devil appeared to him when he was heavily in debt and agreed to finance him for seven years in exchange for his soul at the end of that period. Next morning, there stood on the banks of the Liffey a fine mill with a huge stone inside bearing the Devil's finger-prints. From the exploitation of the mill, Simon made a fortune.

Then came the night of reckoning when, during an orgy in the lodge, Satan materialised to demand settlement. But the debtor had a glib tongue and managed to persuade the fiend to take instead of himself the last man out of the place. 'Run for your souls!' he shouted and his cronies helter-skeltered for the door. But, as a result of his debauchery, Luttrell was out of condition and lost the race for freedom. 'So, me fine lad, I have you after all!' the Devil chortled, seizing him by the shoulder. 'Not yet—look who's over in that corner!' cried his wily prisoner and escaped as the other turning, momentarily relaxed his hold. But Simon's shadow was slower than he was and that the fiend caught, which is why neither Simon nor his descendants had any shadows, so claims the tale. The Devil kept them under lock and key, awaiting their owners who have always come to be reunited with them at the end.

In 1744 Luttrell married the daughter and heiress of Sir Nicholas Lawes, Governor of Jamaica, and thereafter lived most of his time in England, where he played political poker so adroitly that he gained first in 1768 an Irish barony from Grafton for dubious services, becoming Lord Irnham, then in 1781 a viscounty from Lord North, and lastly the earldom of Carhampton from Pitt the Younger four years later. Horace Walpole considered he had 'parts, wit and boldness', but Lady Louisa Stuart regarded him as 'the greatest reprobate in England' whilst Junius branded him as 'this hoary lecher'.

Simon had four sons: Colonel Henry Lawes Luttrell (1737–1821); Temple Simon Luttrell (*c.* 1738–1803) M.P. for Milbourne Port, 1775–80; John Temple Luttrell (*c.* 1740–1829) M.P. for Stockbridge, 1774–5 and 1784–5, then Commissioner of Excise, 1785–1826; and James Luttrell (*c.* 1751–88) M.P. for Stockbridge, 1775–84, and Dover, 1784–8. The eldest, compensating for his lack of inches with aggressive arrogance, spent two years at Christ Church, Oxford, which, according to the *Town and Country* for December, 1771, were 'commemorated for many feats of buckism and gallantry' and an affair with one Arabella Bolton, daughter of his father's best friend's gardener. Commissioned in the army, he served with distinction in America during the latter part of the Seven Years' War, indulging also in amorous exploits. Though without culture and a complete sybarite with wild habits, he had character, a certain native wit and was fearless. His father once challenged him to a duel, and he replied that if the Earl could prevail on any gentleman to be his second, he would fight him with all his heart.

Many ladies of rank and fortune tried to win him for husband, but he preferred a bachelor's freedom, having seldom 'less than three females on his hand who figured in life in a servile capacity; and he generally had as many obscure lodgings where he met them occasionally, as their time and convenience would permit'. In George III's conflict with John Wilkes, he consented to stand as the Tory candidate for Middlesex in 1769, though people predicted he would not live to see the result of the polls but would be lynched by the mob. Policies of insurance were taken out on his life at Lloyds Coffee House. The Colonel, however, was undeterred by such pessimism. He had the reputation of being the best shot in the country. The Whigs, unable to scare him, did all they could to denigrate him.

Colonel Luttrell supported the Duke of Cumberland anonymously in a pamphlet over the Grosvenor affair, but the identity of the author leaked out, as is evident from the following which appeared in the *Public Advertiser* for September 7, 1770: 'The defence of H.R.H., so often advertised as written by an M.P., is quite a catchpenny, the writer being Col. L-----ll, who is no member at all. We are told his defence will be speedily followed by a new publication, entitled *The Letter of an Elder Brother to a Fair Quaker*, which will entirely retrieve the literary Fame of an illustrious family, which has been lately endangered by a hasty and incorrect writer belonging to it.' This, of course, is a reference to George III's association with Hannah Lightfoot, and is of interest as probably the earliest reference to the affair in a newspaper of the period.

The Colonel had three sisters, of whom Lady Louisa Stuart disapproved, writing that they were 'vulgar, indelicate, and intrepid: utter strangers to good company . . . never to be seen in any woman of fashion's house, though often leaders of riotous parties at Vauxhall or Ranelagh'. Anne, born in 1743, was the most beautiful, and married in her teens Christopher Horton, a sporting squire of Catton Park in Derbyshire. According to the *Town and Country* for April, 1772, they were sitting by the fireside when in play he pulled back her chair causing her to fall, which brought about a miscarriage. This so upset him that he became extremely ill and 'his grief was so violent that he never afterwards quitted his bed till his death'.

The twenty-four-year-old widow then went to stay in London with her brother, the Colonel. Here she met with considerable success. From the portraits painted later of her by Gainsborough, Reynolds, Romney, and Cosway, one's chief impression is of a tall, slender beauty with a lovely neck and thick, golden hair, dressed high, with little curls and tendrils. The large eyes are green and fringed with extraordinarily long eyelashes. It was said that she had a trick of raising her eyes and then lowering them to draw attention to the length of those lashes, and that she was the most amusing woman in the capital.

In his *Reign of George III*[2] Horace Walpole, no friend of Anne's, was later grudgingly to write: 'There was something so bewitching in her languishing eyes, which she could animate to enchantment, if she pleased, and her coquetry was so active, so varied, and yet so habitual, that it was difficult not to see through it and yet as difficult to resist it. She danced divinely, and had a great deal of wit, but of the satiric kind.'

Some claimed that the Duke was originally attracted when he met Anne at dances on the lawns at Sunninghill Wells. Others alleged that the affair began at the ceremony already described, when he was installed as a Knight of the Garter in the summer of 1771, that, admiring how she stood out among the spectators, he made enquiries and discovered she had rented a house in Datchet Lane, Windsor, where he first visited her.[3] Another source asserts he then fell so desperately in love as to declare his passion the same evening but that the lady refused to take him seriously. Her amusement turned to alarm when to prove his ardour he went on visiting her daily until she informed her eldest brother, who immediately called on the Duke and told him that, whilst he could not expect him to offer his sister marriage, he was determined to protect her honour and therefore must insist on no more visits. For a time, the Duke stayed away, then he sent for the Colonel and said his happiness depended on possessing Anne, so was ready to marry her forthwith. Luttrell took him at his word and a secret wedding was arranged.[4]

This version hardly satisfied those who liked their scandal highly coloured. According to them, the match was a forced one and from the start the widow planned to make him her second husband: first he was her lover and then when in September, 1771, she told him she was expecting his child and he did not offer marriage, the fiery Colonel called and challenged him to a duel unless he made an *amende honorable*. A cartoon in the December issue of the *Town and Country* depicts Luttrell threatening him with a horsewhip whilst Anne Horton cries: 'I will be a Royal Duchess.'

One thing is certain—the actual ceremony took place between the hours of six and eight on the evening of October 2, 1771, at Anne's house in Hertford Street, with her eldest sister, Elizabeth Luttrell, as the only witness. They were married by the Rev. William Stevens according to the rites of the Church of England. John Heneage Jesse states that he inspected in the Privy Council office the proofs of the marriage obtained by order of King George III in May, 1773. 'The only document of any interest is their joint declaration that they were man and wife, signed by the Duke and Duchess on the night of their nuptials ... The signature of the Duke—'Henry Frederick'—is traced in singularly tremulous characters, while nothing can be neater or steadier than that of the Duchess.'

When rumours began circulating that she was the Duke's new mistress, the bride insisted on her husband telling the King of the marriage, which with misgivings he did. The groom waited until November 1 before going to Richmond Lodge. As he rarely visited the King there, the latter was surprised to see him. George recorded exactly what happened: how he went with his brother for a walk in the wooded grounds—how Henry, obviously nervous and ill at ease, chatted inconsequentially about trivialities—and how at last he jerked out a sheet of paper from a pocket and, thrusting it into the King's hand, requested him to read it.

George's earlier surprise changed to dismay and growing anger, for what Cumberland afraid to voice aloud had written down was a clumsily-expressed statement revealing his marriage.[5] The upstart widow of a commoner was now, after the Queen, the second lady in the land. The King in his account[6] relates that, after walking on for a while in silence to control his feelings: 'I without passion spoke to him to the following effect. That I could not believe he had taken the step stated in the paper, to which he answered that he would never tell me an untruth. Upon which I continued that, if that was the case, it would only be wasting my time to put before him the reason that any of his family must have stated if he had confided in them previous to his taking this disgraceful step ... That to the indelicate method of notifying this to me I hoped he would not add the cruelty of speaking to my mother in her bad state of health. That though it would be a terrible task on me, yet for her ease I would break it to her. I told him as the step was taken I could give him no advice for that he had irretrievably ruined himself. But that it appeared to me after such disgraceful conduct any country was preferable to his own.'

The King gave instructions that the guards which usually attended the Duke on days of state should henceforth be discontinued. On November 3 he wrote to his mother telling her about Cumberland's marriage, and ending: 'The more I reflect on his conduct, the more I see it as his inevitable ruin and as a disgrace to the whole family'.[7] On the 6th he sent the Duke an ultimatum that if he never mentioned the step he had taken and did not allow Mrs Horton to be styled 'Duchess of Cumberland', then the King would receive him again, but if the Duke did not agree to this there would be no further communication with him.[8]

On the next day, which was the offender's birthday, George deliberately held no levee, and sent an order at five a.m. to St Martin's-in-the-Fields forbidding the customary ringing of bells.[9] A few hours later the Duke and his wife set off for their honeymoon in France and on reaching Calais gave a ball to the officers of its garrison (which was also attended by two disreputable wives, Lady Ligonier and Lady Fenoulet, the latter accompanied by her lover, Captain Sutherland).[10] From here the Duke wrote to the King stressing his intention to remain loyal to his bride, 'a most amiable and worthy lady', whatever the consequences. It was indeed in the other's power 'to deprive me of several thousand pounds a year, but not of the inexpressible happiness I feel'.[11]

When the King heard of his brother's departure, he summoned Colonel Luttrell and questioned him regarding his involvement in the affair.[12] Anne's eldest brother insisted that the marriage had come as a complete surprise. Had he received any foreknowledge, he would have warned the King. That he was probably telling the truth is supported by the fact that he was not present at the ceremony. The sole witness was Elizabeth Luttrell, the bride's sister, and in view of her character and subsequent history it is much more likely that she was Anne's adviser and abettor.

That arch-purveyor of scandal, Horace Walpole, wrote at once on November 7 from Arlington Street to his friend, Sir Horace Mann, in Florence, saying that the Duke had left the country after writing to the King that he was married to Mrs Horton, and that she was *enceinte*. 'But think what a bitter pill to the Royal Family when you hear it is the sister of the very Colonel Luttrell whom the Court crammed into the House of Commons in the room of Wilkes—so fatal is that man to the Crown, and such triumphs start up for him even whenever he is at the lowest ebb. Think how he will exult at the Court's being lashed with the instrument they prepared for him! No mortification can equal it!

'But what will you say to this mad boy when you know, that if the world says true, his mother [the Princess of Wales] was thought at the point of death at the very instant he chose to make his declaration. All last week it was affirmed that she has a cancer in her mouth and that it was got into her throat . . .'[13]

In the same letter, Walpole draws a comparison between 'this mad boy' and the King's eldest brother the Duke of Gloucester who was 'all prudence and amiability'. What concerned Horace most was the effect this match might have on the future of his niece, Maria, who was *sub rosa* the wife of the Duke of Gloucester, and consequently implicated in the same disgrace. 'I need not hint to you how unfortunate an event this is at the present moment, and how it clashes with the situation of another person.'

Sir Nathaniel Wraxall wrote of Cumberland's wife: 'This lady, like every member of her family, by no means wanted talents; but they were more specious than solid, better calculated for show than for use, for captivating admiration rather than for exciting esteem.'

Lady Louisa Stuart, who thoroughly disapproved of such characteristics and was also jealous of the new Duchess described her as belonging 'to that disgusting class of women who possibly spread wider corruption than many of the more really—or let me say—more *nominally* vicious: women who have never blushed in their lives; who set modesty and decency at defiance in cold blood; and because they have *done* nothing, take the liberty of saying everything; as if desirous to proclaim that it is not principle, but want of sufficient temptation alone, that hinders their walking the Strand.' She goes on to add that Lady Mary Fordyce, after hearing her talk for half an hour, felt that 'one ought to go home to wash one's ears'.[14]

'Junius' seized the opportunity to lash the Duke in a letter dated November 13 published in the *Middlesex Advertiser*: 'I beg Your Royal Highness's acceptance of my sincere compliments upon your auspicious union with the daughter of Lord Irnham and the sister of Colonel Luttrell. For the present you will have so few of these compliments paid you, that mine, perhaps may be thought worthy of your attention. I do assure Your Royal Highness, with great sincerity, that when I consider the various excellencies which adorn or constitute your personal character—your natural parts—your affable, benevolent, generous temper—your good sense, so singularly improved by experience—and, above all the rest, the uncommon education which your venerable mother took care to give you—I do not think it possible to have found a more suitable match for you than which you have so discreetly provided for yourself. What you have done will, I am sure, be no disgrace to yourself or to any of your relations. Yet I must confess, partial as I am to you for the sake of that good prince of whose resemblance you carry some cutting traces about you, I could wish you did not stand quite so near as you do to the Regency and the Crown of England. God forbid I should ever hear your Royal nephew say, as Edward the Fifth does in the play, *But why to the Tower, Uncle!*—or, *Why should you lock us up, Aunt?*—I mean their Uncle Luttrell and Aunt Horton.

'But, my good youth, let no consideration of this sort interrupt your pleasures. Your amiable spouse is as much Duchess of Cumberland as our Gracious Queen is Queen of Great Britain; and of course she is the *second* woman in the kingdom. Your papa Irnham must at least take rank of Lord Mansfield; your brother Henry [Luttrell] of the Princess of Mecklenburgh; and your sister Miss Luttrell of Madame Swellenburgh.* As to the King's not acknowledging the Duchess, or forbidding her the Court, it signifies nothing. Her marriage is good in law, and her children will be legitimate. She may order plays, keep a court of her own, and set the Princess Dowager at defiance. But you need have no fear of being ill-used. Your brother Harry has a dagger at the throat of a certain person, and swears he will let the cat out of the bag about the Middlesex election. So far from offending Harry, I should not wonder to see him aide-de-camp to the King, and in a little time, commander-in-chief.

'Whenever you want a divorce, you need only leave your spouse alone for an hour or two with ——. When he performed the office of father to Poll Davis, and gave her to his infatuated friend, he contrived to send the young man upon a fool's errand, and that very night consummated with her himself. You, I know, Sir, will never go upon a fool's errand, and I suppose it may be equally certain that your papa, if he had an opportunity, would not ...† Cumbriensis.'

The name left out in the last paragraph of this letter is that of Simon Luttrell, then Lord Irnham, the Duke's father-in-law. He was notorious for his love affairs and this allusion is to one he had with Poll Davis, a well-known frail lady. Feeling it was time she settled down, he persuaded her to marry a young man named Nesbitt and

* The Queen's Keeper of the Robes, and her favourite lady-in-waiting—usually spelt 'Schwellenberg'.

† The omitted words are probably 'commit incest'.

when the latter had to go abroad on business the day after the wedding Irnham is said to have taken the bridegroom's place.

To Mrs Bayley's growing annoyance, paragraphs had been appearing in the press about her 'inconsolableness' since learning of the Duke's marriage. The *General Evening Post* for November 16 published a statement from her that such reports were 'entirely fictitious' and that 'the Lady's amorous passion had long since been sated, pride alone supported the connexion for these many months'. The paper added: 'She has now turned her attention to a youthful surgeon, her neighbour, with whom she almost every night flaunts it in the boxes.'

That other recorder of rumours, Lady Mary Coke, who was abroad in Vienna, noted in her *Journal* for Sunday, November 24, that Lady Greenwich had written to her from England about the Duke of Cumberland's marriage 'with the additional circumstance of Mrs Horton being two months gone with Child before he married her. I'm impatient to know how His Majesty will act'.[15] As there is no conclusive evidence of the couple ever having a child, it is probable such a story was based only on the malicious gossip to be expected in the circumstances.

The King remained unmoved and unforgiving, and in a letter to his mother on November 28 he describes Cumberland's conduct as 'the performance of a Newgate attorney' and adds: 'I now wash my hands of the whole affair and shall have no further intercourse with him.'[16] It was reported that he had ordered the Duke's horses 'to be taken away from his meuse' and that Princess Amelia had cut her wayward nephew out of her will.

It will be recalled that some three months previously, the King's ailing favourite brother, William Henry, Duke of Gloucester, had set out on a sea cruise followed by a visit to Italy. Unfortunately his health, instead of improving, had steadily deteriorated and he had been racked by violent attacks of asthma. After almost dying in Leghorn, he rallied and was taken to the hospitable home of Sir Horace Mann, the British Envoy, in Florence where he came under the care of two physicians, Dr Richard Jebb and Mr Robert Adair, sent out by the King. They and the local medicos disagreed, however, as to the remedies that were most likely to cure the patient and each when he had the opportunity flung the drugs which he had not prescribed out of the window. Mann in a letter to Horace Walpole gave it as his opinion that it was thanks to the Duke's thus being kept free of medicine that he slowly recovered. The British Envoy also complained that the invalid's attendants turned his house 'upside down and behaved with an insolence that an inkeeper would not have tolerated' whilst he himself had 'no refuge but my own garret'.[17]

On November 9, the King wrote to his brother expressing relief on hearing that he was still alive. Then, with the preamble, 'You are the old friend to whom I can unbosom my thoughts,' he proceeded to tell him about Cumberland's marriage, enumerating the reasons for his wrath. 'In any country a prince marrying a subject is looked upon as dishonourable, nay, in Germany, the children of such a marriage cannot succeed to any territories; but here, where the Crown is but too little respected, it must be big with the greatest mischiefs. Civil wars would by such measures be again coming in this country, those of the Yorks and Lancasters were greatly owing to intermarriages with the nobility. I must therefore on the first occasion show my resentment. I have children who must know what they have to expect if they would follow so infamous an example.'[18]

There was some justification for the King's attitude. The Duchess of Cumberland's father was in the House of Lords and her four brothers were in the Commons. How after this, George bitterly regretted, could the Crown claim to be above politics?

The Duke of Gloucester must have learned of his brother's reactions to the Cumberland marriage with considerable disquiet, as they made it clear that he must expect similar disapproval should his own to the widowed Lady Waldegrave ever have to be disclosed. In his replies, he diplomatically supported the King's views. Writing from Pisa on November 22, he described their younger brother's conduct as 'a series of follies and inconsistencies'.[19] A month later, again from Pisa, on December 20, his comments were even more critical: 'His behaviour in this last instance is inexcusable and weak beyond measure. He has got into very bad hands and we know is easily led to anything. I own I greatly fear for some subsequent follies ... But he never did act for himself, and certainly does not now.'[20] Gloucester spent Christmas in Rome where he had an audience lasting twenty minutes alone with the Pope and, recorded Mann, pleased him by sending 'a large quantity of chirurgical instruments to the principal hospital' there. Then, in February, he sailed for home from Naples.

Two months previously, in early December, 1771, the Cumberlands had ended their honeymoon, passed travelling under the assumed names of Mr and Mrs Thomas Johnson, and, avoiding London, went straight to their Lodge at Windsor. Mrs Delany tells a friend, 'The vulgar say the Duchess is to have four ladies-in-waiting, a beautiful one has been recommended, no less a person than a cook's daughter! You may say what you please of her Royal Highness, but she has acted discreetly, and has kept up a dignity equal to any prince in romance, for she has kept her love a humble suppliant to the last moment.'[21]

Horace Walpole wrote from Strawberry Hill on December 4 to the Countess of Upper Ossory that the Duke was 'privately forbidden the Court—for of she there is no question; Lord Hertford is told to tell everybody as a secret, which they are desired to tell everybody, that there is no road from Windsor or Cumberland House to St James's. There is a good-natured exception for the Duke's own servants, who, having been placed by the King and having no hand in the wedding, are allowed to go backward and forward.'[22]

In the Fortescue papers J. Blenkett, corresponding with Captain the Hon. William Cornwallis, writes on December 15: 'The Duke of Cumberland, who has long diverted the town, is just arrived in Pall Mall with his Duchess; they are forbidden the Court, but that probably won't last long.' The *Morning Herald* for the previous day thought it amazing how, when he appeared in public, 'the populace thronged to his chariot, as if the circumstances of his marriage had made the most surprising alteration in his person'.

Mr Blenkett proved wrong in his prediction, although Anne immediately following her marriage had engaged Joseph Edmundson, Mowbray Herald Extraordinary, to prepare her pedigree showing her, if possible, to be of royal descent. She hoped that this might help to placate the King. The *Herald*, however, failed to find any such connection, though he compiled a genealogical table professing to trace her descent from the time of William the Conqueror through the evidence obtained from family deeds and the like. It was an elaborate and sumptuous document, written on a roll of fine vellum more than sixteen feet in length and adorned with eighty shields richly illuminated.[23] For the last three centuries covered, the pedigree has every appearance of being authentic. The early part is less satisfactory.

Anne's niece by marriage in the fifth generation, the Duchess of Windsor, was likewise to claim Norman descent, and, in her case, on both sides of the family. In other ways, too, they had much in common. No sooner had the Cumberlands returned to their home in the Mall than what was alleged to be a true copy of what Anne had written to the King was 'handed about the West End'.[24] In this she asked for an opportunity to throw herself at his feet to beg for pardon, and claimed that she deserved forgiveness for endeavouring 'to reclaim a generous, but heedless youth from levities which were more the effect of a good nature, than of bad principles' and 'to regulate his passions and lead him finally to virtue'.

A week later, on Friday, December 14, the Duke paid an evening visit to his mother next door at Carlton House and spent three hours with her,[25] and the *Evening Post*[26] published a copy of 'a letter of felicitation' from Mrs Bayley to the Duchess 'bandied about by people of *Ton*', in which she wrote that 'though a vulgar mind may be much incensed at the object that deprived it of its happiness' she was free of such pettiness and cordially congratulated her on choosing a husband with such accomplishments. As Anne hardly knew him, she would like to enumerate these.

Although the Duke had been brought up at Court, his behaviour and conversation were common and familiar. He loved humour so well that he was 'all laugh without a joke, and mirth was so much his motto that he never thought at all'. He was 'so exceeding amorous that it would require some art to keep his royal heart from wandering'. This, however, Anne could achieve by changing her complexion and dress 'so as to become what the dear creature calls *new*', and he would then become 'as passionate and amorous as one could wish'. There were other things Mrs Bayley could reveal about him, but would leave Anne to make these 'many pleasing discoveries' for herself.

The *Town and Country* for December, 1771, lists among the publications received for review: 'Love Letters which passed between his Royal Highness the Duke of Cumberland, and the Hon. Mrs H----n within a few weeks preceding their Marriage in which the whole process of this important Amour is plainly delineated. 8vo. Price 1s. Swan.' These were obviously fictitious and the Magazine dismisses them with the comment: 'The unparalleled impudence of a Grub-street garreteer.'

All this must have proved very irritating to Lady Grosvenor. One wonders if she may have regretted not allowing her husband to have divorced her. Could she then have persuaded the Duke to have married her? It was in fact most unlikely for although after the affair at St Albans, he had not immediately dropped her and rented for her that house at Barnes, his ardour from then onwards had rapidly cooled. Now she reacted to news of her former lover's marriage by returning not only all his presents, including a pair of diamond shoe-buckles, but also an elegant post-chaise on which he had arranged to have her coat-of-arms painted, and which he had given her when she went to live at Barnes. On the Monday afternoon before Christmas that year, she hired a postillion and a pair of horses to take the vehicle and a letter to Windsor, where the boy was to spend the night, go early next morning to the Duke's Lodge, take off the horses, leave the chaise, deliver the letter, then ride away without waiting for an answer.[27]

Some eight months later, Lady Grosvenor was seen in the neighbourhood of St James's in 'a most superb equipage at a magnificent entertainment, at which was none but persons of quality'.[28] The following month, it was disclosed that Lord Grosvenor, attempting a reconciliation, had sent her the new *vis-à-vis*, complete with proper attendants, and a letter desiring her return home. 'She kept the equipage, but sent his Lordship word they were best asunder.'[29]

But, despite this splendid conveyance, Henrietta did not immediately re-enter society, for the following spring it was reported that she had fallen in love with a doctor of divinity and had become so fanatically religious that it was feared she would lose her reason if the clergyman's wife and his ecclesiastical superiors did not interfere.[30] This must have happened, for in early July Henrietta announced her intention to live in future in a monastery.[31]

But the Duke of Cumberland's former sweetheart did not renounce the world and all its temptations. Instead, for a time, she captivated Lord Cholmondeley, regarded as the most eligible bachelor in the House of Lords, a huge, ungainly youth of great physical strength, nicknamed by satirists 'Lord Tallboy' and 'Lord Torpedo'. Then we learn, that her aristocratic friends had dropped her and that she was in debt to a banker and a mercer, to whom she paid interest in kind,[32] and was reduced to frequenting Mrs Cornely's masquerades with only a female attendant.[33]

Although Lady Grosvenor had refused to return to her husband, the couple were reunited for one night in 1778 without knowing it, if we are to believe the anonymous author of *Nocturnal Revels, or a History of King's Place*, a curious work in two volumes, published in 1779, which throws much light upon the seamy side of the period. According to this, shrewd Mrs Prendergast, who kept a fashionable 'nunnery' in St James's had a brainwave which she hoped would draw the smart set to her establishment, and so she wrote to all her customers and others likely to be interested informing them that on

Wednesday evening, November 12, she would hold a '*Bal d'Amour*, where some of the finest Women in Europe would make their appearance, masked indeed, but in other respects *in puris naturalibus*'. Everyone who wished to attend had to subscribe at least five guineas in advance. In this way, she collected about 700 guineas, enabling her to make lavish preparations to ensure the diversion's success.

The night of the Gala saw Pall Mall thronged with chairs and carriages, whose occupants seemed to vie with one another to be the first to arrive. Lady Grosvenor and Lady Ligonier (a notorious beauty who was William Pitt's daughter and separated from her husband) came together and were naked except for large fig leaves covering their faces. The moment this was noticed 'there was such a hue and cry for fig leaves, that it was necessary to send for a cargo from Covent Garden Market'.

After the company had danced for some two hours, the serving of refreshment was announced, and 'each Gentleman conducted his partner to the festive board; where having ... drunk about half a dozen toasts to the honour of the Cyprian Goddess and all her Rites, the scene changed, and presented a *camera obscura*, with a proper number of sophas, to realise those Rites which had been celebrated only in theory'.

A mask whether of fig-leaves or of more conventional material had become an indispensable item of dress for a sex-seeking fine lady at a ball, as it provided her with a shield of anonymity giving her the courage to break the Sixth Commandment with the beau she fancied.

The account continues that 'the fervency of the devotion upon this occasion could scarce be parallelled, and it is somewhat extraordinary that Lord G[rosveno]r and Lord L[igonie]r enjoyed their own wives without knowing it, and, strange to tell, pronounced their imaginary LAIS's most excellent Pieces. It was thought, upon the discovery, which was made the ensuing morning, that this would have been the means of promoting a reconciliation between the parties. Indeed, a rumour was circulated throughout the Town, that all misunderstanding had ceased between Lord Grosvenor and his Lady, and that they actually cohabited again together.' But this proved a false rumour.

We learn that the *Bal d'Amour* was such a success that it was soon repeated by Mrs Prendergast. The two functions put nearly a thousand pounds profit in her pocket, and she was pronounced to be the 'proper successor of Mrs Cornelys as the Empress of Taste and Luxury'.

The pages of *Nocturnal Revels* also provide further details regarding the private life of Lord Grosvenor. He would appear to have strong claims to be regarded as the inventor of the modern spring mattress. We are told that a brothel in Berkeley Street was run by a Mrs W—st—n, sister to his Lordship's head groom and 'chief Pimp'. The latter set her up in business, and at the same time promised his employer's custom, protection and recommendation. 'In this respect he has fully compleated his promise; for though his Lordship may sometimes wander in the purlieus of King's Place, or the environs of Marylebone, his chief attraction is in Berkeley Street. Here he constantly meets Miss Hayw[ar]d twice a week, and sometimes oftener.' The 'laughter-loving' Clara Hayward, as the papers dubbed her, started a career as an actress at Foote's theatre in the Haymarket, followed by Drury Lane, after that actor had enjoyed her other charms in Charlotte Hayes's establishment. According to *Nocturnal Revels*, Clara 'figures off and on the Stage in various parts and attitudes, and generally meets with applause, particularly on her under parts'.

Mrs Hayes's 'Nunnery' in Duke Street, St James's, has already been mentioned as one patronized by Lord Grosvenor. Later she retired from business and 'no sooner did Mrs W—st—n learn this than she immediately called on her and purchased all her Elastic Beds, invented by that great creative genius Count O'K[ell]y and constructed by that celebrated mechanic and upholsterer, Mr Gale.' Dennis O'Kelly, owner of the famous horse, Eclipse, was an adventurer who made his money from the turf and from being Charlotte's partner in her uppercrust bawdy-house.

Not satisfied, however, with being in possession of these beds, which gave 'the finest movements in the most extatic [*sic*] moments, without trouble or the least fatigue to either Agent or Patient, she requested Lord Gro[svenor] (who has also a fine mechanical genius, and has already made a great improvement upon Mrs Phillips's machines, by securing them in such a manner that they can never break in action) to throw out some hints for the improvement of these Elastic Beds; and he immediately conceived an additional spring, to the amazing gratification and sensation of the Actor and Actress as Clara Hayward can well testify. To this additional spring we may, in a great measure, ascribe the vogue that Mrs W—st—n's house is now enjoying, being frequented by Peers and Peeresses, Wanton Wives, and more Wanton Widows.'

Nocturnal Revels in addition gives us more information regarding Lady Grosvenor's affairs up to 1779. We are told that she was very bountiful of her favours, and that 'sated at length with Lord Cholmondeley's charms, Captain Turner would be her favourite man did not her avarice compel her to fly to the arms of his elder brother, Sir G[regory] P[age] T[urner], and others, whose purse-strings are more easily dilated'. The baronet known as the 'Eel' lived at Blackheath with an attractive housekeeper who eventually weaned him away from Henrietta. By 1781, the latter appears to have tired of men of her own age or older and to have taken a young lover with whom she lived in Hampstead.[34]

In 1784 Lord Grosvenor, who had been created a Baron in 1761, was advanced to the dignity of Viscount Belgrave and Earl Grosvenor. Lady Louisa Stuart's comments in a letter dated July 27 that year were: 'So my Lady Grosvenor is a Countess and may in all senses be called the *first in her profession* as I remember Lady M. said of some other famous lame beauty. I wonder her consideration did not cool his Lordship's longings for a higher title.'

On August 5, 1802, the new Earl died, appropriately, at Earl's Court, London. Less than a month later, on September 1, his widow married General Porter, M.P. for Stockbridge. Her only regret was that she could no longer call herself a Countess. However, she persuaded her second husband to petition the King to be allowed to assume the title of Baron de Hochepied, granted to his maternal great-grandfather in 1704 by the Emperor Leopold I. This was eventually allowed in 1819.

Henrietta died at Ealing on January 2, 1828. When her grandson's wife, Lady Elizabeth Belgrave, (to whose wedding she had not been invited) heard the news, she commented that she believed the Dowager 'had so little mind as not to be unhappy. ... She was, I believe, dreadfully stingy and has left her money, which ought to be a great deal to General Porter who I fancied was dead but is, I believe, only in gaol'. The remark concerning the latter is intriguing, but according to the obituary notice in the *Gentleman's Magazine*, he died less than three months after Henrietta on March 28, 1828.

The year 1772 opened auspiciously for the Duke of Cumberland. He won the Jockey Club cup, worth £1,500, and 'it was carried down to Windsor Lodge, filled with money won on the same occasion by his having the best horse in the whole catalogue of subscribers'.[35] But the Duchess was not so fortunate. Far from the King showing any signs of recognizing her, she was offered £10,000 in money and £4,000 a year if she renounced her public title, which proposal she rejected. Some disapproved of his attitude, and when he was on his way to morning service one Sunday at St James's a well-dressed man thrust into his hand a piece of paper on which was written the text: 'First go and be reconciled to thy brother, and then come and offer thy gift.'[36]

Also in January, 1772, there opened in London what was rapidly to become the most exclusive centre for routs and masquerades, taking away so much of Mrs Cornelys' trade that she went bankrupt and was reduced to selling asses' milk for a living. This was the Pantheon in the Oxford Road, designed by James Wyatt. Horace Walpole, an early visitor, called it 'the most beautiful building in England' and wrote to the Rev William Mason: 'All the friezes and niches were edged with alternate lamps of green and purple glass that shed a most heathen light, and the dome was illuminated by a heaven of oiled paper well painted with gods and goddesses.' It was so glorious a building in the Grecian style that he thought he was in the old Pantheon itself. 'Even Henry VIII had so much taste that were he alive he would visit the Pantheon.'[37]

In an attempt to keep the Pantheon respectable all known prostitutes were refused admission. The Duchess of Cumberland became a subscriber and wrote before her name 'Her Royal Highness'. Then, when the Lord Chamberlain, preparing for the Queen Charlotte's Birthday Ball to be held there, invited Peeresses wishing to attend to send in their names, she announced her intention of applying.

Once news of this reached St James's Palace, there was general alarm at the possible consequences. If allowed to attend, Anne would have to be given precedence over all other peeresses. The alternative was to refuse her application. Neither course was judged advisable, and at last the Lord Chamberlain sent the Duchess a letter appealing to her 'for the present' to waive her intentions, and hinting that if 'Her Royal Highness' agreed to do so, it might pave the way to restoring her to the King's favour.

Until then, the Duchess had always been officially termed 'Your Grace', so tempted by the Lord Chamberlain's conciliatory note, she yielded and, making the excuse of being indisposed, did not attend the Queen Charlotte's Birthday Ball.[38] But the Lord Chamberlain had acted on his own initiative without consulting the King, who was to remain obdurately opposed to recognizing Cumberland's wife.

In the twentieth century, the Duchess of Windsor, whose situation was similar to that of the former Mrs Horton in some ways, was never to gain the precedence she coveted and which was debarred by King George VI's Letter Patent under the Great Seal of the Realm dated May 27, 1937, when instructions were given that she must be addressed as 'Your Grace' and was not entitled to 'Your Royal Highness' or a curtsy on formal occasions. The Duke of Windsor, nevertheless, insisted on female staff curtsying to his wife, and so did his ancestor, the Duke of Cumberland, much to George III's annoyance, which grew when he learned that ladies visiting Cumberland House were doing the same.

Those mischievously inclined did their best to denigrate Anne in the King's presence. To try and counteract this and please him, she encouraged her husband in cultural pursuits and to read on average for two hours a day books she had chosen for him. Publicity to this was given in *The Craftsman* which added that the Duchess was 'besides an accurate geographer' and that the couple amused themselves 'in the evening in this pleasant study'.[39]

Anne was determined that her husband should confound those who had belittled his mental powers. Thanks to her encouragement, he persevered in his studies, and three months later we read that he has 'a 'gentleman of great eminence in daily attendance upon him from whom he is learning jurisprudence in general' and that he was also 'paying particular attention to the study of civil law'.[40]

CHAPTER TWELVE

Queen Caroline Matilda

King George III also had a black sheep sister whose trial for adultery and imprisonment were to cause him considerable concern and bring Britain to the brink of war with Denmark. Five months after his father, Frederick, Prince of Wales, had died in March, 1751, the widow, Princess Augusta, gave birth to a daughter in Leicester House. Christened Caroline Matilda, the new Princess first appeared at Court when aged thirteen-and-a-half and contemporaries describe her as having almost flaxen hair, large soft blue eyes, a fine mouth (except for a full underlip), an arched nose, the figure of a woman twice her age, and an easy and dignified carriage. She was to become very plump.

Caroline's great-aunt, Princes Louisa, daughter of King George II, had married the King of Denmark, Frederick V, who died on January 14, 1766, and was succeeded by his son, Christian VII, to whom Caroline had been betrothed a year earlier and to whom she was married by proxy at the Chapel Royal, St James's on October 1, 1766. Two days later she sailed from Harwich to Rotterdam and thence to Altona and Roeskilde where her bridegroom met her. On November 8 the marriage ceremony proper was held in the Palace of Frederiksberg. The populace gave her a friendly reception but Christian, who was besotted with his favourite, Count von Holtke, treated her with icy indifference fulfilling her earlier fears about this forced marriage to a complete stranger. Before leaving London, she had sat for her portrait which proved an ordeal both for her and Sir Joshua Reynolds, who commented afterwards that he had found it impossible to do her justice as she wept all the time. Mrs Carter corresponding with a friend disclosed that for this unwilling bride: 'It is worse than dying; for die she must to all she has ever known. . . . May it please God to protect and instruct and comfort her, poor child as she is. They have just been telling me how bitterly she cried in the coach.'[1]

All Caroline's English and Hanoverian retainers had left her at

Altona, so she was now completely without any friend to whom she could turn for comfort. Instead, she had to face the undisguised hostility of the late monarch's second wife, the Dowager Queen Juliana Maria, whose son would succeed to the throne should Caroline be childless, which was likely as Christian had strong homosexual inclinations. In an attempt to wean him away from his pages and Holtke, Caroline started wearing male attire. 'If only she were well made,' wrote a lady of the Court, Madame von Gramm, 'I could understand her walking about in the costume; but just think of her hips, her—quarters!'[2]

The King, however, approved and made her ride astride, attired like a cavalry officer. On a visit from England, the Princess Dowager was horrified to be met at the frontier by her daughter in military uniform with beaver hat, top-boots, spurs, and bulging buckskin breeches. It had become a popular joke among the Danes to tell one another when they saw King and Queen together that she was 'the better man of the two'.

On January 28, 1768, to many people's surprise, a son was born to Caroline, then, that May, Christian left her alone at Frederiksberg until the following January while he went off with Holtke to enjoy himself travelling in England and elsewhere. Horace Walpole's letters provide vivid accounts of the royal visitor's activities. One to George Montagu reads: 'He is as diminutive as if he came out of a kernel in the fairy tales. He is not ill made, nor weakly ... and though his face is pale and delicate, it is not at all ugly. ... Still, he has more royalty than folly in his air, and considering he is not twenty is as well as any one expects a King in a puppet-show to be ... struts like a cock-sparrow, and does the honours of himself very civilly. There is a favourite, too, who seems a complete Jackanapes; a young fellow called Holtke well enough in his figure, and about three-and-twenty, but who will be tumbled down, long before he is prepared for it.'[3]

Corresponding with the Earl of Strafford, three days later, Walpole wrote about Christian: 'The mob adore him and huzza him ... for he flings money to them out of his windows; and by the end of the week I do not doubt but they will want to choose him for Middlesex as M.P. His court is extremely well ordered; for they bow as low to him at every word as if his name was Sultan Amurat.'[4]

Eight days later, Walpole tells his friend Mann: 'The poor little King is fatigued to death and has got the belly-ache. He was to have set out on Monday to hear bad Latin verses at Cambridge and to see the races at York but is confined at St James.'[5] Starved of home gossip away in Florence, Mann replied asking for more and was told that Horace could add nothing to what the other would read in the papers of the King 'hurrying from one corner of England to the other, without seeing anything distinctly, fatiguing himself, breaking his chaise, going tired to bed in inns, and getting up to show himself to the mob at the window. I believe he is a very silly lad ... he has neither done nor said anything worth reporting, but he gives them [the mob] an opportunity of getting together, of staring, and of making foolish obervations. Then the newspapers talk their own language and call him a *great personage*; and a great personage that comes so often in their way seems almost one of themselves raised to the throne.'

Walpole follows this with a titbit about the little King's behaviour at a performance of *The Provoked Wife*. 'He clapped whenever there was a sentence against matrimony; a very civil proceeding when his wife is an English princess.'[6]

During the King's absence, Caroline Matilda had gained confidence and began to take an active role in the government of the country. When the Russian minister treated her with lack of courtesy, she had him recalled and even when Christian returned she retained her hold on affairs, instigating the dismissal of the pro-Russian chief minister, Bernsdorffe, as well as succeeding in getting rid of Holtke. Her mother, the Princess Dowager, who considered the former a wise statesman, told her that she considered his downfall regrettable, to which Caroline retorted: 'Pray, Madam, allow me to govern my own kingdom as I please.'

Such a remark must have sounded vainglorious but there was a large element of truth in it, for Christian was rapidly deteriorating both mentally and physically until he was compared with Caligula. When Caroline feared that her stoutness might be caused by dropsy, she consulted a handsome and ambitious young physician, John Struensee, on whom her husband had become dependent. This brilliant son of a poor clergyman assured her that all she was suffering from was lack of exercise and prescribed more riding which reduced her weight.

From then onwards, Struensee's ascendancy over the royal couple accelerated. He was assiduous in his attentions to both. They enjoyed listening to his reading aloud to them which he was ever willing to do in his attractive, soothing voice. Proud of his fine, blonde hair he had it dressed in the same style as the Queen's which pleased the homosexual King who raised no objection to their dancing almost every dance together at balls and was happy to sit and watch admiringly his wife's cicisbeo's grace and skill in quadrille and minuet. But Struensee was more than a Queen's poodle and soon his undoubted talents in the political arena lead to his becoming Prime Minister. Encouraged by Caroline, he embarked on a policy of radical reforms. He abolished torture—the first absolute monarchy to do this. He did his utmost to obtain freedom for the enslaved husbandmen and allowed all religious denominations to worship without any constraints. He set up a hospital for old and incapacitated soldiers, fostered agriculture, commerce, and manufacturing industries.

Other measures of Struensee's were controversial and aroused considerable opposition. On grounds of economy, he disbanded the regiments of guards and alienated the military—and also the nobility by abolishing the Privy Council and the straitlaced among the people by repealing an ancient law that made capital punishment the penalty to be suffered by convicted adulterers. This lent credence to the rumours circulated by his enemies that he himself led a licentious life.

With the intention of preventing the heir to the throne from becoming as self-indulgent and depraved as his father, Struensee had him brought up in Spartan fashion. He was given an ordinary soldier's son named Edward as his companion and to place the boy on an equal footing he had to be addressed as 'Prince'. He wore a uniform similar to that of the young royal, ate the same food which consisted of bread, rice, milk, vegetables, and fruit, all cold. Both slept on the same mattress, bathed in cold water, were forbidden to wear shoes or stockings in winter, and lived in a fireless room.

Struensee's autocratic attitude and unpopular measures led to mounting opposition against him. The fact that he and the Queen were clearly lovers ensured that a revolt would receive popular support. The conspirators were headed by an army general, the Count of Rantzau-Ascheberg, and the Dowager Queen, and the occasion chosen for action was a masked ball on January 16, 1772. Caroline and Struensee danced together most of the evening and remained until three a.m. though the King had retired to his apartments soon after midnight. Taking advantage of this, Rantzau an hour or so later slipped into his room and rousing him alleged that his wife and the Prime Minister were planning to murder him and that he risked such a fate if he did not sign a document ordering their arrest without delay.

Despite his weakness of mind and body, Christian was not easily deceived and intimidated. The charges against Caroline and his best friend sounded like complete fabrications by their enemies, so he refused to comply with Rantzau's request. The latter than conferred with the Dowager Queen and she joined him in the efforts to force the King to sign the warrant which eventually, bewildered and confused by lack of sleep, he did. Struensee was then dragged from his bed, put into fetters and imprisoned in the citadel, whilst Caroline was taken to a fortress and locked in a cell-like room with her second child, a baby daughter.

When the following month, Struensee had to submit to intensive interrogation he broke down under the strain and with the misguided hope that siding with those now in power might save his life he admitted that he had lain with the Queen but claimed that it was she who had seduced him. A special commission next visited Caroline and confronted her with this evidence. Unable to credit that Struensee should have betrayed her, she cried that it must be a complete forgery. But her questioners insisted that the confession was genuine, and one added that there was no death cruel enough for 'this monster who has dared to compromise you'.

There can be no doubt that Caroline was deeply in love with Struensee and so was horrified by these words. Her ruthless inquisitors sensing her feelings pretended that he might be spared death if she signed a statement admitting that his confession was true. Her sole concern was to save his life and, with foolish impetuosity, she seized the pen held out to her and appended her name to the document. Unwittingly, she had thus rendered herself to forfeit her own life, as that was the prescribed punishment in Denmark for an adulterous Queen.

Arraigned before thirty-five men of mark and found guilty, Caroline was declared divorced from the King and stripped of her title as Queen Consort. She took her own downfall with resignation and her whole concern was over Struensee's fate, and she wept when told that he would surely die on the scaffold, a barbarous death. After a charade of a trial, this took place on April 28.

The authorities were unable at first to find carpenters to erect the grim structure as there was a superstition current among them that it would bring bad luck, so soldiers had to force them to comply. But no wheelwright could be dragooned into providing the wheels on which the quartered corpse was to be displayed, so, in desperation, they were removed from ancient carriages in the royal stable. A mob of over

30,000 watched Struensee's execution, gloating over the excess of butchery, while from a watch tower of the Christiansborg Palace the Dowager Queen Juliana Maria kept her eyes riveted on the scene through a strong telescope and commented that the only thing that spoilt her rejoicing was that Caroline Matilda's corpse had not been flung into the cart as well.

King George III and his family had long been aware of Caroline's love affair and both her mother, Princess Augusta, and the Duke of Gloucester on visits to Denmark had warned her of the risks she was taking through her wilfulness. Though the news of his sister's arrest and disgrace had disturbed the King, he felt that she was largely responsible for her plight and he could not feel sorry for her. His wife, Queen Charlotte, fumed with moral indignation and complained that her sister-in-law's shameless liaison following so closely Cumberland's had so tarnished the royal family's reputation that she dare not make a public appearance for fear of being insulted. Her mother-in-law, the Princess Dowager Augusta, who was dying, reacted even more strongly, saying that no one must refer to Caroline Matilda while attending her for she could never again regard such a person as her daughter.

Fortunately for the divorced and degraded Queen, she had a staunch friend in the British Envoy, Robert Murray Keith, and he pleaded her cause ceaselessly in his despatches, stressing that if King George continued taking no action, Caroline was in grave danger of being incarcerated in the grim fortress of Aalborg and even of being murdered. Queen Charlotte proved wrong for public opinion increasingly supported her sister-in-law. It was thought that she had been misjudged, and Junius in one of his letters attacked the King for unbrotherly harshness, demanding: 'Is our pious monarch cast in a different mould from that of his people?'

Keith had sent the King a detailed account of Caroline Matilda's trial, drawing attention to how it had been stage-managed, how he had discovered that most of the evidence was suborned and perjured, and the manner in which she had been inveigled into making that 'confession'. George was at last moved into having these papers considered by the chief law officers of the crown and they reported that in their opinion the case against her had not been fairly proven.

These conclusions stirred the King into strong measures. He ordered Keith to inform the junta in Denmark that unless Caroline Matilda were released forthwith war between the two countries would follow and British ships would bombard Copenhagen; and in belated recognition of the Envoy's endeavours he appointed him a Knight of the Bath. Horace Walpole wrote to Sir Horace Mann on March 2, 1772: 'Mr. Keith's spirit in behalf of the Queen has been rewarded. The red riband has been sent to him, though there was no vacancy with orders to put it on directly himself, as there is no sovereign in Denmark to invest him with it.'[7]

The new Sir Robert had already pointed out to the clique in power in Copenhagen that by stripping Caroline of her regal rank and Danish citizenship she had become once more an English subject of King George III. Faced with this fact and the unexpected ultimatum, the Danes yielded, but the frigate accompanied by two sloops on board which she left in May did not take her back to England. Queen Charlotte had threatened to leave that country herself if the sister-in-law she still believed to be a wanton were allowed to set foot in it. When Hanover was suggested as an alternative haven she objected to that, too, on the grounds that it was too pleasant and worldly a place for someone of weak character and wayward ways. So George, to preserve marital peace, gave way to Charlotte. His great-grandmother had been the unhappy Sophia Dorothea whose affair with Königsmark had caused a similar scandal in its day. Ever since her father, the Duke of Celle, had died, the castle there had remained uninhabited and it was to this solitary environment that Caroline was sent.

George ordered that his exiled sister should be given all the consideration and comfort due to a Queen who was also an English Princess and despatched a kindly letter to her. 'Dear sister, continue that circumspection in your behaviour that has gained great credit during your misfortunes. It is the most effectual means of showing what a blessing you might have been if those that surrounded you had possessed any principle of honour and integrity.'[8]

Kept away from her children, Caroline grew increasingly miserable. Her only hope was that a rebellion would overthrow the regime in Denmark hostile to her, but King George was doubtful about this and wrote: 'Whenever the present horrible people that manage that kingdom are either removed by death or the intrigues of some new party, it cannot avail anything in your favour; but your leading an exemplary life will by degrees turn the cry in your favour and will hereafter make your son step forward in defence of his mother. I doubt but many dissatisfied people will try to make up to you, but I trust you will not give ear to their proposals. Others will be encouraged by the Danish court to sound you with no other view but to pry into your thoughts. Believe me, dear sister, the only dignified as well as safe part for you is give up all thoughts of that country, at least till your children can be in a situation to come to your assistance.'[9]

Some two and a half years later, there was sufficient unrest in Denmark for the disaffected to start plotting a coup d'état which they thought might have more chances of success if Caroline were associated with it. Any scheme that would reunite her with her children appealed to the ex-Queen, but when approached in secret for his support George would have nothing to do with it. He wrote to his 'dearest sister' that it was not by calling himself an honest or an honourable man that he could deserve either of those epithets, but by a correct conduct. When promising to see that she was allowed to leave Denmark, he had stressed that he would not assist her to return there later. What he had said, he would 'scrupulously fulfil'.

George continued: 'Indeed, I cannot, dear sister, say any more than if the Danish nobility shall at any time bring the King to recall you with that éclat and dignity that alone can make it advisable for you to return to his kingdom, I shall not only not prevent your going but support those who have been accessory to it; but from what I have declared I cannot either enter farther into the affair or be entrusted with the plan on which they mean to act.'[10]

But the plot never reached fruition. The climate of Celle did not suit Caroline and her health deteriorated. Three years later, an epidemic of what was called the 'military fever' broke out in Germany and she caught it. Her resistance was low and, only aged twenty-four, to quote the words of an attendant 'like a weary wayfarer' she sank into her final sleep, and was entombed next to her great-grandmother, Sophia Dorothea, whose tragic fate was so similar to hers.

CHAPTER THIRTEEN

The Royal Marriage Act

The passage of time did not diminish the King's anger over the Cumberland marriage. The death of his mother must have helped to maintain his unforgiving mood. He resolved that no other member of the Royal family should follow the Duke's example and that the law should in future prevent it, and so, at his bidding, the Crown's most dependable lawyers, Mansfield, Wedderburn and Thurlow drew up the Royal Marriage Bill which came before the House of Commons on February 20, 1772, when Lord Rochfort and Lord North delivered the following message from the King: 'His Majesty, being desirous from paternal affection for his own family, and anxious concern for the future welfare of his people, and the honour and dignity of his crown, that the right of approving all marriages in the Royal Family (which ever has belonged to the king of this realm as a matter of public concern) may be made effectual, recommends to both Houses of Parliament to take into their serious consideration whether it may not be wise and expedient to supply the defect of the laws now in being; and, by some provision, more effectually to guard the descendants of his late majesty King George the Second (other than the issue of princesses who have married or may marry into foreign families) from marrying without the approbation of his Majesty, his heirs or successors, first had and obtained.'[1]

The Bill had a reception in both Houses as icy as the weather without, and caused controversy throughout the country. The Bishop of Oxford declared that by giving the King powers to keep young Royals celibate it would encourage them to have mistresses. But Warburton, Bishop of Gloucester, saw no harm in that. Charles James Fox resigned from his post as Junior Lord of the Admiralty, and a Captain Phipps described the Bill as 'a measure giving the Princes of the Blood leave to lie with our wives, while forbidding them to marry our daughters'.[2]

Horace Walpole tells us in his *Journals* that 'Lord North and the

Ministers were 'ridiculously alarmed, and so much terrified by the defection of Mr Fox and disapprobation of others' that they obtained a modification of the Act and brought it in the next day with an alteration, exempting Princes from 'positive prohibition of marriage after twenty-five years of age, and enabling them, after a declaration for a year before the Privy Council to marry, unless Parliament made an objection'.[3]

The Duke of Cumberland was present in the Lords on the first day the Bill was debated there. Only the Duke of Richmond spoke to him. Henry Frederick had notes in his hand which he appeared to browse over as if planning to speak.[4] The other asked him if he took exception to being mentioned in the discussion. He replied that he had no objection and that he was there to defend his Duchess in case anyone should suggest making the Bill apply retrospectively, thus invalidating his own marriage. (He had wed Anne on October 2, 1771, before his twenty-sixth birthday on the 7th of the following month.) But as no peer went so far as to demand this, he told Richmond that he thought he had better leave, which he did and remained absent for the rest of the discussion.

The King made the Bill a personal matter, and in his message to Lord North after the first debate, he wrote: 'I cannot say the management of the debate in one House of Lords this day edified me. I hope there will be a meeting tomorrow to settle the mode of proceeding on Friday. I do expect every nerve to be strained to carry the Bill through both Houses with a becoming firmness, for it is not a question that immediately relates to Administration, but personally to myself, therefore I have a right to expect a hearty support from everyone in my service and shall remember Defaulters. Queen's House, February 26, 1772, 3 minutes past 11 p.m.'[5]

That same night the Bill was read a second time in the Lords. During the debate, doubt was expressed as to whether the King could have the right in law to prevent his grandfather's children from marrying as they wished. Two days later, on the 28th, the Judges unanimously gave it as their opinion that whilst 'the care and approbation' of the King's own children and grandchildren 'do belong to this realm, they could not find it anywhere precisely stated what other branches of the Royal Family were also included'.[6]

The House of Lords then went into Committee to resolve whether the Judges should be asked further questions, but it was decided not to test further what Fox described as 'the glorious uncertainty of the law'.[7]

On March 2, when the first enacting clause of the Bill was read in Committee, the Marquis of Rockingham attacked it, saying that if King George III's own fertility were inherited by his descendants, thousands might in the course of time find themselves affected by such an Act.[8] Gouty Lord Camden (who had acted for Lord Grosvenor in the arbitration over his wife's alimony) went further and asked earnestly for an answer to the question: 'Who are the Royal Family?' He saw no reason to confine the matter to the King's descendants. All those of Edward III of which there were at least a thousand were members of the Royal Family, and so were those of Charles II. The Act should cover the whole Royal Family, past and present, so that half of England might become wards of the Crown.[9]

But Lord Chancellor Thurlow allowed no amendment of any kind. 'The King cannot make a bad use of this power,' he said, 'because Parliament would punish any minister advising him ill.[10] So, next day, the Lords passed the Bill by 90 votes to 26, and on March 4 it reached the Commons, where debate was heated and protracted. One of the best speeches came from Lord Folkestone, who pointed out that the Bill imposed the right of prohibiting a marriage without means of punishing disobedience. This was in law 'as in commonsense, a non-existent'. It was insulting to the people because it implied that 'an alliance of a subject with a branch of the Royal Family is dishonourable to the Crown'. He had heard that the Duke of Cumberland on applying to have his registered was told it could not be done unless a herald attended.[11]

Charles James Fox considered it 'very probable' that the ten-year-old Prince of Wales would eventually marry a woman without his father's consent and live with her notwithstanding an act of parliament which forbade this. 'As the lady would not suffer in her reputation and would be thought his legal wife by the greatest part of the world, when he came to the throne he would marry her again. And in that case the children he had by her during the life of his father would be illegitimate by act of parliament but legitimate in the eyes of the rest of the world.'

The bill would not prevent a future King from marrying an apple girl, but it might bar his heir 'from making the most proper match'. In such a case, asked Fox, where would be the dignity of the Crown? It was claimed that if a subject were to become the monarch's consort, her relations might be favoured by him. 'We will suppose that a future King should have a mistress. Is it not probable he will be as partial to her friends as to his wife's?'

The Hon. Nicholas Herbert, M.P. for the pocket borough of Wilton, moved that the bill's sitting should be amended by the addition of the words 'an act ... for the encouragement of adultery and fornication'.[12]

But despite logic and ridicule the measure was passed on March 24 by 168 votes to 115 much to the King's relief. According to what the Whig John Almon, wrote in his in his *Political Register*, the bill became law at a cost to George III of six peerages, one blue ribbon of the Garter, three red of the Bath, one baronetage, three reversionary patent places, £25,000 in occasional gratuities, besides innumerable promises of lottery tickets.

The King had apparently succeeded in his purpose which was, as he put it in a letter to the Duke of Gloucester, 'to let my children know what they have to expect if they would follow so infamous an example' as Cumberland's. But legal prohibition often fosters what it seeks to prevent and the Prince of Wales was to marry Mrs Fitzherbert long before he reached the age of twenty-five, encouraged and abetted by his Aunt Anne whom George had alienated by his relentless refusal to acknowledge her as a Royal Duchess.

In January that year reports had twice appeared in *The Craftsman* that the Duchess of Cumberland was pregnant. On the very day the Royal Marriage Act became law, March 24, 1772, the *General Evening Post* declared: 'We are assured that Her Royal Highness the Duchess of Cumberland is in a state of pregnancy. In the same issue, it was also mentioned that she and the Duke had 'set off for Windsor on Monday morning from their house in Pall Mall'. Then, on March 28, the paper informed its readers that: 'On Wednesday night, Lord North waited on the Duke of Cumberland at Cumberland House in Pall Mall, with whom he had a long conference.'

What brought the Duke back so soon to London and caused the King's first minister to pay him so lengthy a visit? The records of the period do not tell us and we hear no more of the Duchess's pregnancy. Years later, one Olive Wilmot Serres was to claim that she was the Duke's daughter. The date of her birth she gave as April 3, 1772, but her story must be left to the final chapters.

After waiting for the furore caused by the Royal Marriage Act to die down, the Duke of Gloucester returned to England from Italy and rejoined his wife. They decided that in the circumstances their secret union would have to be revealed to the King. It was arranged that the Duchess should first tell her father about it. On June 15, her uncle,

Horace Walpole, informed his friend, Mann, in Italy: 'On the very evening of his return the Duke of Gloucester allowed my niece to acquaint her father that they have been married ever since September, 1766. Lady Waldegrave which I think very modest does not take the royal title, but her father has shown the letter so much that even copies of it have got about. For my own part, I have not at all changed my sentiments from the event, but still think her prudence to have been perfect.'[13]

'My dear and ever honoured Sir,' wrote Maria. 'You cannot easily imagine how every past affliction has been increased to me by not being at liberty to make you quite easy. The duty to a husband being superior to that we owe a father, I hope will plead my pardon; and that instead of blaming my past reserve, you will think it commendable.

'When the Duke of Gloucester married me, which was in September, 1766, I promised him upon no consideration in the world to own it even to you without his permission which permission I never had until yesterday ... To secure my character without injuring his is the utmost of my wishes, and I daresay that you and all my relations will agree with me that I shall be much happier to be called Lady Waldegrave, and respected as Duchess of Gloucester, than to feel myself the cause of his leading such a life as his brother [the Duke of Cumberland] does, in order to be called Your Royal Highness. I am prepared for the sort of abuse the newspapers will be full of. Very few people will believe that a woman will refuse to be called Princess if it is in her power. To have the power is my pride, and using it in some measure pays the debt I owe the Duke for the honour he has done me. All I wish of my relations is that they will show the world they are satisfied with my conduct, yet seem to disguise their reasons. If ever I am fortunate enough to be called Duchess of Gloucester, there is an end almost of all the comforts I now enjoy, which if things go on as they now do, are many.'

Sir Edward sent his brother the letter to read, describing it as 'one of the sweetest samples of sense, language, and goodness of heart I ever saw'. But cynical Horace Walpole was not taken in by such protestations, and soon he was writing to his crony in Florence: 'My niece the Duchess has not written in the same strain of self-denial to her sister Dysart. To her she recounts the magnificence of the presents the Duke has given her; and many other expressions show me that her ambition, which is her prevailing passion, would not long be smothered.'[14]

But the Duke himself delayed over breaking the news to the King. Then, in early September, Maria told him that she was pregnant. He could procrastinate no longer, so on September 13, 1772, he summoned up the courage to write to the King: 'I am grieved at finding myself obliged to acquaint Your Majesty with a thing that must be so disagreeable to you, but I think the world being so much acquainted with my marriage whilst Your Majesty is still supposed to be ignorant of it is neither decent nor right. I will not pretend to justify the action: it is now six years since, being in September sixty-six, and I hope you will believe it, Sir, it would never have been made publick had it not been for a variety of accidents which have made it necessary for me now to declare it to you.'[15]

The King, who disliked Lady Waldegrave and thought her extremely vain, was stunned by this letter. He was deeply hurt to learn that the rumours were well-founded, and that his favourite brother had deliberately misled him for six years by pretending that Maria was no more than a mistress.

Horace Walpole, corresponding with Sir Horace, comments '*The* marriage – my niece's marriage is formally notified to the King by the Duke of Gloucester. Last Wednesday I received a letter signed "Maria Gloucester" acquainting me that the declaration had been made and received by His Majesty with grief, tenderness and justice. I say justice, *tout oncle* as I am, for it would have been very unjust to the Duke of Cumberland to have made any other distinction between two brothers equally in fault, than what affection without *overt* acts cannot help making. This all implies that the Duke of Gloucester must undergo the same prohibition as his brother did, which I am told is to be the case, though the step is not yet taken.'[16]

The King, in fact, showed far less resentment towards the new offender than towards the Duke of Cumberland. Maria wrote: 'He must be displeased but his behaviour has been such upon the occasion that we have all the reason in the world to be grateful to him.' However, he had to appear fair, so he offered Gloucester the same terms as he had their younger brother. If he insisted on publicly acknowledging Maria as his wife, then both would be forbidden the court. The alternative was a left-handed marriage. The Duke of Gloucester remained loyal to his wife, so he and the King agreed to differ. 'It was said that the King wept all night,' wrote Lecky, 'but it was in sorrow rather than in anger.'

The revelation of the Duke of Gloucester's secret marriage

infuriated Lady Mary Coke. Lady Louisa Stuart wrote that she 'lost her rest and appetite and ran some risk of losing her wits upon these royal misalliances. She foamed at the mouth as she declaimed against them. Knowing the whole affair, certainly one can conceive nothing more irritating to a great lady, duchess-dowager of York by her own creation, yet with the Campbell blood in her veins, unable to prove herself so, than to behold two such persons authentically Duchesses of Gloucester and Cumberland.'[17]

As for the two Dukes' remaining Aunt, Lady Mary wrote to Lady Strafford on Sunday, September 27, that Princess Amelia was 'more shocked than I can describe to you with the Duke of Gloucester declaring this miserable marriage. She thinks it in all the circumstances so much worse than the other, that She cannot speak of it with patience. ... The Princess told me that She hears the Duke of Cumberland is taken again to his old ways, & Horton, She says, is very violent & treats him very ill. "But," she added, "I am not sorry for it." ... You are in the right in thinking the Princess Amelia retains all her liveliness & spirit: even the other day, miserable as She was, & upon a subject that I feel little less than herself, She once made me laugh. When one is very much shocked 'tis not uncommon to apprehend the most unlikely things: to this I attribute her R.H.'s imagination that one day or other the King would acknowledge these extraordinary marriages. "And then," said She, "they will be placed in the vault. If you live to see it, scratch me up, for I would not lie in the same place with Horton & the bastard [the Duchess of Gloucester] for all the world.'[18]

Both marriages were eventually acknowledged, but Princess Amelia was spared the fate that she feared. She was buried in Henry VII's Chapel, Westminster Abbey, in 1786, the Duchess of Gloucester at St George's, Windsor, in 1807, and the Duchess of Cumberland died near Trieste in 1808 (not 1803 as some authorities say) and was probably buried there. She was at least not buried with the Duke, who lies in Westminster Abbey, *in the vault*, with Princess Amelia.

The Duke of Cumberland certainly received more punishment than Gloucester. When in early June, 1772, he wrote to the King asking permission to retire with his wife to her homeland, Ireland, he was forbidden to do so.[19] At a chapter of the order of the Garter held on June 18, 1772, at St James's, Lord North was invested with the ensigns of that order as a reward from the King for the admirable adroitness with which he had secured the passage of the Royal Marriage Act; and the Duke of Cumberland was the only knight not summoned to attend the chapter. 'He was privately forbidden the Court,' wrote Walpole, 'for of she there was no question. They were invited to none of the Court festivities, and when there was an installation of the Knights of the Bath, the Duke received a hint not to occupy his stall in St. George's Chapel.'[20]

The Duchess consoled herself by sitting for her portrait in the studios of leading painters – Gainsborough, Reynolds, Romney and Cosway – and going everywhere in great state. Corresponding with Lady Strafford on June 26, 1772, Lady Mary Coke claimed having heard from the Duke of Bolton that Anne drove to Ascot races with her husband in a chaise 'but then got out & went into a Coach & six horses that follow'd with Miss Luttrell & a Mrs Hodges, who, immediately upon her coming in, both stepp'd backwards. The Duke informed us that when he came near the Coach, he pull'd off his hatt, & made her a bow, upon which She just moved, but much less he said than the Queen wou'd have done on the same occasion.'[21]

That other purveyor of gossip who moved in royal circles, Mrs Delany, wrote to her niece, Mrs Port of Ilam, in October, 1772, that to celebrate their first wedding anniversary, the Cumberlands gave 'a grand entertainment to all their attendants, a ball and supper for fifty people, and all the *valets des chambres* and abigails within their compass graced the entertainment, whilst their Royal Highnesses condescended to be put to bed by a housemaid and a footman. She has her state coach following her wherever she bestows her presence, with three or four ladies (or rather *misses*) called her maids of honour. She wears a sack sometimes white, sometimes other colours, trimmed with roses of ribbon, in each a large diamond, no cap and diamonds in her hair, and some gewgaws hovering over her head; a tucker edged with diamonds, a little twist with a jewel dangling, and no more of a tippet than serves to make her fair bosom conspicuous than to hide it.'[22]

The Duchess was certainly fond of diamonds. Two years later, on September 4, 1774, we find the Hon. William Legge writing to his father, the Earl of Dartmouth, about a masked ball he attended in the Assembly Rooms at Southampton where she was decked 'all over diamonds, but did not pull off her mask'.[23]

On Sunday, November 22, 1772, Lady Mary Coke for once has something favourable to say about the Duke himself: 'Her Majesty has a new chair making, that is said to be the prettiest thing of the kind ever seen. The Duke of Cumberland had bespoke one of the same

Chair Maker for his Lady. 'Tis said he proposes she should go to publick places this winter, in which I think he judges ill, tho' in other respects his behaviour is far more proper and more respectful to the King than the Duke of Gloucester's, who notwithstanding the excessive obligations he has to His Majesty, in open defiance of his positive orders, trys to prevail with people to come to his House, that not only go to Court, but are even in the King's service.'[24]

John Brooke states in his excellent life of King George III that, although Anne may not have been the ideal wife for the Duke of Cumberland, she made him very happy, kept him straight, so that after his marriage he never looked at another woman. This is probably very near the truth, though at variance with what Princess Amelia told Lady Mary Coke and passed on by the latter to Lady Strafford in her letter of September 27, 1772, already quoted in this chapter. But Lady Mary was repeating gossip at third-hand, so it was no doubt embroidered. One can similarly discount Walpole's caustic comment that, according to what he had heard, the Cumberlands' honeymoon had waned to half a moon before they left England. The Duke was weak and he needed a strong-willed wife like Anne. He may at times have tried to stray, but she with her Irish temperament would have soon destroyed any butterfly that attempted to alight in her garden of love. Certainly in his correspondence with the Prince of Wales, his nephew, he sounds genuinely fond of her.

Through his love of music, the Duke became a patron of Mrs Billington, the popular *prima donna*, who had a voice of remarkable compass, three octaves from A to A in altissimo, and who held at her house in Fulham by the river, musical conversaziones almost every night that she was not singing at Covent Garden. Cumberland went there regularly and scandal tattled that he was often the last to leave. However, when he introduced his nephew, Prinny, to her, she tried her hardest to make the youth her lover, but with short-lived success. It appears that she specialised in some perversion of which George soon tired. After he had ended the affair, he told his uncle that the only satisfaction he enjoyed in her society was when he shut his eyes and opened his ears.

It was the Duchess who gave the orders at Cumberland House. There were the male Luttrells, too, always dropping in – the crack-shot Colonel and the three other brothers, all M.P.s. The house had been built for the Duke of York, eldest of George III's brothers, according to the designs of Matthew Brettingham, a very competent

Lady Grosvenor and Henry Frederick, Duke of Cumberland surprised by the Countess of D'Onhoff, 1771. British Museum

William Henry, Duke of Gloucester, by Francis Cotes.

Maria, Duchess of Gloucester, engraving by H. Bryer. British Museum

Henry Frederick, Duke of Cumberland from a portrait by Gainsborough, photograph by John R. Freeman. British Library

Anne Horton, later Duchess of Cumberland, by Gainsborough 1766. National Gallery of Ireland

Henrietta, Countess Grosvenor, by Gainsborough 1767.

Edward Augustus, Duke of York, engraving after J. Macardell.

The Duke and Duchess of Cumberland strolling in the grounds of Cumberland Lodge, Windsor Great Park. Reproduced by gracious permission of Her Majesty The Queen

but dull architect. It was of red brick and on three floors, with the staircase in the centre and with two rooms on the west, two on the east, one north and one south. Judging from the opinions of writers of the period, its appearance was regular and substantial but 'void of architectoric Excellence'.[25] On his death in 1767, York left it to his brother the Duke of Gloucester, who allowed his younger brother Cumberland to live in it, then, on the latter's marriage, assigned to him the Crown lease in 1772.

Between then and 1790 the Duke and Duchess did their best to improve the place through the profits obtained from gaming at their faro-table. They planned to give the courtyard of the main entrance in Pall Mall a more imposing appearance by demolishing the houses on either side, which hemmed in their own by projecting a good distance beyond it, and then to replace them with elegant wings set further back. The property on the west had been left to the Duke of Cumberland by York, and this was demolished and replaced soon after 1773, with Adam as architect, by a wing where the Duchess's sister, Lady Elizabeth Luttrell, resided. The Duke was unable to buy the house on the east until 1788, and a wing in its stead was not erected until after his decease.

The Cumberlands commissioned Robert Adam to prepare plans for refurbishing the interior. He prepared 55 drawings in all from 1780 to 1788. Most of these were never put into execution owing to the Duke's precarious financial position. They are preserved in the Sir John Soane's Museum.

In 1780–1 the two smaller ground floor rooms on the south front were converted by Adam into an impressive oblong-shaped 'Great Drawing-room' with five windows in its south wall. The Duke was genuinely fond of music, and at the same time the ceiling in the adjoining Music Room was made infinitely more attractive with a decorative scheme of oval painted medallions fringed with fanciful festoons, acanthus scroll-work and pendant musical trophies. Both rooms overlooked St James's Park and many thought they had the finest view in London.

To the Duchess's grief, their finances never permitted the realisation of Adam's best designs for the richly elegant restyling of the large south-west drawing-room, and the transformation of the ante-chamber to the state bed-chamber into a boudoir for her, with four semi-domed apses containing sofas.

Lady Louisa Stuart wrote that the Duchess of Gloucester

maintained a degree of state, approved of by the Duke, that gave some stiffness to her parties, which were commonly rather select. On the other hand, at Cumberland House unbounded freedom reigned as its mistress 'laughing forms and etiquette to scorn, was better pleased that tag, rag and bobtail ... should flock in, than that numbers should ever be wanting. This did not spring from humility. She was not honestly indifferent to the honours she affected to undervalue; but she had sense enough to know that nothing could ever place her upon the same level with persons born in the purple: therefore she bore them an inveterate hatred, and made whatever appertained to rank, birth or dignity the object of her contemptuous sarcasms.

'Her sister, Miss Betsy (or Lady Elizabeth) Luttrell, who had a great deal of real though coarse wit, and was more precisely what the Regent Orleans entitled a *Roué* than one would have thought it practicable than anything clad in petticoats could be, governed the family with a high hand, marshalled the gaming table, gathered round her the men and led the way in ridiculing the King and Queen. Buckingham House served as a byword – a signal for the onset of "Ho! Ho! Ho!" – and a mighty scope for satire was afforded by the Queen's wide mouth and occasionally imperfect English, as well as by the King's trick of saying "What? What?" – his ill-made coats, and general antipathy to the fashion. But the marks preferably aimed at were his *virtues*, his freedom from vice as a man, his discouragement of it as a sovereign; the exclusion of divorced women from his court, beyond all his religious *prejudice* – that is to say, his sincere piety and humble reliance upon God. Nothing of this scoffing kind passed at Gloucester House: the Duke respected himself and his brother too much to permit it, and the Duchess how ever sore on her own account, saw nothing ridiculous in conjugal fidelity, nor yet in going to church and saying one's prayers.'[26]

In contrast to Lady Louisa Stuart, Lady Mary Coke wrote to Lady Strafford on August 13, 1773, repeating opinions already expressed in her letter of November 22, 1772: 'The Duke of Cumberland's conduct since his unfortunate marriage has been proper, sensible and respectful to the King. The Duke of Gloucester's has been the reverse of all the three, but then the Person who he calls his wife is a foolish, insolent woman, and the Duchess of Cumberland appears by her conduct to be sensible.'[27]

The two Duchesses had one thing in common. They were both beautiful, but, whereas Anne seemed to grow more beautiful with the passing years, Maria's looks began to fade, which brought out the defects in her character, made her meaner and domineering and turned her into a shrew. Like Anne, she was fond of having her portrait painted. Romney alone finished no less than seven. When she visited Reynolds for the same purpose, he was amused by the contrast between husband and wife, and he told his pupil, James Northcote, that if the Duke of Gloucester came to watch he would tumble about the studio at 47, Leicester Fields in his awkward manner without speaking to the artist. Such bad behaviour annoyed the Duchess who on one occasion chided William below her breath, whereupon he leaned on Sir Joshua's chair while he was painting and said! 'What! You always begin with the head first, do you?'

Once on his own public day, the Duke was told by Maria that he ought to speak to Edward Gibbon, which admonition drew from him the remarks: 'So I suppose you are at the old trade again - scribble, scribble, scribble?'[28]

In May, 1773, the Duke of Gloucester again fell ill. His wife was near her time and, not having told the King that a child was expected, he was worried as to what response the news would bring. Unable to put off the task any longer, he wrote announcing the approaching event and requesting that the great officers of state might be alerted to be present at short notice. To his dismay, no answer came, so after a few days he wrote a second letter, which also was at first ignored.

Eventually, the King was persuaded to send a message of frigid formality that after the child's birth he would arrange to have 'your marriage, as well as the birth, inquired into, in order that both may be authenticated'. This was all he would undertake to do, as he disapproved of the match. The King could not be blamed for taking this attitude, for rumours were rife that Maria's approaching confinement was feigned to gain sympathy.

The Duke was much concerned by this message, and he wrote back in protest demanding immediate action to authenticate the marriage on the grounds that the Privy Council might be unwilling to attend at the birth without this first having been proved. He threatened that if the King did not grant his request, he would go to the House of Lords 'tell my case and beseech despatch'.

After further delay, at last, on May 23, the Archbishop of Canterbury, was sent to call on the Duke and make arrangements to investigate the matter. In the evening, he returned with the Lord Chancellor Apsley and was received by the Duke and his Duchess, the

Bishop of Exeter, John Dunning and another lawyer, Dr George Lee, former legal adviser to Frederick, the late Prince of Wales. Apsley produced a statement regarding the marriage and asked Gloucester to sign it. He took exception to this and insisted that they should first listen to his account of what had transpired.[29] He told them how he had been married by Lady Waldegrave's chaplain, now dead, and that 'there were no witnesses'.

Gloucester went on: 'Your lordships remember that I was once at the point of death at Florence. At that awful moment I called for Colonel Rainsford [his equerry]. I told him I was married. I then enjoined him on his duty to a dying master, as soon as he should have closed my eyes, to hasten to England, and repair to the King, and declare my marriage, and say that my last request was that His Majesty would allow a small pittance to the widow of his favourite brother. My lords, Colonel Rainsford took notes of what I said; he has them in his pocket, and shall read them. And now, my lords, your lordships will not wonder that the last thoughts of a dying man turned on the woman he loved.'

The Duke then asked the Bishop of Exeter to tell them what he knew. 'When the Marriage Bill was brought in,' said the Bishop, 'I thought it right to question Lady Waldegrave then on a visit to my deanery [at Windsor]. I went into her, and telling her my reasons for inquiring, I asked whether she was married? She burst into a flood of tears, and cried: "I am! I am married!" and then falling into a great agony, she wrung her hands and exclaimed: "Good God, what have I done! I have detrayed the Duke, and broken my promise to him!"'[30]

After this hardly conclusive evidence was taken down and sworn to, the Duke pleaded that his questioners should lose no time. 'Look,' he cried, 'at the condition of the Duchess.'

It seemed to the two that Gloucester was on the verge of a nervous breakdown, so to placate him they went off to report their findings to the King and soon came back with his reply that, though satisfied, he would agree to his brother's being married again if so wished. But the Duke wanted clear, unconditional acceptance of the 1766 ceremony, and at last on May 27 George agreed to this. It was only just in time, for two days later the Duchess gave birth to a daughter, Sophia Matilda, in the presence of all the great officers of state.

The King had also taken steps for the legality of the Cumberlands' marriage to be investigated at the same time. On May 21, by Order in Council, he appointed the Archbishop, the Lord Chancellor, and the Bishop of London to do this forthwith, and two days later, on a Sunday afternoon, they called on the Duke of Cumberland and, after being questioned, he signed a declaration that he had married Mrs Anne Horton on October 2, 1771, in her Hertford Street house. The Duchess, the officiating clergyman William Stevens, and the witness Elizabeth Luttrell having confirmed this on oath, the three men then said they were convinced and informed the King to that effect.

CHAPTER FOURTEEN

The Wandering Royals

Late in the summer of 1773, the Cumberlands went abroad. All the London newspapers informed their readers that on Friday, August 17, the Duke and Duchess, Lady Elizabeth Luttrell, the Hon. James Luttrell, together with General Prevost, Colonel Deaken, Colonel Garth and others, set out in eight carriages from Cumberland House for Dover with the intention of visiting most of the European Courts during the next two years.[1]

To Anne's delight, on arrival at Calais she and the Duke were greeted with royal honours and so stayed there a few days, again giving a ball to the officers of the garrison. The pair went twice in state to the theatre, and, on the morning after their last visit, two of the players called to thank them for the compliment paid their company and to receive the usual gratification. The Duke handed them three guineas which they regarded as 'a shabby guerdon'.

Horace Walpole was quick to garner all the gossip regarding this episode and corresponding with the Countess of Upper Ossory told her that the mummers retaliated by sending their candle-snuffer – a 'dirty fellow' – to present a faded bouquet to the Duchess. He was rewarded for his impudence with 'a volley of *coups de bâton*'. This did not intimidate the actors who then sent one of their party after the Duke to St Omer with a letter asking if it were really true that his Royal Highness gave so small a sum for they suspected their two representatives had pocketed most of what was given. 'The man who went with the letter has been put in prison, and the whole troop has been ordered to leave the town – *voilà qui est bien tragique pour les comédiens*. This matter is as much talked on at Calais as if it was an affair of state.'[2]

After this rather unpleasant episode, caused no doubt through funds being low, 'the wandering court', as Walpole labelled them, resumed their journey to Italy. The *Annual Register* recording events in October quotes an account from Paris that as the Cumberlands were travelling incognito as Earl and Countess of Dublin, they desired that no public honours be shown them. This was based on a statement issued on their behalf by General Prevost, which was actually a face-saving device in case the British Ambassadors' orders from home to allow the couple no precedence were observed by the Courts of the various countries through which they passed. The Duchess was in fact longing for ceremonious recognition, and the General discreetly dropped hints in the right quarters.

On October 5, the Cumberlands reached Strasbourg, where the Baron de Wurmar, who was in command of the garrison, arranged, after a visit from the persuasive Prevost, for the Duke next morning to review the troops and for a gala performance at the comedy theatre in honour of the visitors, followed by supper with the Baron and the city's principal personalities.

On October 9, when at ten in the morning, the Cumberlands resumed their journey via Basle to Italy, troops lined the streets the length of the route from their lodgings to the city's gate, through which they passed to the salute of all the cannon on the ramparts, then detachments of the Corsican legion accompanied them as far as Kerich.

The *London Evening Post* reported on October 16 that a letter received from 'a gentleman in the Duke's retinue' mentioned that his Royal Highness and wife had been given all the honours due to their rank and escorted by a detachment of the military on every stage of their journey through France. This was through the express orders of King Louis XV. The correspondent was probably General Prevost, who may also have been the source of a piece in *The Craftsman* a week later disclosing that the Cumberlands had delayed their departure from London to give all tradesmen time to send in their bills for immediate settlement. 'To their honour, the Duke and Duchess pay their household as exactly as the quarter becomes due and at the same time keep house becoming their Princely dignity – an example not unworthy of imitation in many who at this time mingle in the great world.'

As might be expected, Lady Mary Coke's letters written from Florence where she was staying to her sister, Lady Strafford, comment disapprovingly on the continental progress of the Cumberlands. Lady Mary, too, had her *folie de grandeur* and believed she ought to be treated by foreign courts as though she were the Dowager Duchess of York. Sir Horace Mann wrote to Walpole: 'She has talked to me for hours of ... the bad usage, nay affronts, which she had received from the Empress of Austria which she supposes influenced the Arch-Duchess of Parma to whom she could not get admittance.'[3]

In his next letter, Mann complains that 'the height and violence of Lady Mary's temper led to her attacking servants and being summoned before the public tribunals. He had been able to save her from being convicted only by hinting that she was mad.[4] Her rage was undoubtedly caused by resentment that the Express had taken a great liking to the Duchess of Cumberland and had treated her as if she were of royal birth when in Vienna. On December 18, Lady Mary told Lady Strafford that she blamed General Prevost for this as he had played 'all sorts of tricks to have her acknowledged as the King's sister, very contrary to His Majesty's intention'.[5] Then in the New Year, on January 5, the obsessed correspondent returns to the same grievance in another letter: 'As His Majesty had never notified the marriage to any foreign courts, the Empress ought never to have known there was such a person as the Duchess of Cumberland.'[6]

Later that month on the 18th, *The Craftsman* again published part of a letter from Italy claiming that the Duke had 'already made such proficiency in the Italian language, without the help of Latin, that he can read Ariosto in the original. He has an Italian preceptor constantly with him, from whom, he says himself, that he learns more in one hour, than he did under his English masters in a whole year. This gentleman, it is said, will come to England with him.'

On New Year's Day, 1774, the same paper disclosed that the Duke had sent orders to his major-domo at Windsor Lodge for it 'to be kept open three successive days during Christmas for the neighbouring poor inhabitants to be entertained with roast beef, puddings, pies, etc.'.

In a letter dated January 15, Lady Mary wrote in reply to one from Lady Strafford: 'How could you give credit to those who pretended to say they knew his Majesty's Ministers abroad had orders that the Duke of Cumberland and his Duchess should be received with distinctions and honours: it is the very contrary ... Their having obtained those honours contrary to the King's intention was entirely the Stratagem of the Duchess and her friend Prevost ... The last accounts from Milan mention their still being there, where She had taken state upon her in a very extraordinary manner, even to the not allowing any other card table in the room where She play'd.'[7]

Favourable news about the Duke, however, continued to appear in *The Craftsman* which on January 21, after reporting the death in

London of Mr Flowers, his butler, continues: 'A gentleman just arrived from Italy, who has been frequently with the Duke of Cumberland, says that His Highness is so captivated with the curiosities he meets with that he hardly affords himself the usual time to enjoy his dinner; that all his conversation at table is of the several beauties in art and nature he has seen that day; for which his taste is enlivened by a person of very extraordinary genius and a great virtuoso, who constantly attends him on his researches, in the diversified treasures of a world unknown to him before.'

As a result of adverse dispatches reaching the King in England concerning Prevost's activities, he was ordered home in February. Sir Horace Mann in Florence immediately informed Horace Walpole: 'General Prevost has quitted him [the Duke] under pretence of going to Switzerland to see his relations, but a total disapprobation from England of his conduct seems to be the cause of his dismission.'[8]

In London *The Craftsman* for April 2, 1774, contained better news for the absent pair. 'We hear that every step towards a reconciliation between the Duke of Cumberland and his Royal brother is at last agreed on, principally through the mediation of Lord Mansfield; and that their Royal Highnesses the Duke and Duchess will make their appearance at Court, for the first time, on the ensuing birthday, being about the time they are expected home (attended with the usual state).'

Before travelling back, the Duke visited the Pope, who, arranged for St Peter's to be illuminated in his honour,[9] and who when they were about to part, politely told him: 'Though your country's customs laugh at some of our ceremonies, an old man's blessing could certainly do you no harm.' And he laid his hands on the Duke's head and gave him and his suite the Papal benison. It was said that the Young Pretender on hearing of this declared he would never go to the Papal Court again or stay in Rome.

The Duchess of Cumberland returned to England determined that the success achieved abroad should be repeated in London. She and the Duke spent the summer first at Windsor, then in a house they rented at the Polygon in Southampton. Nothing came of the rumoured reconciliation. *The Craftsman* for June 11 reported there was no Court on the King's birthday and added: 'It is said his Royal Highness meant to present his compliments to his Majesty on that day, but was dissuaded by his brother the Duke of Gloucester, who observed the impropriety of entering another's apartments *unasked*.' Anne, like her sister-in-law the Duchess of Gloucester, continued to be treated as if she were a mistress. At Cumberland House in the autumn, fifty persons came to her first weekly reception, but when Queen Charlotte let it be known that anybody who frequented the functions of the two repudiated Duchesses would not be invited to Court, no one of any distinction visited them.

However, according to Lady Louisa Stuart, the ban was not strictly observed. 'It overawed people for the first month, in the second they stole a visit to Gloucester or Cumberland House, went to Court early in the third, and being spoken to as usual troubled their heads no more about the matter.'[10]

Adversity brought Anne and Maria together at the start. When the Duke of Gloucester revealed his secret marriage, the King's forbidding his presence at Court did for a while unite the couples. The *St James's Chronicle* reported on September 26, 1772, that the two Dukes and their wives 'took an airing in one coach and all dined at Cranbourn Lodge' – the Gloucesters' Windsor home. Then on May 1, 1773, *The Craftsman* stated: 'The Dukes of Gloucester and Cumberland live in the utmost harmony in their rural retreats; when the former was ill, the Duke of Cumberland attended him from nine o'clock in the morning till nine at night; the same union subsists between their ladies, who seldom omit a day of seeing each other.' But, as we shall learn later, such harmony could not last between the two Duchesses who were temperamentally so dissimilar.

Undismayed by the King and Queen's refusal to recognize her, Anne made up for it by parading on public occasions with all the trappings of royalty – so much so that those in Court circles ridiculed her. For example, Lady Mary Coke, writing to Lady Strafford, on December 14, 1774, described how she had dined with Princess Amelia and 'the usual company' in Cavendish Square: 'We had a good deal of conversation upon the folly of the Duke of Cumberland, who in complaisance as it is thought to his Lady, has order'd his Box at the Opera to be magnificently decorated; a white satin festoon curtain drawn up with cords and tassels of gold upon the front, and on the outside to the House white satin with a shining gold fringe, and two Chairs of the same silk. The box being so furnished, on Saturday last, every body expected the Duke and Duchess to have made their appearance, when behold the Mountain brought forth two mice, and Mrs Hodges and Miss Luttrell placed themselves in the two white satin Chairs; this 'twas thought was adding redicul to absurdity.'[11]

Then, a week later, Lady Strafford is told: 'The Duke and Duchess of Cumberland produced themselves at the Opera on Saturday last; he led her in and out of the House, but She and Miss Luttrell sat on the white satin chairs, and he behind for some time; after he went into the pit and conversed with Ld George Germain and Mr Greenville, who was attending his Lady, and who he probably wish'd rather to talk to ... Somebody told the Princess that the Duchess of Cumberland went with eight footmen before her chair.'[12]

Anne's passion for pomp had irritated her sister-in-law, Maria, and we find Lord Rochford writing to the King on November 27, 1774, that according to Gloucester's equerry, Colonel Rainsford, the two Dukes and their Duchesses had not seen one another that summer and there was 'a great coolness between them'.[13]

Maria had given birth to a second daughter, christened Caroline Augusta Maria, and the Duke of Gloucester, concerned about their financial position, asked the King to safeguard the family's future by making them an adequate allowance. George replied that he did not feel it right to request Parliament to support William's children while there was no provision for his own. He had good grounds for such an attitude. On ascending the throne, he had in a public-spirited act relinquished the Crown's right to its hereditary revenues in exchange for a Civil List of £800,000 per annum, which was £76,000 less than his predecessor had been receiving. With an ever increasing family, which eventually totalled fifteen, three brothers dependent on him, and dowries to be found for two sisters, it is not surprising that by 1769 he was forced to apply to Parliament for £513,000 to pay off his debts. Although this was allowed without a division, there were some questioning speeches. 'Considering the system of economy established in His Majesty's domestic concerns, he ought not to be in this situation,' declared one M.P., and another hinted that part of the money might have been spent in *douceurs* 'to influence the freedom of this House'.

The King's refusal to help so worried the Duke of Gloucester that he had a severe attack of asthma and was advised by his physicians to go abroad. In the early New Year, he wrote to George for permission to do this offering to sell him two houses on St Leonard's Hill so as to obtain funds for travelling, and repeating his plea for a family allowance.

On January 16, 1775, the King instructed his first minister, Lord North, to inform the Duke that he had no objection to his going abroad but would not buy the houses, and as regards providing for his family he saw no reason to give a different answer than previously. 'I cannot deny that ... my heart is wounded. I have ever loved him with the fondness one bears to a child than a brother. His whole conduct from the time of his publishing what I must ever think a highly disgraceful step has tended to make the breach wider. I cannot therefore bring myself on a repetition of this application to give him hopes of a future establishment for his children, which would only bring on a fresh altercation about his wife whom I can never think of placing in a situation to answer her extreme pride and vanity. Should he be so ill advised as to have a provision for her and her children moved in Parliament, the line of conduct to be held is plain as my conduct is proper. I am not unwilling that the whole world may know it, and all the answer to be given by my minister is that it is natural the King should not apply to Parliament for provision for the children of a younger branch of his family when he has not as yet done it for his own numerous offspring, and totally avoid mentioning the lady. So far for the public, but for yourself you know my way of thinking too well to doubt that should any accident happen to the Duke I shall certainly take care of his children.'[14]

Eleven days later, Horace Walpole wrote to Sir Horace Mann that the Duke of Gloucester was slightly better. 'It is a constitution that will always give alarms; it has radical evils, and yet amazing stamina. They now talk of his going abroad in April. He will take the Duchess and his daughters ... His mind will be more at peace, and he will be free from all who would distract it for their own ends. The Luttrells are every day, I believe, writing impertinent paragraphs in the newspapers, as if in behalf of the Duke of Gloucester, which only tends to incense the King against him, that they may involve him in their own views; but he knows it, and will not be their dupe.'[15]

On the 15th of the following month, Walpole informs Mann that the Duke's cough is very bad. 'I think he falls away. He will not leave England till April, because he will inoculate his children before he carries them abroad. I trouble at the delay, and have said all I dare to the Duchess against it, as I am impatient to have him set out, and think no time should be lost.'[16]

In March, the two Princesses were inoculated, and the youngest, Caroline, a sickly infant, died the very next day, March 14, and was buried six days later at Windsor. As a result, the sorrowing parents deferred their departure for Italy till the late summer. A report in the *London Evening Post* claimed that the Duke was 'so distressed, previous to his leaving England, that he had an execution on his house for £5,000 and it is further confidentially asserted that the Duke of Cumberland absolutely mortgaged his own house in Pall-mall, in order to supply him with that sum; an instance of fraternal affection not very common nowadays in the royal circle'.[17] Later, it alleged that his total debts amounted to £60,000, mostly to tradesmen.

The new King of France, Louis XVI, invited the Gloucesters to stay with him in Paris, but the Duke declined as he was anxious to reach the south before the bad weather set in. On September 7, Walpole mentions their arrival in Venice to Mann and then confides: 'I own I am in pain about the Duchess. She has all the good qualities of her father, but all his impetuosity; and is much too apt to resent affronts, though her virtue and good nature make her as easily reconciled; but her first movements are not discreet ... She has admirable sense, when her passions do not predominate.'[18]

On reaching Padua, the Duke and four of his staff fell violently ill with enteritis and it was some days before they were well enough to resume the journey to Rome which was reached on December 12. Here on January 15, 1776, a son, Prince William Frederick, who lived to manhood, was born to the Duchess in the Teodoli Palace, but this did nothing to soften the King's obduracy.

A year passed and the family's financial position deteriorated. Their social status caused them to maintain a sizeable staff, which even when they were travelling, according to Captain Pleydell the Duke's new equerry, included 'six women, six pages and seven living servants'. In the Sackville papers, there is a letter dated February, 1777, from the Duchess's father, Sir Edward Walpole to Lord George Sackville (later Germain) appealing for his assistance in getting the Duke's allowance augmented, but he replied that he could not see any possibility of parliamentary help before the King forgave his brother.[19]

When he heard this, the Duke wrote to Lord George on March 12, stressing that all he wished was provision for the Duchess and his children in the event of his death and did not expect the country to pay his debts. Sackville then asked a Captain Jennings, one of the Duke of Cumberland's Grooms of the Bedchamber, who was also a friend of Gloucester's, and who was about to leave London for Italy, to visit him and report on the state of his finances.

Although the Duke had enjoyed excellent health in Rome, he had found the heat of summer somewhat trying and therefore arranged to spend that of 1777 in Venice and by Lake Garda. On April 21, the

Gloucesters and their entourage started on their way, pausing at Florence, Bologna, Ferrara, and Verona where the Duke was suddenly taken so seriously ill that he changed his plans and decided to travel straight home to consult English physicians as he had no faith in foreign ones. Explaining this, Captain Pleydell informed John Strange, the British Resident Minister in Venice: 'His constitution is most delicate. Mr Bryan, his Domestic Surgeon, has advised his going immediately to save his life. He fully intends being in Italy again by the end of November or beginning of December and staying six months at Rome – a large house is taken there for his reception. Perhaps a few months in England may quite set him up again. The Duchess as you may easily believe is full of care and trouble.'[20]

The Gloucesters and their entourage, however, had only gone some twenty-five miles when the Duke collapsed on arrival in Trent and was carried into the *palazzo* of a Baron Crepaer and put to bed. Three days later, on June 25, Pleydell wrote to Strange: 'He is extremely emaciated ... the pain accompanying that constant irritation wears him to a skeleton. He will listen to no advice of the Foreign Faculty. I can only say while there is life there are hopes. The Duchess is ever with him inconsolable.'

In view of the gravity of the situation, an urgent message was sent to the King regarding his brother's critical condition and asking for doctors to be sent out from England to treat him. This George arranged at once. Pleydell's correspondence with Strange concerning the Duke describes the subsequent course of events. On June 25: 'He is so very weak that some alteration must soon happen for the better or surely he can't hold it out. He is indeed this a.m. rather easier, but still the Flux continues (tho' not bloody) and a constant irritation that teazes him much. He keeps his bed entirely.' On July 5: 'He is better than for some time'. Then two days later: 'He wishes much for the Physicians from England. The Duke begs you will send him as many pounds as you can (six or eight if possible) of Sago. He can procure none here, and it is the only Nourishing thing he can eat.' On July 15, the equerry thanks Strange for the sago, but the physicians still have not arrived and the Duke is weak and impatient. Then on the 16th, Dr Jebb and Mr Adair reached Trent with a King's messenger, their journey having taken eleven days.

On July 26 Strange is thanked for his offer to send the Duke a few potatoes which were unobtainable in the town. 'If you can spare a few, they will be very acceptable. The Duke would also like a dozen bottles of the best Claret as the physicians think a little would be of use to Him and the Duchess prefers it to all other wine. He is very weak and the additional complaint of the Piles kept him from sleeping.'

Pleydell's letter of July 30 suggests Jebb and Adair feared their patient to be consumptive: 'In all human appearance the poor amiable duke can live but a very short time. This is the opinion of the doctors. ... He has sucked the breasts of some healthy country women that were sent for to the Mountains – this last resource, however, seems to have little effect.' But this unusual cure did benefit the sick man, for, on August 2, his equerry writes that he slept 'tolerably well' the previous night and that 'the Phisical Gentlemen begin to think there must be some stamina left'. Seven days later, they are 'more sanguine in their hopes' and Pleydell indulges in a little self-pity: 'What a dull gloomy uncomfortable life I pass.' He also mentions the arrival of Captain Jennings.

Prior to his departure, this old friend of Gloucester's had visited the King in an attempt to persuade him to send a message of reconciliation to the Duke. Afterwards, he wrote to Lord George Sackville: 'I just caught the King's eye, and was honoured with a slight salute, and then His Majesty follow'd the Queen into the Garden while Ramus [the King's black page] coming up to me told me exactly these words: "Sir, the King orders me to tell you that he is much obliged to you. He desires you to give his love to his brother, and he heartily hopes you will find him quite recover'd" ... I trust your Lordship's generosity to put the best interpretation on what may have perhaps rather imprudently escaped from my pen, yet if it produces any good to the Duke I care very little for its consequences to myself.'[21]

Captain Jennings was obviously shocked with what he found on arrival in Trent for he wrote to Sackville: 'Consider, my Lord, and paint it in those natural and affecting colours which you can do, that the King of England's brother, once his favourite, his friend, now hangs in a cot and at the point of death in a mean apartment in a little insignificant town, a thousand miles from home.' He goes on that if it had not been for 'the romantick generosity of a private gentleman' who had insisted on giving them shelter in his house the Duke and Duchess and their two children 'would have been lying now in an inn far worse than any subaltern officer was ever quartered in England. His Royal Highness is so emaciated that Dr Jebb and Mr Adair declare that no living person that they saw ever equall'd him. His appearance is quite shocking, he has been above six weeks on his back without the strength to move himself. ... His Royal Highness said to me with the most affectionate look and tone of voice: "I am indifferent about myself, I have scarce a wish to live ... but what is to become of the Duchess, what of my children when I am gone?" '[22]

The circulation of this letter in Court circles, together with the two physicians' own reports to the King must have helped the Duke's cause, for on August 23, Pleydell tells Strange: 'We hear many confirmations of His Majesty's great concern and attention to His Royal Highness's recovery – this looks well. This very illness may be the means of reconciliation between the Royal Brothers. I write every post to General Harvey. I know His Majesty sees all my letters as well as those I write to some other friends.'

Then, on August 27, we learn that after a recent improvement the Duke is in the 'utmost danger' having been taken 'extraordinarily ill on Monday evening – so low that the Physicians expected him to expire – one thigh & leg swell'd much. Last night I expected him to die. Thank God he is still alive. Wrote yesterday to England that he was in the most imminent danger.'

When this news was received at Court, the King wrote at once to his brother. This letter is not in the Royal Archives so one can only guess at its contents, but Pleydell tells Strange on September 6 that the Duke immediately started to get better and was able 'to answer it with his own Hand – every likelihood of a happy reconciliation'.

In England, on September 15, the Duchess's father, Sir Edward Walpole sent a note to Horace Walpole to say that he had received two letters, one from his daughter and the other from Dr Jebb, from which it was clear that the Duke was really recovering. 'He sat up four hours, dined three times at a table out of bed, gathered strength and flesh. He was merry, talking and laughing while she [the Duchess] was writing.'[23]

Sir Edward claimed the credit for this, believing it due to his having suggested that the Duke be given 'a Medicine to be found in Bates' Dispensatory' consisting of 'mulled Wine with Yolk of Egg' to which was added 'three drops of Chemical out of Cinnamon'. But there can be little doubt that it was the psychological effect of the King's letter that wrought the miraculous cure, and all the patient now wished to do was to travel back to London as soon as possible. On September 23, they set out and from Augsburg on October 2, Pleydell wrote to Strange: 'His Royal Highness is in good spirits and supports the journey much better than I would have expected. This is the ninth day he has travelled without stopping. He proposes staying here a couple of days and setting forward the 5th.' Then, on the 26th, the equerry gave the news of their arrival in London after a very pleasant journey: 'The Duke is very hearty and strong, considering everything – can walk about the room with a crutch.'

The next letter from Pleydell to the British Minister Resident in Venice is dated a month later, November 25, and tells of the Duke getting stronger – 'more flesh, able to go to the Opera, talks of going soon to Bath for a few weeks'. He ends: 'Between ourselves ... how ever approaching the great reconciliation seem'd to be, there has as yet been no meeting of the Royal Brothers. The King is most anxious for the Duke's health and welfare. But has not seen Him Yet. We trust it may be soon ... tis unlucky to be so long delay'd. There is company every evening at Gloucester House but few or no courtiers.'

Possibly, the Duke may have wondered whether he had been wise in hurrying back home, and the King hearing of his astonishingly swift recovery may have asked himself if those piteous reports from Trent had been purposely exaggerated and that the Duchess he so disliked was responsible. He relented sufficiently to allow Parliament to vote the not yet two-year-old Prince William an annual allowance of £8,000 and his sister, Princess Sophia Matilda, £4,000. But, as regards their mother, he remained firmly convinced that she was an unscrupulous widow, who having been born on the wrong side of the blanket to a plebian mother, was quite unfit ever to be accepted as a member of the royal family. He told Lord Hertford he could not receive her at Court 'without affronting all the sovereigns of Europe by countenancing a *mésalliance*'.[24]

When the Duke pressed for Maria, also, to be given an allowance, the King wrote to Lord North on November 29: 'I should have thought the handsome proposal delivered by you to the Duke of Gloucester would have deserved at least the civility of not applying for a public provision for a person who must always be odious to me.'[25] As as result of this wounding rebuff, the Duchess in retaliation persuaded her husband to ally himself with the Whig opposition.

CHAPTER FIFTEEN

The Cumberland Fleet

Some two years earlier the youngest royal black sheep brother had also joined the Whigs. 'He has erected his standard in opposition,' wrote Horace Walpole on January 25, 1775. The *St James's Chronicle* for March 18, that year, stated that 'ever since his attachment to the minority, the Duke constantly attends his duty in the House of Lords'. Lady Louisa Stuart considered that they made much of the Cumberlands and the Gloucesters because it was 'a cheap and safe way of showing disrespect to the Crown'. 'A great Whig,' a contemporary labelled Cumberland, who referred to all of that party as 'our friends' and did his best to persuade his nephew, the Prince of Wales, to support them. It was at Cumberland House, which became a centre for all who opposed the Government, that the Prince first met Charles James Fox.

In 1775, in his speech from the throne, the King set out his proposals for sending troops to crush the American rebellion. Feeling ran high, and even the royal family were divided upon the expediency of the war. When a minister told Cumberland that his brother hoped he would support the proposed measures, he replied: 'God forbid that a prince of the house of Hanover should violate those rights in America which they were raised to the throne of England for asserting'—and he voted with the twenty-nine other peers supporting Lord Chatham's plan of reconciliation.[2]

Contrary to what might be expected in the circumstances, the Duke of Cumberland's political activities did not at this time prejudice his naval advancement, for in February of the following year he was appointed Vice-Admiral of the White, a promotion which placed him in a senior position on the flag list to such distinguished officers as Howe and Rodney. Then, a month later, on March 5, the Duke made his maiden speech in the House of Lords when he supported the Duke of Richmond's motion to countermand the use of German mercenaries against the American colonists and to suspend hostilities immediately.

The Duke ended by stressing that his views were not motivated by any disrespect for his brother, the King, but from concern at the prospect of Brunswickers being sent to 'assist in destroying and overturning the constitutional rights of America'. According to the *St James's Chronicle* of March 15 at this point: 'He seemed to be much affected and abruptly sat down.' The motion was defeated.

In 1777, rumour linked the Duke's name with that of an attractive and amoral actress with sad eyes and shapely limbs Mary Robinson. Surprisingly, that usually rich source of scandal, the letters of Horace Walpole, contain but one reference to this. Writing on October 8 that year to the Countess of Upper Ossory, he admits: 'I neither know whether Lord Harcourt's dog broke its heart, nor whether their Royal Highnesses of Cumberland are going to part.'[3]

In her *Memoirs*, Mrs Robinson alleges that if she were to disclose the identities of all the men who had made proposals of a certain kind to her, it would cause 'consternation in fashionable families'. The only name she revealed was that of the Duke of Rutland, who offered to settle £600 a year on her if she would leave her husband. She then goes on to mention a similar proposal 'from a Royal Duke' which she claims she scorned. There can be little doubt that she was referring to Cumberland, who, as a connoisseur of acting and actresses, had admired her and her artistry since that promising début as Juliet at Drury Lane.

In February, 1777, Mary Robinson first appeared in the role of Amanda in Sheridan's *A Trip to Scarborough*. The audience supposed the play to be an entirely new piece, and when they found it was only a new version of Vanbrugh's *The Relapse*, there was a disturbance. She wrote later: 'I was terrified beyond imagination when Mrs Yates, no longer able to bear the hissing of the audience, quitted the scene and left me alone to encounter the entire tempest. I stood for some moments as if I had been petrified. Mr Sheridan, from the side wing, desired me not to quit the boards; the late Duke of Cumberland from the stage box bade me take courage: 'It is not *you*, but the play they hiss,' said his Royal Highness. I curtsied; and that curtsey seemed to electrify the whole house, for a thundering peal of encouraging applause followed. The comedy was suffered to go on, and is to this hour a stock play at Drury Lane Theatre.'

From that night onwards, Mary Robinson was established as an actress, thanks to the Duke's words of support. It is not surprising that he should have delighted in her triumph and have been attracted by her. Sensing this may be why Anne suddenly decided to take him abroad to join his elder sister, Augusta, and her husband, the Hereditary Prince of Brunswick, in Spa.[4] They left in mid-May for what was then the foremost watering-place in Europe with its cures for rheumatism, gout, constipation, and even barrenness, and where to distract one's attention from brooding on such ills there were concerts, dances and facilities for gambling at the Levoz, the Redoute and the Vauxhall.

Despite these attractions hardly had the Cumberlands reached the resort pleasantly situated in the forest of Ardennes than the Duke left his wife with the Brunswicks and went back to London. According to the *Post* of June 5, his sudden reappearance in the capital was 'to arrange his affairs and take measures for the discharge of his debts in this kingdom, then with such household as his income will support, without running into debt, retire to some obscure Barony in Germany, being determined, that if he must *unprince* himself, it shall be in a corner, and not in the face of his country....'

Another reason for the Duke's return was so that he could be present at the third Annual Boat Race of the Cumberland Fleet Society, which he had founded, and to the winner of which he presented every year a silver cup. The Duke diplomatically always arranged for the event to take place either on the King's birthday or near it.

The earliest reference to these races in the press of the period the author has discovered was in the *Public Advertiser* for July 6, 1775, which reads: 'A Silver Cup, the gift of His Royal Highness the Duke of Cumberland, is to be sailed for on Tuesday, the 11th instant, from Westminster Bridge to Putney Bridge and back, by Pleasure Sailing Boats, from two to five tons burthen, and constantly lying above London Bridge. Any gentlemen inclined to enter his Boat may be informed of particulars by applying to Mr Roberts, Boatbuilder, Lambeth, any time before Saturday Noon.'

Owing to bad weather the race had to be postponed until July 13, when there were probably about twenty competitors. It was won by a Mr Parkes 'late of Ludgate Hill' with *Aurora*, and *Fly* came second.[5]

No member of the House of Hanover before the Duke had shown any interest in sailing. He enjoyed it and is perhaps best remembered by the club he started, the first of its kind, which was later to become the famed Royal Thames Yacht Club, whose members' boats are still collectively known as the Cumberland Fleet.

The late Earl Mountbatten was for a quarter of a century the Fleet's Commodore, then in 1970 he became its Admiral and was succeeded by his nephew, the Prince of Wales, in whose presence five years later at a Thanksgiving Service in Westminster Abbey to commemorate its Bicentenary he laid a wreath on the tomb of the founder, Henry Frederick, Duke of Cumberland. The celebrations included an impressive review in the Solent by Earl Mountbatten from the training vessel, *Royalist*, of over one hundred and sixty yachts belonging to the Fleet.

The first silver cup presented by the Duke and the Fleet's original colours are still the possession of the Royal Thames Yacht Club today. The latter consist of a white ensign and a white burgee with a red cross (that does not extend to the fly of the flag).

By the time the Duke's third annual boat race took place on the exceptionally fine afternoon of Saturday, June 7, 1777, the event had become so popular that the shores between the bridges at Westminster and Blackfriars were crowded with spectators and the river, too, with sightseers in boats, some with musicians aboard. One of the rules was that every competing craft had to be steered by its owner, known as the Captain, who was permitted to have two assistants and probably no other crew. At half-past two, seven sail flying the Fleet's colours and with swallow-tailed pendants curling from their mastheads came to their moorings by Blackfriars Bridge—the starting place from 1776 onwards. Here they waited until three o'clock, when the Duke arrived in his barge, accompanied by his attendants and a brother-in-law, Captain John Temple Luttrell, R.N., and preceded by another barge bearing his band of music. Then, a quarter of an hour later, the boats slipped their cables on the firing of a pistol.

A neat, well-built little craft, the *Duchess of Cumberland*, took the lead and kept it up to within a few yards of the previous year's winner, the sturdy *King's Fisher*, which, gaily decorated with flowing colours, was moored just below Putney Bridge and round which the competitors had to sail. But the *Duchess*, upon putting about, lost time, enabling the *Eagle* and the *Sea-horse* to get ahead of her. The former kept the lead all the way back to Blackfriars Bridge where, clearing the centre arch, it reached the finishing line off Smith's Gardens at a quarter to six. The Duke must have been relieved that his wife was not present to witness the defeat of the craft named after her.

The winner was saluted by the Duke's barge, and by all the boats near by, with three general huzzas. The bargemen then lay on their oars, and Captain Kitchingman, the owner of the *Eagle*, getting alongside, the Duke's butler, filled the prize cup with claret and handed it to the royal donor, who drank the health of the victor and then presented him with the trophy. The Duke and his party dined on the water, and then in the evening went to Vauxhall Gardens for entertainment.

'What afforded a pleasing reflection on the whole was that not a single accident happened in the course of the day,' commented the *London Evening Post*. Then, a month later, the Duke travelled back to Spa to rejoin his wife, and at the end of August they returned to Windsor Lodge. Shortly afterwards, on September 13, the *Post* published the impressions of an anonymous contributor who had also spent the season at Spa and which must not have pleased the Cumberlands. The company there had been 'remarkably numerous, chiefly consisting of Irish, many English of rank having given up the houses they had engaged to avoid meeting the Duke and Duchess of Cumberland, who have nevertheless scraped together a medley to make a circle, mostly of those who have not been received in any other. Among these, Lord and Lady K-rr-y have distinguished themselves and resented the frequent repulses they have met with at St James's by giving a sumptuous entertainment to the Royal couple, trumpets and kettle-drums with crackers, proclaiming the names of Anne and Henry, by which appellations they announce themselves there—"Princess" Elizabeth is representative for her sister, returning her visits. This place, long frequented more for its ease and general intercourse than for its waters, is now ruined from the diversions that are made among the company, by the vanity and folly of a few, who cannot distinguish themselves by their virtue or understanding.'

Charles Pigott in his lampoon of high society women, *The Female Jockey Club*, published in 1794, has this to say about how Elizabeth Luttrell behaved. 'The Duchess herself was obliged to preserve the dignity of her exalted station, but she most condescendingly allowed her sister to relax and to partake promiscuously in the different amusements of the towns and countries where they fixed their abode. In the rooms of Spa, her ladyship was the life and soul of the place; the very quintessence of English gaiety, polished manners, and elegant dissipation. Morning and evening her spirits were inexhaustible; the first to attend the faro bank on its opening; the last to leave it on its settling. With the Bankers and Croupiers she was a distinguished favourite, contriving by the laudable punctuality observed in her payments to maintain a most excellent credit amongst them, of which she often generously availed herself on behalf of her princely brother-in-law, when in consequence of a bad run, both his purse and his credit have been unfortunately exhausted.'

Although partial to faro, Elizabeth was not averse to *rouge et noir*, much played at Spa, and could rattle a dice with 'a noble, manly grace not surpassed even by Colonel Fitzpatrick, a veteran and a most determined hazard player'.

In the meantime, the 15-year old Prince of Wales had fallen in love with Mary Robinson after seeing her as Perdita in *The Winter's Tale*, and then later he confided his feelings to his favourite uncle, who realized that the one person whose friendship he dare not risk losing was the Heir Apparent's. He therefore not only withdrew as a candidate for 'Perdita's' favours but did much to further his nephew's wooing of her.

The crisis had passed and Henry and Anne were united again. The *London Evening Post* for Saturday, November 1 mentioned a visit of the Duke to Drury Lane that Thursday to see Mr Henderson in *The Roman Father*. Mrs Robinson was not in the cast. 'He was accompanied by his brother-in-law, the Hon. James Luttrell, which is another proof that the reports relative to a fracas between the Duchess and him have no foundation.'

The *Post* also published a report from Brussels that 'the consort of the Duke of Cumberland intends to pass the winter in this city. She has provisionally hired two boxes at the playhouse for two months.' Then, a fortnight later, it reported that the Duke had arrived and proposed to stay there with his Duchess for some time. It would seem as if she had decided it would be best to keep the Channel between him and Mrs Robinson. Later he wrote approvingly to the most politically active of his brothers-in-law, Temple Luttrell, congratulating him on a speech in the House of Commons on December 10 in which he attacked the Government's policy of paying 'savage Red Indians to murder and scalp colonists', and urged higher wages for naval ratings who were receiving only £4 a month.[6]

We read no more about the Cumberlands in the press until early April, 1778, when their return, accompanied by Elizabeth Luttrell, was reported. The Duchess was said to be perfectly recovered from the indisposition which occasioned her tour abroad for the change of air.

That same month, when grievously ill, Lord Chatham heard that the Duke of Richmond intended to move in the House of Lords an Address to the Throne recommending military evacuation of America. The great statesman, ignoring the advice of his physicians, left his sick room at Hayes to answer the Duke. Exhausted by his perorations against surrender to his old enemies, the Bourbons of France and Spain, he had an apoplectic seizure. Had it not been for the timely assistance of the Duke of Cumberland and Lord Temple, who caught him in their arms, he would have fallen to the ground.[7]

Since General Burgoyne had surrendered with his army to the Americans at Saratoga on October 17 of the previous year, and the entry of France into the war on their side, things had gone badly for the British. Although he supported reconciliation with the colonists, the Duke now felt he should be on active service in the Navy. He applied to the King for some command at sea, but was told there was none suitable for him, so was forced to limit his nautical exploits to holding his Annual Boat Race. There were again seven entries, including the *Duchess of Cumberland*, which was once more narrowly defeated, this time by a Captain Newton's *Tartar*.

Where the Duke met with success was on the turf. His stud of horses was remarkable for their blood. His *Sulphur* was not only very successful as a racer but also sired *Little Isaac*, *King Priam*, and *Don Joseph*, all of which won sweepstakes for him in 1778. He himself was no mean horseman. For example, five years earlier, on February 19, 1773, he and Sir Edward Hales, riding their own horses, had raced each other on Ascot Heath and the Duke had won a hundred guineas. It was with Hales that Mrs Bayley once flirted in a vain attempt to rekindle her royal lover's ardour.

On July 20, 1778, the Duke narrowly escaped death when walking in a grove near his home in Windsor Forest. Lightning shivered two limbs from the trees a few yards from where he stood. Later he told his equerry: 'I shouldn't have minded dying had it been a French ball from a mizzen-top.'

Shortly after this, there were rumours that the King having relented, had agreed to the Duke's appointment to a command in the fleet, but these were soon proved false. 'The same influence in the Cabinet which precludes him from the *presence*, equally precludes him the command of the Royal George,' the *London Evening Post* informed its subscribers on September 2. Still, he had better luck at Abingdon Races that day when his brown colt, *Pompey*, won him £50.

A month later, the *Post* reported that offers from the Dukes of

Cumberland and Gloucester to serve respectively in the Navy and in the Army had been rejected. Next, on October 20, it stated that Cumberland was to go abroad the Admiral's ship of the fleet about to sail for the Mediterranean, but he was to have no command. As a sop, however, the Duke was promoted to be Admiral of the Blue. But the King would take no further steps towards a reconciliation for some time. 'The whole political sentiments and conduct of the Duke of Cumberland are so very adverse to what I think right,' George wrote to Lord North on May 9, 1780, 'that any intercourse between us could only be of a cold and distant kind and consequently very unpleasant.'[8]

CHAPTER SIXTEEN

Temporary Reconciliation

It is, of course, one of the ironies of life that the appearance of a common enemy does more to reconcile and unite opposing factions in a nation or members of a family than anything else, and one direct consequence of the Gordon Riots that broke out in London on June 2, 1780, was to do just this. On that day, a mob some 60,000 strong, led by the Protestant fanatic, Lord George Gordon, tried to break into the House of Commons and force the repeal of Sir George Savile's Catholic Relief Bill which had been passed in 1778. They destroyed the few chapels of that faith belonging to foreign embassies, broke open Newgate prison, attacked the Bank of England, wrecked the distillery at Holborn, and sacked the house of Lord Mansfield, now Lord Chief Justice, who favoured Catholic emancipation. London was set ablaze with nearly forty fires. The timorous magistrates took no active steps to quell the violence. It was the King himself who mastered the crisis by issuing orders in Council for the military to suppress the insurrection.

Gloucester and Cumberland immediately sent George messages offering their active services, which pleased him.[1] As a result on June 9, he wrote to the former expressing a wish to be on excellent terms with him in the future but that so to avoid disagreement when they met. 'I hope it will be understood that nothing is to be mentioned in the conversation between us about the Duchess of Gloucester. I shall be happy at any time to see the children.'[2] Horace Walpole, Maria's uncle, says that the Duke threw this letter into the fire declaring: 'It is not fit this letter should ever be seen.' He then had a long private audience with the King, who, according to Walpole, 'wept over him, and told him he had ever loved him the best of his family and hoped to see him often' and 'heard with great patience very strong things the Duke said to him'. Nevertheless, all such plain speaking failed to make George change his mind. At least, from then onwards, relations between the two brothers were friendly.

On the Saturday after this meeting, the Duke of Cumberland visited the King by invitation to talk things over. Then, on the following Thursday, all three dined together, and on Monday, June 19, the two Dukes attended a meeting of the Privy Council.

Anxious that nothing should upset the peace-making, the Prince of Wales had written to the King on June 12: 'I think it my duty to acquaint your Majesty yt. upon our return through Hyde Park, the Duke & Duchess of Cumberland passed us in their carriage. The Duke alighted, & sending the Duchess forward, joined us and accompanied us through the Park. His Royal Highness expressed that he had been under some embarrassment in what manner to behave on meeting us, but hoped that what he had done was for the best, & said at the same time that if yr. Majesty disapproved of the step he had taken, that you would please to suppose it never had passed. I thought it my duty to acquaint your Majesty with what had passed, & shall reserve further particulars till I have the honour of seeing you tomorrow'.[3]

The King replied the same day: 'The more open you are in your conduct towards me, the more cordial will always be mine in return. Nothing could be more proper than your writing me word of your meeting this day in Hyde Park with the Duke of Cumberland. Your conduct has been most proper; I say nothing of others.'[4]

The Queen, too, apparently played her part in the rapprochement. When the Duke of Cumberland arrived for dinner on the 15th it was reported that he asked if he might be allowed to see her, and that immediately the King agreed, a side door flew open and his lady hurried in and embraced her brother-in-law. 'Two or three moments after, she rose from her Seat, and again embraced him, while the Tear of Joy, the Pearl of precious, of inestimable Price, stole down and ornamented her Royal Cheek'.[5]

On Wednesday, June 20, there was, as the papers put it, 'a most crowded levee' at Cumberland House. At this were present all the Foreign Ministers in London, the Dukes of Northumberland, Dorset, and Queensberry, and a host of peers, including Lord North. The Senior Service was represented by Admirals, Lord Howe, Lord Edgcumbe, Keppel, and Pigot, and the Army by Generals, Lord Amherst and Sir George Howard. Everyone appeared pleased that harmony had been restored, and the levee did not break up until three o'clock.

'The reconciliation of the King to the Dukes of Gloucester and Cumberland is now made public,' wrote Mary Hamilton also in June. 'They were introduced on Tuesday to the Princes and Princesses with the restriction that their Royal Highnesses were not to enquire after the Duchesses of Gloucester and Cumberland. They are to be at the Drawing Room today, and the elder Princes are to meet them.'[6]

On July 13 it was announced in the *Court Miscellany* that 'the Duke of Cumberland will reside part of this Summer at his Lodge at Windsor at the express Request of their Majesties'. The Duchess was not mentioned.

The fifteen-year-old Duke of Clarence (later William IV), who was at sea, wrote to his mother to ask if the nor'-easter of royal disapproval no longer blew upon his uncles. Queen Charlotte replied from Kew on July 28: 'The report of the King's being reconciled to his brothers is true; it seems to give universal satisfaction in public, but makes no difference in our way of living at Windsor. The Duke of Cumberland comes to court, and walks Sundays upon the Terrace ...'[7]

The Prince of Wales, as rigorously disciplined when young by the King as he himself and his brothers were by the Dowager Princess, had not been permitted to attend balls until mid-1779 or to hold a commission in the army. As a result of these prohibitions, the Prince had become restive.

When, on August 12, 1780, his eldest son reached the age of eighteen, George III realized that he could no longer withhold his liberty, and therefore allowed him his own establishment in a wing of the Queen's House so that he could still keep him under surveillance. The Prince celebrated his birthday by holding his first levee in the Audience Chamber. Among those who came 'on Purpose to pay their Compliments were the Duke of Cumberland who was dressed unusually elegant, and went in a new Chariot, and his Servants in new Liveries'.[8]

The Duke took advantage of the relaxed relationship between him and the King to further his own friendship with the heir apparent. Writing from his Lodge on September 6, he enclosed a key of the Windsor Great Park (of which he was Ranger) for the Prince, declaring: 'Shall be happy at all times that the Park may afford you every amusement you can wish.'[9]

Then on October 11, the Duke enquired on what day his nephew intended hunting in three weeks' time because he wished to accompany him.[10] The Prince of Wales replied giving the date, and on the 17th his uncle wrote back: 'I shall certainly do myself the pleasure of waiting upon you next Sunday soon after one o'clock ... I hope we shall have some good hunts together as I shall devote my time to you whenever I am not thought troublesome ... Permit me to conclude with assuring you how sincerely & unalterably I am attached to you & that nothing in life can ever make me differ in these sentiments.'[11]

On the 31st of that month when the new Parliament was opened, the Duke, thanks to his improved relations with the King, received the honours customarily paid to a Prince of the blood when he attended the House of Lords. This caused a hitch in the proceedings. A salute was supposed to be fired as usual when the Sovereign left St James's. As the Duke's equipage accompanied by mounted guards appeared, the gunners mistook him for the King and discharged their artillery long before the latter set out. When the salvo sounded, the noblemen in the House of Lords imagined the King had arrived and hastily put on their robes a full hour before necessary.

Hoping that in time the ban on the Duchess would be lifted, the Duke did all he could to please his eldest brother. He went stag-hunting with him in Windsor Forest, attended every Drawing Room at St James's, and, when in London, Sunday service in the Chapel Royal and saw that the Prince of Wales came as well.

Then, towards the end of January in the New Year, the Duke was shown by his nephew a detailed letter of directions, dated December 22, a month earlier, giving instructions regarding the young Prince's future conduct. In it, the King forbade him to go to Balls, Assemblies or Masquerades in private houses, and went on: 'When I mentioned your not going to private houses I should have added the impossibility of going either in town or the country to those of your uncles, had you not known that on my reconciliation with them in the beginning of the summer, the saying the women will not appear will not be admitted by me as a reason to relax on this head.'[12]

Cumberland read this with dismay. Nothing, it now seemed, would make the King recognize the Duchess or even allow his son to have contact with her. This provoked the Duke into writing on January 31, 1781: 'As I supposed that every mark of attention on my part to the Prince could not but be agreeable to your Majesty, it was with the utmost astonishment and mortification I learnt your Majesty had forbidden the Prince's Establishment to dine at Cumberland House.

'After this publick proof of your Majestie's intention to exclude me from the benefits of society enjoy'd by the rest of mankind, it is impossible to receive with satisfaction those attentions (however flattering) all your Majestie's subjects wish to pay me when I am conscious they thereby mean your Majestie's displeasure.

'Thus, Sir, condemned by your Majesty to a situation so repugnant to my own feelings, all that remains for me is to request permission to withdraw from your Majesty's dominions and as a citizen of the world seek an asylum in some other part of the globe.'[13]

There is no record of the King's answering this letter, but the Duke did not leave the country. On March 13 that year, Horace Walpole tells Mann in Florence: 'Their Highnesses of Cumberland have turned short from the King, and court the Prince of Wales, and the opposition, and the *ton*, and the mob.'[14] And, shortly after this, he writes to the Hon. Thomas Walpole: 'The youngest uncle has got possession of the eldest nephew, and sets the father at defiance.'[15] For the rest of 1781 the Duke continued to attend Drawing Rooms at St James's, services in the Chapel Royal, and stag-hunts with the King, and always, week after week, in the newspapers reporting this, occurs the phrase—'the Prince of Wales and the Duke of Cumberland'. The pair soon became inseparable.

Despite their incompatible characters, the Duchesses of Gloucester and Cumberland had preserved the appearance of friendship. On the evening of Sunday, February 14, a 'grand entertainment was given at Gloucester House to the Duke and Duchess of Cumberland and divers of the principal nobility of the first Rank.'[16] Then twelve days later, the quartet, together with the Gloucesters' two children, dined with Princess Amelia at Cavendish Square.

But Maria had become jealous of the Prince of Wales's growing fondness for his other Aunt and indifference to her own beauty, and this now led to an open breach. When Anne suggested that the two women and their husbands should appear together in the same box at the opera, so as to demonstrate their solidarity, Maria scorned the idea, saying rudely: 'I could not smell at the same nosegay as her in public.'

Such a snub did not worry Anne. The Prince of Wales's response to his father's obdurate prohibitions had been to invite his Uncle Harry to call on him as often as he wished, which led to the King's complaining: 'I am ashamed to see my brother paying court to my son.'

When the Cumberlands gave a ball and grand routs, the Prince defiantly patronized them. As soon as the news spread that he was frequenting Cumberland House, the Duke and Duchess's social functions became crowded with the most fashionable of London society. A levee held by the Duke on March 5 attracted more than five hundred carriages full of guests.[17] (In many of the vehicles, the fine ladies squatted on the floors, the reason for this being not to hide and keep their visit a secret but because had they sat on the seats the tall plumes in their hair would have crushed against the roofs.)

Prinny's affair with Mary Robinson had ended, but he had difficulty in extricating himself from it, having given her a promissory note for £20,000 to be redeemed when he was twenty-one. Not satisfied with this, she threatened to publish his love letters to her, and the King had to provide £500 for their purchase. Unknown to the latter, on the Duke of Cumberland's advice, the services of Charles James Fox had been procured and in exchange for an annuity the note was surrendered. It was Fox who, according to Robert Huish, was 'the most active pander to the passions of the Prince'.

Frederick, Duke of York, who had left for Hanover in December to further his military training, wrote to his brother on March 30, 1781, urging him in view of the reports he had heard to take care of his health. 'You cannot stand this kind of life, and I am afraid it is the Windsor Lodge Duke who leads you into it. I have no doubt but that he means you exceedingly well, but believe me, he is not the best adviser you can follow.'

The Prince replied on April 10: 'You mention in your letter as if you apprehended yt. the Duke of Cumberland had in some manner been ye cause of my disorder, by raking & rioting & other things of ye same sort. You are really much mistaken. I have never seen ye D ever since you have gone when anything of that sort has been going forwards, quite ye contrary. He has acted as my firmest, staunchest & best friend would have done, as you or Lake would have done, had you or he been present, in an affair wh. I wanted ye advice of such a friend, wh. has lately happened; & wh. I hope now will be speedily put an end to. It originated from ye old infernal cause Robinson ... You shall hear everything concerning it the moment it is settled, but it is too long to be mentioned now. You will therefore perceive how much you are mistaken concerning him, when so far from rioting and raking with me, he is always advising me to take care of my health.'[18] Lake was Lt-Colonel Gerard Lake (1744–1808), the Prince's equerry, who had left for military service in America that January.

Although the Duke of Cumberland was now 35, he was certainly still addicted to schoolboyish pranks. One morning soon after having bought a pair of spirited horses, he invited Baumgarten, his favourite musician, to ride with him on the box of his phaeton to try them out although he knew him to be of a nervous nature. 'Had it been any one else, Baumgarten would have refused, but, unwilling to offend his patron, he climbed apprehensively up onto the driver's seat. It was not long before the Duke began whipping the horses till they almost broke free of their harness. Meanwhile, Baumgarten was trying to hold tight to the box, but his companion's tormenting shouts of 'Take care—or you'll be off!' eventually so terrified him that he threw his arms round the other's waist, crying: 'If I go, so will you!' And he refused to release his grip before they reached the stables.

It was customary among writers of memoirs of the period to blame Cumberland as partly responsible for the deterioration in his nephew's character, but most of it was based on hearsay and, in view of the letter quoted earlier, one ought to discount much that is condemnatory.

John Heneage Jesse wrote his *Memoirs of the Life and Reign of King George III*, in Victorian times and in cases of doubt took the side of the monarch. He alleged: 'Under the auspices of his weak and frivolous uncle, the Prince's conversation is said to have been a compound of the slang of grooms, and the wanton vocabulary of a brothel. The Duke—who, in allusion to his nephew's Welsh principality, had the bad taste to style him familiarly "Taffy"—kept a faro-bank for his amusement at Cumberland House, in Pall Mall; carried him to the lowest scenes of debauchery, and even introduced money-lenders, and still worse characters, into the Prince's apartments at Buckingham House. Moreover, it was under the Duke's influence that the Prince's conduct towards his father became marked, not only by disobedience, but by the most undutiful contempt. The fact of the King's constant attendance in the hunting-field at this period was attributed, by those who knew him best, to a double desire to enjoy more of the society of his son, and to keep him out of the way of evil companions.

'The King's hour of dining, when resident at Windsor, was at this time three o'clock, and when in London four o'clock; yet the Prince, as if with the purpose of exposing his father to the comments, if not the derision, of the royal household, rarely made his appearance at the former place till four o'clock, or, at the latter till five.'[19]

Walpole, no friend of the Cumberlands, reports the King, in 1781, as saying to the Duke of Grafton: 'When we hunt together, neither my son nor my brother speak to me; and lately, when the chase ended at a little village where there was but a single post-chaise to be hired, my son and brother got into it, and drove to London, leaving me to go home in a cart if I could find one.'[20] He also wrote that within earshot of the King 'the two men spoke of him in the grossest terms'.[21]

In view of this it is not surprising that the trio did not often hunt together. On October 22, 1781, the Prince informed the Duke of York in a letter: 'I now hunt four times a week, twice with ye King & his hounds & twice with our friend ye Duke of Cumberland and his hounds.'[22]

The faro bank mentioned by Jesse was actually begun by the Duke as a means of supplementing income as he and the Duchess found it impossible to live on £20,000 a year, the same as he had received when a bachelor. There was also the interest to pay on a mortgage of £15,000 he had raised on Cumberland House.

Among the manuscripts of the 5th Earl of Carlisle preserved at Castle Howard is a letter to him from the wit and gambler John Hare, dated February 11, 1782, which reads: 'The Prince of Wales has been to the Duchess of Cumberland's public nights and sups there every Saturday with about twenty people. ... The Duke holds a Pharaoh Bank, deals standing the whole night; and last week when the Duke of Devonshire sat down to play, he told him there were two rules; one was "not to let you punt more than ten guineas;" and the other "no tick". Did you ever hear a more princely declaration? Derby lost the gold in his pocket and the Prince of Wales lent him 50 guineas; on which the Duke of Cumberland expressed some surprise, and said he had never lent 50 guineas in his whole life. "Then," says the Prince of Wales, "it is high time for you to begin." I am sure you will like this reprimand. I have always by some accident been prevented from going to the Duke's levee, which I am sorry for, as I am told his dealing at Pharaoh is the most ludicrous thing that can be conceived.'[23]

A letter to the Earl from man of fashion, Anthony Storer, dated the 24th of the same month contains this comment: 'London is but a *triste séjour*, everything disjointed and falling to pieces; eternal politics and squabbling; nothing to enliven us but the Duke of Cumberland's Pharaoh Bank. There are now so many banks that the market is overstocked.'[24]

By 1787, faro had become a matter of business as well as a game of chance in the so-called polite world. When Fox was out of office and out of cash, he with a crony set up a faro bank at Brook's Club, which, on return to power, he assigned to a syndicate of three, headed by Lord Cholmondeley, one of Lady Grosvenor's favourite men. Like the Duke of Cumberland, they did not trust any employees to act as croupiers, so dealt the cards themselves for which service their charge was three guineas an hour. As banker, Cholmondeley himself raked in between £300,000 and £400,000, ruining half his fellow members.

The Prince of Wales caught the gambling craze and, when he did not go to Cumberland House, rumour had it that his uncle brought other addicts to his quarters in the Queen's House. He was to lose such huge sums that when he died, a wag suggested 'I.O.U.' should be carved on his tomb.

Horace Walpole, sending London news to Mann in Florence, wrote that the young men gaming at Almack's lost on average £15,000 there in an evening. Play was high as can be seen from this entry in the Club's records: 'Mr. Thynne, having won only 12,000 guineas during the last two months, retired in disgust, March 21st, 1772.' The gamblers before starting to play either turned their embroidered coats inside out for luck or donned instead frieze great coats. Then they slipped leather shields over their lace ruffles, and masks over their faces to hide their feelings if playing *quinze*; and to protect their eyes from the light they wore straw hats with high crowns and wide brims, decorated with ribbons and flowers.

According to Walpole again, the Duke of Cumberland took his nephew on drunken escapades. Yet in the example he gives it was thanks to uncle's attentions that Prinny came to no harm. He says that shortly after the latter's coming of age, Lord Chesterfield invited them both to a roistering at Blackheath. The evening ended with some revellers unchaining a mastiff and fighting it. Several were bitten before the animal could be overcome. When they left, the intoxicated Prince jumped into his phaeton and promptly fell asleep, leaving the reins to his uncle, who, having remained sober, managed to bring him safely to town.

In early 1781, there was trouble over the loan of £13,000 the King had made the Duke so that he could pay Lord Grosvenor his damages and the costs. For some reason it was made through the intermediary of the Duke's former governor and treasurer, Edward Le Grand, to whom he was to remit quarterly instalments of £500, but he became a late payer and when Le Grand died half was still owing.[25]

The King had instructed the deceased to hold all the monies received until the full amount was repaid, and then to return it to the Duke as a gift from his brother. Following Le Grand's decease, George decided to cancel the outstanding debt and instructed the Executrix, a Mrs Frances Colleton, to pay the £6,500 held by the Estate to the Duke, which she did.

The Cumberlands then claimed from the Executrix £2,100 as interest on the grounds that as Captain James Luttrell, who acted as their representative in the matter, maintained: 'Mr Le Grand actually had put the money out to interest and drawn considerable profit from it, and that the Duke conceived it to be the intention of His Majesty that such profit should not belong to Mr Le Grand's executor but to himself and that Mr Le Grand having died a very rich man, there seemed no reason why the Duke should sacrifice any right of his to the heirs of Mr Le Grand.'

When the King heard of this, he was annoyed and directed Lord North to ask Captain Luttrell to call upon him. Following the meeting, the minister had the following communication, dated April 8, 1781, sent to the King:

'Upon the whole, Lord North believes that the Duke is now sensible that he has no legal claim to the interest of the money. Lord North gave it as his opinion that the money in Mr Le Grand's hands belong'd to his Majesty, and not to the Duke of Cumberland, which opinion Mr Luttrell did not dispute but said that his R.H. brought his claim on behalf of his Majesty, & in pursuance of what he conceived to have been H.M.'s intention & that he did not found it on any original claim & right of his own.

'Lord North imagines that H.M.'s declaration will put an end to the business.'

It did.

CHAPTER SEVENTEEN

The Cumberlands Discover 'Brighthelmstone'

The popular belief that it was the Prince Regent who discovered the charms of Brighton for himself, and made it fashionable, is not strictly correct. It was through visits there to the Duke and Duchess of Cumberland that he became increasingly attracted by Brighthelmstone, as it was then called.

At the beginning of the eighteenth century it had been no more than a fishing village, in peril of vanishing completely through the sea's erosion of its shores. Two ferocious storms had ravaged its mean dwellings, and a visitor in 1724 records that the inhabitants were living 'almost underground'. It owed its revival to a quackish physician from Lewes, Richard Russell, whose book, *Dissertation on the Use of Sea Water in Diseases of the Gland*, earned him a wide reputation. Sea-bathing and sea-water drinking were his cure for almost any complaint. 'A little draught of the sea-water is convenient immediately upon coming out of the sea,' he wrote, 'because by purging the body, it prevents the blood from flying into the Head.'

In 1751 he started sending his patients to Brighthelmstone. He obtained such a high proportion of cures, and his practice grew so large in consequence, that two years later he moved there himself, buying some land and having built an impressive house of stone and brick, with many bedrooms therein to accommodate those who came for treatment. Today the Royal Albion Hotel stands on the site. The doctor's waiting-list became longer and longer, for he maintained there was no human ill he could not cure, from madness to sterility. To have made his treatment too simple might have led to competition from other physicians; he therefore concocted his own special pills prepared, so he claimed, from the bones of cuttlefish, the eyes of crabs, coral, burnt sponge, snails, the flesh of vipers, and even 'prepared wood lice'. This, taken last thing at night, was followed first thing in the morning by a pint of sea-water.

When the Doctor died, others were quick to take over his work.

The most successful of these was an Irishman, Dr Pelham, who, improving on Russell, proclaimed in his *Short History of Brighthelmstone, with Remarks on its Air and Analysis of its Waters* that its chalky ground had 'no perspiration, and therefore must be extremely healthy', that the nearest river was six miles away, and as no other maritime town was 'equally remote from one, I may venture to affirm that the soil here is extremely dry, and that the air of this place must be proportionately purer'. There was no 'noxious steam' from perspiring trees, and no 'insalutary vapour' from 'stagnant water'.

Determined to give the place the merits as well of an inland spa, he extolled the virtues of a newly discovered well at St Anne's in Hove, from which sprung chalybeate waters. Shepherds, it appeared, found that sheep drinking there had lambed prolifically. Whilst refraining from suggesting that it might have similar effects with human beings, he believed that partaking of the iron-rich water would increase 'appetite and spirits' and greatly relieve 'bodies labouring under the consequences of irregular living and illicit pleasures'.

Another physician, Dr Awaiter,[1] astutely exploited the advantages of indoor sea-water addiction, with its consequent greater harvest in fees. And so he had erected a building in classic style with pipes leading into the sea, from which the water was pumped to fill its 'Hot and Cold Baths'. Thus he claimed 'bathing would become more universal, be unattended with terror, and no cure protracted. Moreover, invalids would have the advantage of this bathing remedy all the year round, whereas, on account of the variablement of our climate, it is denied them at present, except in the summer months and then only in calm weather'.

Catering as Awaiter did for the sickly and the squeamish whose constitutions were too delicate and stomachs too weak to bear drinking sea-water straight, he prescribed boiling four ounces each of it and milk in a pan and adding sufficient cream of tartar to turn the mixture into whey. Then, after straining from the curd and allowing to cool, it should be drunk.

Thanks to the publicity thus given to Brighton, London's *beau monde* began visiting it during the summer months to try and restore their health and vigour. It was in September, 1771, that the Duke of Cumberland first visited the tiny town. The church bells pealed in welcome, the Battery fired a salute of twenty-one cannon, the packet-boats at anchor responded by discharging their guns, and in the evening the houses of the leading citizens were all illuminated. In appreciation of this unexpected honour, the Duke stayed a week, gave a public breakfast and a ball, and expressed himself 'highly delighted with the situation of the place and the conveniences attending it'. The ladies found him 'charming', reported the *Sussex Weekly Advertiser*.

Eight years later Cumberland fell ill with ulcers on his lungs, and his doctor suggested that a stay in Brighton might benefit his health, so he rented Dr Russell's old house on the Steine. He arrived just after four one afternoon in August, 1779, to a reception as splendid as that given him on his first visit. Two hours later, the Duchess followed and to her delight a number of young men dressed themselves in white and met her on the road, then ran cheering before her carriage into the town.

During their stay, the Cumberlands attended a performance of *The School for Scandal* and *Three Weeks after Marriage* at the New Theatre in North Street. A box ornamented with the ducal arms was specially fitted up, and shown such deference they responded by being most affable to all and sundry. Here was a domain where Anne felt she would be treated like a Queen. As for her husband his health was much improved by the visit, so for the next four or five years they returned every season. In 1781, they rented a new abode, the larger bow-fronted elegant Grove House, which was only six hundred yards from the sea and gained its name from the adjacent Promenade Grove, a small-scale version of London's Vauxhall Gardens. They invited Prinny to be their first guest.

The *St James's Chronicle* for June 19 reporting this added: 'Some members of the convivial set, whose festive qualities have been lately so alluring to the Heir Apparent, are engaged to be of the Party and everything is preparing that will render manifest the Temple of Jollity.'

The Duke delayed leaving London until his Annual Boat Race had taken place. In the *Morning Chronicle* for May 5, 1781, appeared an advertisement bv the members of the Cumberland Fleet in which, with his permission, they challenged 'all gentlemen proprietors of pleasure sailing boats, within the British dominions, to join with them in the contention'. It was the first time the event was made open, and he generously provided for this special occasion a silver gilt cup costing fifty guineas instead of a twenty guineas silver one as previously.

Such interest was thus aroused that, according to the report in the *St James's Chronicle*, the oldest watchmen declared they had never seen so many boats assembled on the Thames before. At least 30,000 people were on the water and a 100,000 lined the banks from Blackfriars

Bridge to Chelsea. Towards 4 pm that Monday, June 25, the eleven competing craft came to their moorings off the Temple. Unfortunately the Duke, accompanied by the Duchess and her brothers and sisters arrived half-an-hour late in his barge, and when the competitors set out for Putney, the tide was so spent that 1777's winner, Captain Kitchingman's *Eagle*, could not make Battersea Bridge. All then by order of the Duke anchored off Chelsea Church and, after consulting them individually, he postponed the event until Monday, July 9. Despite this setback, festivities followed at the Royal Cumberland Tea Gardens (formerly Mr Smith's and renamed in honour of the Duke the previous year).

The deferred race took place as arranged and was won by a Thomas Taylor's *Cumberland.* Duke and Duchess were saluted from the shore 'both coming and going by several discharges of artillery' and supped at the Grand Pavilion, Vauxhall, while the Captains of the Cumberland Fleet regaled themselves at the Tea Gardens, where later the Duke joined them with his band which played until two a.m.

A few days later, the Cumberlands went to Brighton, hoping that their nephew would soon join them as planned. The King, however, forbade him to do so, but he rebelliously swore that it would be only a celebration postponed and promised to visit them there directly he came of age. Meanwhile, the resort grew in popularity. The following year, a letter from Brighton appeared in the *Morning Herald* for September 28: 'This place is as full as an egg, but the company is a motley group. The Duke is at the head of the whole and condescendingly associates with all from the baron to the blackleg—play runs high, particularly at whist. We have every kind of amusement that fancy can desire for the train of folly and dissipation. . . . Few people think of stirring from hence at present till the stag-hounds come down about the middle of next month.'

That same year, the Duke received an honour which gave him some much-needed prestige, and indicated that many people believe he had reached maturity and had forgiven him his youthful excesses. The Freemasons elected him their Grand Master, an office which he held to his death. Thanks to him, a new Freemasons' Hall was built in London, and he was the original patron of the Royal Masonic Institute for Girls.

At the same time the Duke and his wife continued to make Cumberland House the most popular *rendez-vous* for the *beau monde*. For example, for the night of March 18, 1783, the Duchess sent out a thousand cards—600 were invited to a card party at ten o'clock, and 400 to a ball and supper at twelve. The Prince of Wales, all the foreign ambassadors and most people of fashion were present.[2]

Facts such as these show how inaccurate Jesse was when he wrote of the Duke in his *Memoirs of the Life and Reign of King George III:* 'Avoided by his royal relatives and neglected by the world, his society, during the later years of his life, seems to have been mostly confined to the kinspeople of his Duchess, and a few associates whose tastes and habits were congenial to his own. No single individual of high rank and character appears to have countenanced him. Even the most violent member of the Opposition shunned rather than courted his acquaintance.'

Such assertions are quite unfounded—a year earlier a ball at Cumberland House attracted all London society. George Selwyn in a letter to the Earl of Carlisle, dated March 15, 1782, wrote that when this took place on the previous night the streets leading there were 'filled with chairs, flambeaus, vis-à-vis's, peach-coloured satin, blonde lace, and diamonds'.[3]

In August, 1783, the Prince of Wales came of age and fulfilled his promise. At half-past six on the evening of September 7, his arrival in Brighton was announced by the usual bell-ringing and firing of guns. Later he and the Duke appeared on the Steine, and watched by Sunday's crowds they strolled up and down for about half an hour before proceeding to the Rooms. The evening ended with a display of fireworks before Grove House. Erredge tells us in his *History of Brighthelmstone:* 'The auspicious event was celebrated by the inhabitants with a general illumination, every pane of glass in the town displaying a candle stuck in a lump of clay.'

Next morning the Duke took his nephew stag-hunting on the downs, then in the afternoon the visitor amused himself shooting at his uncle's chimney pots. In the evening the Cumberlands accompanied him to a ball held in his honour at the Castle Inn Assembly Rooms, which the *Sussex Advertiser* described as 'the most splendid ever known at that place'.

It was the Duke who introduced Prinny to the pleasures of the turf. Every year it had been the custom for Lewes Races to be patronized by people from Brighton, but Cumberland thought the latter should have its own meetings, and be sited on the Whitehawk Down, just outside the town; and as a result of his efforts the first races were held under his auspices on August 26 and 27, 1783, on a two mile course occupying the horseshoe-shaped ridge of the hill. They began in a modest way with only three events in two days—and one was for ponies.

With the approach of winter, 'fashion' left Brighton for London and the Cumberlands, whose finances called for economies in order to rehabilitate them, left the country. Lady Bute, writing to Lady Louisa Stuart from London on October 7, 1783, informs her: 'The Duke and Duchess of Cumberland are going abroad for a twelvemonth, which will occasion a considerable blank in the divertion, but I suppose the Prince of Wales's entertainments are to make up for this loss; he is building an immense room at Carlton House for the purpose of balls, etc., which I hear is to be decorated and furnished in the highest taste and magnificence ...'

On coming of age the Prince had decided to move away from his wing in the Queen's House, so inconveniently near to his parents. He chose for a new home Carlton House, the old residence of his grandmother, the Princess Dowager, which had been tenantless since her death. One of its chief merits in his eyes was that it adjoined Cumberland House. A fortune was spent in reconstruction, decorations and furnishings.

Whilst this was in progress, the Cumberlands were in Strasbourg. They had left London in November, 1783. The Duke wrote to his nephew from Calais on the 25th of that month describing their journey there. He goes on: 'Believe me, dear Sir, that nobody could feel more than *we* did at parting with you & were melancholy enough on the road. Your kindness & politeness to us on all occasions can never be forgot. Whenever you have a leisure moment of reflection, consider there is not one more sincerely attached to you than myself ... I cannot help writing the very feelings of my heart to you. Your conduct at all times has been so remarkably good to me that whenever I have it in my power to be of service to you, you have a right to command me. We are just getting into the carriage & both hope we shall not be forgot.'[4]

Then on the 30th, soon after arrival in Paris, the favourite uncle corresponded again with the Prince. The Duke of Manchester, Ambassador to France, had shown them 'every mark of civility'. They had been to the Opera 'the musick noisy and bad, fine shew and the dancing very good ... I hope you are diverting yourself. I feel very severely the loss of you, my dear friend, & indeed after such an acquaintance as I have had with you I find nothing that anywhere can resemble you ... I have no kind of news to tell you here & fear my letter to you, who live in a very gay world, will appear but dull. I hope your *friend* will not be scrupulous & come & partake of your agreeable parties at your house. Be happy my dear Sir is my greatest wish.'[5] The 'friend' referred to Mrs Fitzherbert.

At the end of the first week in December, Henry and Anne reached Strasbourg, from where on the 27th the later wrote at length to the Prince. It would appear that the Duchess had promised him a report on the looks of a certain lady. It is a pity that she omits her name:

'I never can forget anything yr. R.H. wishes me to remember & had it so much at heart that I stay'd a day longer at Paris on purpose to see——[sic] for half an hour at the Duke of Manchester's. The first coup d'oeil is not striking, but yr. R.H. knows that a little beauty accompany'd with strong sensibility & a thousand agrémens constitutes the tout en semble capable of inspiring a forte passion rather than symmetry of form or features; of these however I had no opportunity of judging.

'Here we are at Strasbourg for the winter, much fêté by all the commandants & not ill lodged; the Duke de Crillon offer'd his magnificent house at Avignon, but the Duke's penchant for Germans & music gave the preference to Strasbourg. As to myself, when I had taken leave of yr. R.H. my difficulty's were at an end, or having exausted every painful sensation I felt not at all the fatigues of the journey. The Duke and Dutchess of Manchester did everything that depend'd on them to make Paris agreeable to us; they are both much esteem'd there but I recollect the Friday before I left England & thought I had seen a better.'

This reference to the dinner the Prince had given in their honour before departure is followed by one to Fox's controversial India Bill, a well intentioned measure that would have transferred political responsibilities for that country from the East India Company to Parliament. It was defeated through the King's intervention.

'I am more grieved than surprised at this first proof of great objects sacrificed to the gratification of private pique in the fate of the India Bill. You know, my dear Prince, I ever was of opinion that the prerogative of the Crown ought not to be diminish'd & every struggle for power in the present inauspicious season of republicanism is dangerous to monarchy.'

The Duchess ends that her sister, Lady Elizabeth, was in better health and 'extremely flattered' by the Prince's remembrance of her in his letter. 'Tonight is the first Masquerade at the Theatre but I have no friar to dress or inducement to join the throng.'[6]

The next extant letter we have from the Duke to his nephew is dated Wednesday, April 14, 1784. One senses a certain boredom. 'Our life here is pretty much the same; the Marquis de la Salle, the Commandant, is at home three evenings in the week, at a little after eight, after the Play, parties of cards are made; everybody plays at a very moderate price & indeed in a garrison town it is of the greatest consequence that play for any great sum should be forbid. Supper is over & everybody retires by half past eleven. Every Saturday the Duchess has company to supper & we at our house just do the same as the Commandant.[7]

Again from Strasbourg, on August 23, 1784, the Duke acknowledges 'a kind and affectionate letter' from his nephew. He goes on: 'I am very glad you are on your guard what you write, yet if ever you have anything to communicate, Garth will let me know without mentioning your name. The Duchess is extremely sensible of your attention to her & begs me to assure you of her best compliments & good wishes. We mean the 1st of October to go to the South of France in order to pass a warmer winter than the last. This climate is changeable beyond measure, hot & cold the same day. Our life here is pretty much alike; when the troops exercise of a morning I go out to see them.'[8] They left Strasbourg as he wrote and went to hibernate in Avignon.

The Cumberlands had been very friendly with Mrs Fitzherbert right from the start of her association with their nephew. Alarmed by his stabbing himself in an apparent attempt at suicide, she had gone to live in Paris. Consequently he grew to miss her so much that in a forty-two-page impassioned letter to his 'dearest and only belov'd Maria,' dated November 3, 1785, he begged her to return and marry him. The Duke and Duchess had been on the point of going abroad again to stay in Italy, after returning to England for the summer, but they agreed to postpone their departure and to be present at the secret wedding.

The Prince wrote in his spidery fist that Maria must set out for England 'almost ye very moment after you receive this express & to be married ye very night of yr. arrival, & not to say a word either of ye day of yr. return or of our marriage to yr. family till it is over, as you will then be received by y.m. all with open arm.'

Maria's lovesick suitor went on to tell her how he had sought the support of the only members of his family he could trust in an emergency, the Cumberlands.

'They have behav'd in ye handsomest manner possible, & tho' they had settled their departure for Tuesday next & have business of the utmost consequence of their own they have said if it was for my happiness they wd., if they possibly could, postpone their journey till after ye return of ye courier from Paris with yr. answer, & yt. if you intend to follow very close they will endeavour to remain here in order to give a sanction by their presence to our happy tho' secret union. Everything will be done as private as possible; no one else besides the Duke & Dss. will be present unless it the Duke & Dss. of Devonshire; in short, everything is settled. We want nothing but yr. arrival.'[9]

Deeply touched by this letter, Mrs Fitzherbert nevertheless did not return until December 3, so the Cumberlands left on their travels, pausing in Paris, where they saw Maria and no doubt did their best to persuade her to marry the Prince. Anne would have seen in the situation a repetition of what happened in her own case. She had been a widow when she married the Duke whilst Maria was twice a widow. It must have given the former Mrs Horton immense satisfaction when she later heard of the secret marriage, performed like her own in the bride's house and which the Royal Marriage Act forbade because the Prince of Wales was under twenty-five years of age.

The Duchess and her husband spent the winter in Naples, where they were entertained by Sir William Hamilton. His wife, the famous Emma, wished to help Romney, who was staying there and who had never received any royal patronage, so she suggested to the Duchess that he might paint her portrait. Anne needed no pressing, and the result was a half length painting of great charm.

Elizabeth, Duchess of Devonshire, mentions in her unpublished journal in the Dormer Collection the presence in Naples of the Duke 'with his vixenish Duchess'. She goes on: 'He seems to be in love with me—one cannot be suspected of encouraging him.' The application of the adjective 'vixenish' to Anne suggests that she might have suspected the old Adam was stirring in Henry, and have made warning noises to the other duchess to keep off her preserves.

In a letter to his nephew, dated February 8, 1786, the Duke wrote: 'I do not at present see any happy prospect in returning home to see you, for I must keep strictly to what I told you at parting that until I am clear England must be the most improper place in the world for me ... I own I am much tired of this country, finding nothing so comfortable as my friends in England, but if I have no good news must bear things quietly and remain here certainly till I am able to set off straight for home again.' The Operas were the only amusements 'for the natives themselves do not open their houses'. The place would be 'shockingly dull when the English leave us'.[10]

On April 15 the Duke wrote to the Prince that the Duchess, fearing the summer would be too hot in Naples, had decided to leave, which they had done on Friday the 7th. Since then they had been in Rome where they would remain for another three weeks, before proceeding to Florence for about a week. After this the Duchess, who did not care for travelling by sea, would go with Lady Elizabeth and an equerry, Captain John Braithwaite 'through Turin over the Mont Cona'. The Countess of Ferrers, he and some of the servants would embark at Leghorn for Marseilles to join the Duchess at Besançon on their way to Spa, which they hoped to reach by the middle of June and where they intended to stay for three months.[11]

The Cumberlands arrived in Florence in mid-May. The British Envoy there, Sir Horace Mann, was ill but wanted nevertheless to pay his duty to them at the inn where they were staying, providing they did not mind his being carried up and down the stairs. However, they would not hear of giving him such trouble and instead 'the Duke immediately came to me, as the Duchess did, in the evening, and put me quite at my ease', he wrote to Walpole. Such consideration pleased him and compared favourably with the curtly condescending attitude of the Gloucesters towards him. They were in Milan and had deliberately avoided coming south so as not to meet the Cumberlands, but once the latter were out of the country they went to live in Rome, where later that year Mann saw them. The Duke of Gloucester was once more very seriously ill, and now Mann detected a distinct deterioration in his relations with Maria. 'I shall not comment upon the state of his mind,' Sir Horace wrote to his friend, Young. 'The Duke and Duchess are unhappy. ... Mutual discontent is so obvious that it cannot be concealed.'[12]

Meanwhile, the two Dukes' nephew, the Prince of Wales, was busily engaged with the building of the Marine Pavilion. Nearly two hundred workmen were employed with the result that it was ready within three months, enabling him to move in on July 6. But he was now heavily in debt, owing over a quarter of a million pounds.

Prinny wrote to the Duke of Cumberland from Brighton on July 21 how, as the King had refused to help, he had dismissed his Household, commenced the sale of his Stud, and would live like a private gentleman. He had decided to follow the Duke's example and live abroad, and intended to join them in a few weeks. He concluded with desiring his uncle 'to lay me at the Duchess's feet, & to believe yt. you ever shall find me through life'.[13]

Henry sent a sympathetic reply. They would be remaining in Spa all August, but he did not recommend the place. The weather was rainy and cold, and the society there dull. They had not decided where to spend the winter.[14]

Shortly after this the Duke fell seriously ill. Pleurisy set in, and he was in danger of losing the sight of his left eye. When the Prince heard, he immediately sent his personal physician, George Blane, out to Spa, and due to the latter's skill and care the sick man recovered. The Duke and Duchess sent a joint letter of thanks to their nephew on September 11.[15] Then on the 18th the invalid wrote that Blane after 'mature deliberations' had decided 'to carry me back to you, as he knows I have no opinion of the foreign physicians & that if I have a relapse I cannot there have immediate relief. The Duchess who agrees in everything that is either conducive to my health or wishes, altho' she fears the climate of England for me, yet gives up her opinion. The agitation of mind she had had during my long & painful illness has given her a pain in her side for which next Wednesday she & Ly Elizabeth set out for Aix-la-Chappelle to drink the waters. The doctor hopes to carry me to her next Sunday & we mean to leave that place for dear England on Sunday, October 15; therefore five or six days will land us safely at Cumberland House where I shall stay another five or six days & then go to the lodge.[16]

Back in England the Cumberlands found, as Sir Nathaniel Wraxall states in his *Memoirs:* 'All the gloom which the disasters of the American war had diffused during successive years over the capital seemed to have dispersed like a dream.' By the end of the year, as he too put it, Cumberland House was 'considered the central point of elegant amusement in the metropolis' and adds: 'A crowd of distinguished persons, male and female, filled the apartments once a week.'

About Anne herself Wraxall says: 'The Duchess, like almost every individual of the Luttrell family, by no means wanted talents, but they were more specious than solid, better calculated for show than for use, for captivating admiration than for exciting esteem. Her personal charms, allowance being made for the injury which they had sustained from time—for in 1786 she was no longer young—fully justified the Duke's passion. No woman of her time performed the honours of her own drawing-room with more affability, ease and dignity. The King held her in great alienation, because he believed that she lent herself to facilitate or to gratify the Prince of Wales's inclinations on some points beyond the limits of propriety, Carlton and Cumberland houses communicating behind by the gardens.'

Wraxall goes on: 'Lady Elizabeth Luttrell, a younger sister of the Duchess—their father having been raised in the preceding year from the rank of an Irish viscount to the dignity of an earl of the same kingdom—was domiciled at Cumberland House. She inherited no portion of the Duchess's beauty, elegance, or prudence. Coarse and destitute of softness in her manners, wanting principle and devoured by a rage for play, she finally closed her life in a manner the most humiliating as well as tragical.'[17]

The King himself was unhappy about the return of the Cumberlands, and when Anne's father, Lord Carhampton, died in the New Year, the Duke wrote enquiring whether he might not wear mourning 'as an indispensable act of propriety, and be allowed to pay my duty in black'. George replied coldly: 'I have received the Duke of Cumberland's letter. He must be the best judge how to conduct himself on an occasion that does not in the least concern me.'[18]

There was much to worry the King at this time, the cumulative effect of which contributed to causing his approaching attack of madness. Apart from the loss of the American colonies and the Prince of Wales's behaviour, he was deeply concerned about the Duke of Gloucester. It is unlikely that his wife had ever really loved him. When widowed, thanks to her beauty, she could have taken her pick of the distinguished suitors of rank and large fortune who longed to marry her. As a man, Prince William Henry had little to commend him, it was the prospect of royal grandeur that had attracted her to him, and frustrated in that ambition she had made him her disappointment's whipping-boy. Although he had never had a mistress, apart from her, now in middle age, William was driven by her shrewish treatment into seeking consolation in the tender embraces of Lady Almeria Carpenter, sister of the Earl of Tyrconnel and Lady of the Bedchamber to his Duchess. Sir Nathaniel Wraxall rated her 'one of the most beautiful women of her time, but to whom Nature had been sparing of intellectual gifts'. He adds that thanks to her charms the Duke of Gloucester 'soon forgot all he had gone through for his amiable wife'. The Earl's own spouse was the mistress of the young Duke of York, Prinny's brother and the Gloucesters' nephew. Wraxall comments that Tyrconnel might be said to have contributed at this time 'more than any nobleman about the Court to the recreation of the reigning family'.

Lest the King should learn first of this liaison and ostracize him for it, William confided how miserable his married life had become owing to Maria's 'very unfortunate turn of mind and temper'. On June 22, 1787, he wrote from Coppet, near Geneva: 'I have told her that if she lets the children from this time alone, and behaves more respectfully to me before the world, she may still remain in my house, though so long since as when my daughter was but a year old she threatened me with leaving me. I hope Your Majesty will forgive my troubling you with all this detail, but my heart is very full. I am indeed severely punished for my juvenile indiscretion by the very ungrateful return I receive at home.'[19]

Later that year when their son went to Cambridge the Gloucesters separated. This was followed by much acrimonious argument over the appointment of a governess for their daughter, Princess Sophia. The King, sorry for the girl, offered to make the choice himself and selected a Miss Dee of Taplow, and also increased the Duke's annual allowance by £4,000 so as to help him to meet the additional expenses caused by these changes.

The records still extant give no indication as to whether the Duke of Gloucester's relations with his wife improved or not with the passage of time, but when he died on August 25, 1803, he left her sole Executrix of his will and with very few debts to pay. Queen Charlotte wrote from Weymouth on the 29th of that month to her friend, Lady Harcourt: 'His sufferings must have been dreadfully Painful; but his good temper and cheerfulness never have left him. I understand that he was not quite open with his Physicians, and that some Complaint He kept a Secret for three days, to which the Medicines which they administered at that time were almost fatal. How unfortunate to deceive oneself, & much more when one wishes to deceive others. This the King is not to know, but the Physicians stand justifyed to the world. ... The dear King was so well prepared for the stroke, & every thing managed with so much delicacy, that I have the satisfaction to say that his health has not suffered ...'[20]

The King was in fact extremely upset at the death of his favourite brother and not only treated Prince William and Princess Sophia as his own children from then onwards, but also became kindlier disposed towards the widow and when she died and was buried next to her husband in St George's Chapel, Windsor, then at last he allowed her the style of 'Her Royal Highness'. This was an honour which her sister-in-law, the Duchess of Cumberland never achieved, chiefly because of the King's conviction that she encouraged the Prince of Wales in dissipation, whereas in reality she restrained him.

An instance of the Duchess's holding her nephew in check is given by Lady Louisa Stuart in her *Letters*. Writing from London on April 6, 1787, she describes her visit to Lady Hopetown's in Albermarle Street where assembled 'the whole town'. There was a sad *contretemps*, she says. 'The Prince had named the day himself, his friends had promised that he should dance with Lady Anne Hope in proper form and behave himself mighty well. But lo! at twelve o'clock in *reeled* his R.H., pale as ashes, with glazed eyes set in his head, and, in short, almost stupefied. The Duchess of Cumberland made him sit down by her and kept him tolerably peaceable till they went down to supper; but then he talked himself into spirits, set all in motion again with the addition of a bottle and a half of champagne, and when we went to supper (for all could not sup at a time) he was most gloriously drunk and riotous indeed. He posted himself in the doorway, to the terror of everybody that went by, flung his arms round the Duchess of Ancaster's neck and kissed her with a great *smack*, threatened to pull Lord Galloway's wig off and knock out his front teeth, and played all the pranks of a drunken man upon the stage, till some of his companions called for his carriage, and almost forced him away. He was so far gone that I daresay he does not remember anything that passed, this morning.'[21]

That June the *Lewes Advertiser* reported that the people of Brighton were in high spirits 'from the flattering prospects of the ensuing season and outvied each other in decorating their houses outside and in'. Of all watering places in the country it had 'without doubt, by far the pre-eminence'. The Prince of Wales arrived as usual in July to visit his new seaside home, and soon after came the Cumberlands, followed by people of fashion from London and abroad.

The balls and assemblies, the theatres and concerts were crowded with company. Never before had the Steine been more thronged on the morning of the Races to see 'the start' to the hill. Led by the

Prince, driving Mrs Fitzherbert in the barouche known as his German waggon and drawn by six bays, filed an impressive cavalcade—next, his Uncle Henry and his Aunt Anne, together with their beautiful French guest, the Princesse de Lamballe, destined to die a terrible death four years later in the Revolution—then the Duke and Duchess of Richmond, the Duke of Bedford and the Marquis of Queensberry, and a host of other peers, including Cumberland's old enemy, Lord Grosvenor, and his gambling crony, Charles James Fox.

Apart from all this, the visitors who felt in need of it followed Prinny's example and sea-bathed for their health's sake. The Duke often accompanied his nephew. He was, however, a poor swimmer. His famous dog, Turk, which closely resembled Lord North facially, always swam further than he. A diarist of the period wrote that this Newfoundland was 'as big as a middling-sized calf, though he is not above eighteen months old ... He hath a familiar way, too of shutting his eyes and appearing to be fast asleep, when he is all the time perfectly awake'.[22]

The Duke that summer became extremely popular with the local fishermen, when a press gang recruiting for the King's Navy seized two young Brighton fishermen. The *Lewes Journal* reported that there might have been bloodshed had it not been for his mediation.

'He went into the midst of the multitude and, by promising to interpose in behalf of the men, induced the mob to desist from further violence; and on the Regulating Captain assuring them that not one should be impressed without a fresh order, and, even in that case they should have twenty-four hours' notice, they repaired cheerfully to their boats. The next evening upwards of forty sail appeared ready for sea, thus furnishing employment to a great number of men who had been shut up in idleness upwards of eleven weeks through fear of being impressed.'

Cumberland, it seems, but for the unforgiving attitude of the King might have become a respected member of the Establishment. He had shown his willingness to conform by becoming Grand Master of the Freemasons, and, presiding in that capacity, he saw his nephew, the Prince of Wales, initiated into the mysteries of masonry at the *Star and Garter*, Pall Mall, on February 6, 1788. *The Times* recorded that the Dukes of Norfolk and Manchester and 'several other noblemen of that respectable order attended at the ceremony'.

It was at this time that the King became seriously ill with what is now believed to have been porphyria. There is a certain irony in the situation that just as his black sheep brother had now settled down, George in his disturbed mental state broke loose from the restraints of respectability. A pamphleteer, Philip Withers, wrote in *History of the Royal Malady, by a Page of the presence* in 1789: 'The Royal mind is *inverted.* The ideas of younger life are now floating on the surface of the imagination; and those principles of dignity and decorum, from the practice of which he has been deemed a paragon of virtue and domestic excellence, are now buried.' The King revealed, for example, his secret passion for a Lady of the Bedchamber, the Countess of Pembroke, kept asking to be taken to visit her and in readiness hid in his pockets some stockings, nightcaps and a pair of drawers.

Taking advantage of the crisis, the Duke of Cumberland was among those who advocated that the Prince of Wales should be appointed Regent. During the winter of that year, when it looked as though this might occur, the Prince began to plan what to do with the patronage he would be able to dispense. He promised his favourite uncle some appropriate advancement to improve his financial position.

But the King unexpectedly recovered, and then all the royal family, including Cumberland but not his Duchess, and both Houses of Parliament went to St Paul's on St George's Day, 1789, to render thanks. An outraged peer, writing to the Duke of Buckingham on April 27, 1789, about 'the pilgrimage to St Paul's' complains: 'The Princes of Wales, York, Cumberland, and, I am sorry to say, Gloucester, talked to each other the whole time of the service, and behaved in such an indecent manner that was quite shocking.' Apparently during the Archbishop's sermon, they all chewed biscuits.[23]

Throughout this period, the Cumberlands were unwavering in their support of Mrs Fitzherbert, whose intimate friends they had now become. The Duchess wanted her to behave as she considered befitted her position as wife to the Prince of Wales. She addressed her in letters as 'my dearest niece'. It was she who persuaded Maria to take a box to herself at the opera, which drew the comment from Lady Jerningham: 'It was a thing which no lady but the Duchess of Cumberland ever did—a hundred guineas a year!'[24]

CHAPTER EIGHTEEN

The Importunate Widow

The Duke of Cumberland was only forty-five but his health was now steadily deteriorating, and though he must have been in great pain and knew that the nature of his illness would lead to an early death, he remained cheerful, never complained and, when he felt better, made much of it. Anne did all she could to maintain his spirits and never were they closer than at this time. Apart from his firm friendship with the Prince of Wales, there was also much affection between him and the Duke of Clarence, later to become King William IV.

In May, 1790, this nephew was appointed to command the 74-gun line of battle ship the *Valiant* in the Fleet assembled in consequence of the Nootka Sound dispute with Spain. Cumberland himself had become Admiral of the White, the senior flag rank in April, 1782. In a letter to the Prince of Wales from Torbay on July 25, William says: 'We are still in suspense about peace or war. Tomorrow, perhaps in the night, the Duke of Cumberland will arrive; we shall then have fine fun.'

On July 28 the uncle wrote to the Prince of Wales from aboard the *Valiant* that William had sent a cutter to Weymouth with an invitation to come down to the Fleet, which he had accepted. He had looked over the *Valiant*. 'I must say a finer ship nor ship's company I never saw so perfectly in the most minutest part exact; it does your brother giant credit ...'[1]

From Weymouth, on August 5, the Duke acknowledged a letter from Prinny: 'I am much obliged to you for all your kind anxieties concerning me, but I assure you I live a very regular life here. I rise by seven every morning, two mornings bathe, miss the third: after breakfast write by the post: musick & then at twelve ride. I am always a bed between 10 & 11; therefore nothing can be more regular, & I mean to continue so all the while I stay here.' He adds that Doctor Blane wished him to be as much at sea as possible and whenever 'any vessel of the King's comes this way I shall embrace the opportunity'.

The Duchess sent 'her kind love' to Prinny. She was in very good spirits though there were few people there. Already Cumberland claimed to find benefit from bathing. 'The throat is infinitely better & I can eat a very hearty breakfast now, my rice at dinner & fish, wich we have very good here, soals in particular.' He sent his compliments to 'Mrs Fitz'.

In another letter, dated August 8, the Duke mentions his belief that the King will review the Fleet. 'If so I should wish both you & the Duke of York would make me of the party professionally. I shall make it a point of duty to attend. We shall have good sport with the Duke of Clarence & it will make fun for two or three days either at Portsmouth or Plymouth.' In a postscript he recommends the Prince to have his hounds taken for a swim at Lymington. 'It will make their coats so fine & equal, if not better, than any physicking. I long for the hunting season.'[2]

The tone of his letters give one no inkling that the Duke was failing fast. A rodent ulcer had entirely destroyed his palate. By the end of August, this prevented him swallowing anything but liquids. On September 14, to please Doctor Blane, he got down the yolks of two eggs, but with such extreme pain that he could not be prevailed upon to try it a second time.

According to the account in the *Gentleman's Magazine*, Cumberland came up to London from the Windsor Park Lodge on the afternoon of September 17, and, so far was he from having any idea of approaching death that his Band were ordered up to town for a concert in the Mall on the same night. He had also arranged to meet his hounds to hunt at Windsor Lodge the next morning. But, on his alighting from his carriage in Pall Mall, he found himself so excessively weak that he exclaimed: 'I feel now that I am going.' He was to die peacefully during the course of that night watched over by the Duchess.

The King, when he heard of his brother's death, wrote from Windsor in precise, matter of fact terms on the 18th to the Marquess of Salisbury: 'Having just received the melancholy news of the death of the Duke of Cumberland, I think it right to acquaint you that this event must suspend all Court days. You must give directions for the funeral; in your office will be found the necessary precedent. I should suppose it may be on Saturday; the mourning to be ordered to Sunday the 26th. The Playhouses will, of course, not be opened till the 27th.[3]

The Duke of Gloucester, who was in London, went at once to Cumberland House, where he found the Prince of Wales already there consoling the widow. Later that day Gloucester wrote to the King describing his visit. The Prince, he confided, had tried to persuade him to join in making a combined request to the monarch that proper provision should be made for the Duchess. He said that he evaded answering as well as he could 'but upon his pressing me hard I did venture to say that I thought any application from him or anyone would be highly improper, yet I rather fancy the Duke of York is to be sent to Windsor tomorrow. *She*, to my astonishment, went alone to the Great Lodge at 7 o'clock this evening, with orders not to be followed by anybody. I found there was a will which the Prince wished to be opened; Lady Elizabeth had it. It was dated in '77, merely appointing *her* whole Executrix. I recommended the paper being put into M. General Garth's hands, who was also present.'[4] The Duke in this will of September 26, 1777, left everything to his widow.

Three surgeons, Gilbert Blane, Pennell and Charles Hawkins conducted a post mortem on the body, and made their report.

'Upon inspecting the thorax the left lobe of the lungs was found in a sound state except that the back part of it adhered slightly to the pleura, or membrane which lines the chest.

'The right lobe was universally diseased with a large quantity of thin putrid matter diffused through its whole substance and it adhered very strongly to the surrounding membrane of the thorax.

'The heart and its vessels were in a perfectly sound state. All the parts contained in the abdomen or cavity of the belly were in their natural state, except the stomach, part of the inner surface of which was in an inflamed state.

'There was a considerable ulcer in the back part of the roof of the mouth, and the uvula was entirely destroyed, but there was no ulceration in the throat beyond what was visible during his Royal Highness's life.

'The brain and its membranes were found in a sound state.'[5]

On Tuesday, September 28, the Duke's remains lay in state in the Prince's Chamber, adjoining the House of Lords, and at ten o'clock in the evening were conveyed by torchlight through the Old Palace-yard to the South-East door of Westminster Abbey for interment in the royal vault of Henry VII's Chapel.

All the pomp and ceremonial for which the Duchess had longed when her husband lived came now. The drums and trumpets sounding a solemn march, the banners proud with naval trophies. The impressive procession filing in macabre majesty—the Sergeant

Trumpeter, the Knight Marshal's men: the gentlemen who had served him; the Pages of the Presence, the Pages of the Back Stairs, the Pages of Honour, Physicians, Chaplains, Equerries, Secretaries, Pursuivants of Arms, Heralds of Arms, the Comptroller and Treasurer of his Household, Norroy King of Arms, the Lord Chamberlain of his Majesty's Household. Next Clarenceux King of Arms, attended by two Gentlemen Ushers, bore the deceased's coronet upon a black velvet cushion. Then the body, in its coffin covered with a pall, adorned with eight escutcheons of the Duke's arms, under a canopy of black velvet, carried by eight Admirals in uniform, with crapes on their hats and on their arms, and supported by two Barons on either side.

Behind plodded Garter King of Arms and two Gentlemen Ushers, the Chief Mourner (a Duke in a long black cloak, his train borne by a baronet, with two Dukes as supporters), next ten Earls, assistants to the Chief Mourner, another Gentleman Usher, Grooms of his Bedchamber and Yeoman of the Guard.

And at the end minute guns were fired as usual.

From aboard the *Valiant* at Plymouth on September 20, 1790, William Duke of Clarence wrote to the Prince of Wales: 'This morning Frederick [the Duke of York] wrote me the melancholy account of the death of our worthy uncle. From the intimacy and friendship that has so long subsisted between you two I can easily figure to myself your grief. His goodness at all times to me I cannot forget. Poor fellow, he certainly had the best heart in the world. I am glad to hear by Frederick the King was so much hurt. But, my dear brother, the Duchess is to be pitied. Her conduct by all accounts was exemplary: indeed, her goodness has been manifested on all occasions. Do, my dear brother, in your peculiar way, say everything for me to this poor woman. I have wrote to her but it was an unpleasant task. See the letter and tell me if it was a proper one, and how she received it. I really esteem the Duchess and feel for her excessively.'[6]

One's first reaction after reading this letter is that the future William IV was following the conventions of being polite about the dead and the bereaved, but if one considers the earlier correspondence between them there can be no doubt that the two men were fond of each other.

The *Gentleman's Magazine* for October published a fair and revealing assessment of the Duke's character. His knowledge of foreign languages had been acquired in conversation 'rather than from any regular endeavour at an attainment of them'. His skill also in musical performance 'and judgement in musical composition, as well as taste in selection must be admitted as evidence of a capacity that, if in early life, it had been directed ... to higher objects might have been proportionately successful.'

To those who were not intimate with him, his conversation seemed to be 'bold, unjointed chat'; but those who enjoyed his confidence had often heard remarks that indicated shrewd observation and knowledge of the world. 'This declaration is so little consonant with the general ideas of the public respecting his character, that it may be treated with ridicule ... let it be considered, however, that the opinions of mankind were adverse to his intellectual repute, and that, whenever he spoke, his auditors were rather prepared to expect something frivolous, than to examine whether what he uttered was really so. The truth is, that he possessed a strong flow of spirits, which betrayed him into conversation before he had sufficiently reflected upon what he was inclined to say.'

Another reason for Cumberland's being misrepresented was due to his indistinct manner of speaking, caused by the condition of his right lung and the ulcer that was eating away his palate. As a result, he was not always understood, and those listening to him, rather than ask him to repeat what he had said, pretended to comprehend his meaning 'sometimes conceiving that what he said would not have deserved attention had it been intelligibly conveyed', but usually assuming that his articulate remarks were 'certain evidences of folly'.

The passing of the brother whose amorous entanglements had caused him so much concern did not soften the King's attitude towards the widow. On Saturday, October 2, Lady Elizabeth Luttrell wrote to the Prince that William Pitt, the Prime Minister, had sent for Major-General George Garth, the late Duke's Treasurer, that Thursday to learn in what situation Cumberland had left the Duchess. Garth had told Pitt that after paying debts, nothing remained for her. 'Today he informed Garth ye King wd. give the Duchess four thousand a year. I shall go to town tomorrow in hopes to have the honour of seeing your Royal Highness.'[7]

The Prince replied from Brighton at 1.30 p.m. the next day that he had received her letter just as he was going to bed and was quite shocked at the 'shabby proposal or offer' made to the 'poor Duchess'. He thought that Garth ought to have an interview with Pitt and represent that it was totally impossible for her to subsist on 'so small an income'. If Garth found 'the Great Billy' was very obdurate, then he, the Prince, would wish the Duchess to write to the King himself, and to say that 'unless he means her to understand by so shabby a pittance that she is to be banished the country, it is totally impossible for her, *as his brother's wife to exist*, so far from living, in the manner she ought to do upon so very incompetent an income'.

The Prince added that he would talk further to Lady Elizabeth about it when he saw her. He would be returning next day to London, when he would go instantly to her at Cumberland House, as he wished very much to see her in order to 'concert some plan' by which they might endeavour to get something more for the Duchess. But he was afraid 'we might as well attempt to whip blood out of a post'. However, he thought 'nothing ought to be wanting on our sides, whether we are successful or not'.[8]

Anne, however, decided that neither a second visit from Garth to Pitt nor a letter from herself to the King would have any effect. The only thing that might would be representations from the Prince himself. So, on October 6, from Windsor Great Lodge, she wrote to him, pointing out first that as the Duke's allowance of £20,000 a year had ceased on his death, the Crown would be saving £16,000. Reports had been circulated of 'some insurance manoeuvre or advantage derived from the Duke's Will. Your Royal Highness knows my sentiments too well to believe I would have consented to the Duke relinquishing any expense his birth or amusements required to make a provision for my present situation, & it will be always a consolation to my mind that he lived free from care, & had no idea of the misfortunes that await me'.

In view of the friendship between the Prince and the Duke and 'the particular kindness' with which he had been 'graciously pleased' to honour her for more than ten years, Anne requested him to send for Mr Pitt and 'state to him the impossibility that I should support, with any degree of propriety, the rank in which the partiality of the King's late brother placed me, unless enabled so to do by his Majesty's munificence'.[9]

The Prince did as the Duchess requested and saw Pitt the next day, the 7th. Then, on the 8th at five p.m. from Downing Street, the Prime Minister wrote to the Prince to say that the King 'after a full consideration of the circumstances of the case' had determined that there were no grounds for altering his original intention.[10]

Prinny had been proved right in his pessimism. To get even the promised pension was like, as he had put it, attempting 'to whip blood out of a post'. Eighteen months passed without the widow receiving any payment. In the meantime, she subsisted from the proceeds from the sale of her late husband's most valuable effects. These throw a favourable light on some aspects of his character. 'No man is a hypocrite to his pleasures,' Dr Johnson has written, 'and no man spends money on things he does not like.' The Duke had always loved music, been the patron of many musicians, and himself excelled as a 'cellist (taking after his father); and with Anne's encouragment he had become a bibliophile. *The Times* states that on February 17, 1791, his immense library of 'almost all the composers in Europe for nearly 200 years past' was auctioned at Christie's, together with his celebrated collection of musical instruments. 'Handel's works, Haydn's, Baumgarten's and a few others sold very high. A beautiful ton'd organ by Green, with a piano-forte stop, went for £76.13s. His Royal Highness was in possession of a violin by Stainer, which had long been the admiration and envy of the amateurs. It is now in the hundred and twenty-first year of its age, and the fortunate purchaser is Mr Bradyll, at the price of 130 guineas! Mr Condell bought the favourite tenor for 50 guineas, and several other instruments sold at high prices. All the great performers in town were present.'

The Times also records that on the following Thursday, the 24th, the Duke's books went under the hammer at Christie's. 'Catesby's *Natural History of North Carolina*, finely coloured, fetched £15.15s., *Magna Britannica et Hibernia* £52.10s., *The Antiquities of Ancient Rome, including the Vatican* by Piraneli, Ross, Aquila, £524.10s. This superb work was presented to the Duke by Pope Ganganelli. Mr Gray purchased it for a Great Personage.'

In mid-July that year the widow and her sister, Elizabeth, travelled abroad to stay at Spa. Here they must have succeeded in rehabilitating their finances, probably through winnings at faro, and consequently decided to return to London. The Duke of York, Anne's nephew, had become engaged to the eldest daughter of the King of Prussia and went there to bring her to England. A revolutionary rabble stormed their coach at Lille and, learning they were not French aristos trying to escape, let them go after tearing from the vehicle all the insignia of royalty. The Duchess of Cumberland had arranged to meet the couple in Brussels and travel back home with them. Sensing an opportunity to gain a useful future ally, she did her best to make the journey a pleasant one for the ill and unhappy little Princess. Rough seas detained the party five days in Calais, then they sailed in the *Cumberland Packet*, and Anne insisted on their landing at Deal instead of Dover because she knew from experience that they would be better accommodated there and would find it easier to procure comfortable carriages to bring them and their suites to town.

On November 23, *The Times* informed its readers that the Duchess of Cumberland 'proposes to keep a great deal of company this winter, and it is said intends frequently to fill all the rooms in Cumberland House. Faro and his host will be very conspicuous'. Her first function was a grand 'Dress Ball' in honour of the Duchess of York held on Monday, December 19. *The Times* for that day commented: 'The Duchess of Cumberland's routs this winter will be conducted in the same elegant style they were previously to the decease of the late Duke. Her Royal Highness's conduct since that melancholy event has been exemplary in every respect and it is now right she should lay aside the trappings of woe, and enjoy the comfort of her exalted station.'

Tuesday's readers received a very full account of the ball. Upwards of 200 cards of invitation had been delivered. The apartments were decked out with 'all the taste and magnificence that fancy and liberality' could produce. 'The Faro Table of Lady Archer formed an agreeable lounge for those whose feet were not "so plagued with corns"—this indispensable article in fashionable furniture was brought to Pall Mall early in the morn ere Justice Hyde had waked from his first sleep.'

The Prince of Wales did not appear till past eleven p.m. and did not seem 'at all displeased with the attention shown to Mrs Fitzherbert'. He and the Duchess of York opened the ball at midnight. 'She was in very elegant undress of blue silk trimmed with silver and was very highly rouged ... The Ladies who did not dance were fully dressed—those who did wore fancy dresses.'

The widow's nephews by marriage, the Dukes of York and Clarence, and her brother-in-law, the Duke of Gloucester, attended, together with the latter's son and daughter, Prince William and Princess Sophia, and his inamorata, Lady Almeria Carpenter. Among others present were the Dukes of Richmond, Bedford, and St Albans, the Duchesses of Richmond and Rutland, Lord and Lady Melbourne, the Countess of Jersey, and the entire *Corps Diplomatique*.

The Times enthuses: 'This splendid Fête seemed to bid defiance to politics - it was in short, open to all parties and influenced by none ... The Servants wore full dress liveries extremely magnificent and reminded us of the splendour which used to be seen here during the life of the late Duke.'

The Duchess's Ball was a brilliant success, and it was followed a month later on January 16, 1792, by another, tactfully held on the night after that in celebration of the Queen's Birthday, to which as in the past she was not invited. She had hoped that the King might at last have softened his attitude, but he showed no signs of doing so. Instead, her taking it upon herself to launch his niece by marriage annoyed him. He had refused to allow Anne to retain the tenancy of Windsor Great Lodge, and when Major-General Garth sent Pitt an inventory of the furniture and other effects left there, valuing them at £8,450, and asking for this sum to be paid her, the King wrote to his minister querying the valuation.

First George pointed out that most of the contents were already his property. When his uncle, 'Culloden' Cumberland, had died, he had bought the furniture from the estate and had only lent it to Henry. He had no intention of paying for it twice. If it were claimed that certain things belonged to the deceased, then definite proof must be provided before he would be prepared to purchase them for the use of the next tenant at a fair independent valuation.

As a result of the King's directive, his widowed sister-in-law received very little from the sale of the Duke's effects in the Lodge. The 'fashionable card parties' she resumed did not yield sufficient profit to meet the expenses of running Cumberland House, although her confident, opulent air gave a totally different impression to the world at large. Charles Pigott in his pillorying of London Society, *The Jockey Club*, published that year, wrote of the Duchess: 'Her palace is the receptacle of all the elegance and fashion in town. Her Faro Table is the best attended; consequently the profits arising from it the most considerable. She with her dexterous and amiable sister, Lady Elizabeth Luttrell, conduct it with all imaginable decorum, never losing sight, however, of the main chance, and a noble harvest they made of the fat pigeons that frequent it.'

There was growing unrest in the country and the French Revolution had given a fillip to radicalism. Outward ostentation was savagely attacked by the cartoonists and ballad-writers in prints and broadsheets. Dr John Wolcot, famous for his satire penned as 'Peter Pindar', unaware that the promised royal pension remained unpaid to the Duchess, wrote in his *Resignation, an Ode to the Journeyman Shoemakers who Refused to Work Except their Wages were Raised*:

Behold a hundred coaches at her door,
Where faro triumphs in his mad career.
We *must* support her – or by hook or crook –
For, lo, her husband was – a royal duke.
We must support, too, her fine gold-laced crew
Behind her gilt coach, dancing molly fellows,
With canes and ruffles goodly to the view,
And (suiting their complexions) pink umbrellas.

But, in reality, the widow's financial position was precarious, and she was secretly trying to sell Cumberland House at the worst of times when the wealthy feared to invest their money in property lest revolution should erupt in Britain. At last, in desperation, on May 2, 1792, she sent her brother-in-law a begging letter: 'Your Majesty beholds at your feet the most unfortunate of your Majesty's subjects who, conscious of having incur'd your Majesty's displeasure, would remain for ever in respectful silence, but that the dread of becoming an object of the charity of individuals can only be averted by your Majesty's gracious interposition.

'I am sir, Sir, the widow of your Majesty's late brother, the Duke of Cumberland. I forfeited a very considerable estate by that marriage & was disinherited by my father, Lord Carhampton, from a mistaken idea that so elevated a situation must insure me a provision.

'From the hour of the Duke's death your Majesty's Minister withheld every part of his income & I became a melancholy instance of the vicissitude of human events after having been the wife of your Majesty's brother nineteen years, deprived of even the necessarys of life.

'Mr Pitt informed me, thro' General Garth, that your Majesty had commanded him to say your Majesty would make a provision for the Duchess of Cumberland, and I humbly beseech you, Sir, that this, your Majesty's most gracious promise may be fulfill'd before the close of the present session of Parliament.

'I have, Sir, with the assistance of my friends, been enabled to gratify the only ambition which has survived the Duke, that of paying all his debts.

'Cumberland House has been offer'd every person likely to buy it, hitherto without success, & unless I can very soon find a purchaser will be seized by the Banker, who, previous to his Royal Highness's marriage, lent fifteen thousand pounds upon it. He will not accept as security for the payment of the interest the warrant for one thousand pounds a quarter sign'd by the Lords of the Treasury: it is upon a tenure so precarious that I am consider'd as having no income. I intreat, Sir, your Majesty to believe that nothing but the extreme horror of the situation I have ventured to submit to your Majesty's Royal breast could inspire me with courage to address my Sovereign.

'I have, Sir, reconciled myself to the melancholy necessity of quitting your Majesty's dominions for ever and shall depart with the consolation of having render'd the Duke of Cumberland's life happy, his death easy, & his memory respected, and in the hope that the unoffending & unfortunate may find friends in every part of the Christian world.

'Presuming, Sir, upon your Majesty's great goodness of heart and affectionate regard to the memory of your Majesty's late Royal brother, I humbly trust that your Majesty will be graciously pleased to relieve my mind from the dreadful apprehension of becoming eventually an object of the charity of individuals by commending that the pension your Majesty's bounty may assign to my support be made permanent.[11]

In August of the previous year the Prince of Wales had tried to help by manoeuvring the Duke of York into purchasing Cumberland House. He was in Berlin and had asked his elder brother to find a suitable London residence for him. But the Duke wrote back at once to say that he was not interested as in its present state Cumberland House was 'but little, if at all, bigger than my own house, and besides, by no means so well laid out, for in my house there are six rooms together to see company in, but in Cumberland House there are only three; besides Cumberland House wants new furnishings and thoroughly repairing before it would be possible to inhabit it, and likewise has no stabling or coach houses belonging to it'.[12]

The Duchess's letter to the King at least had the required effect, the pension was paid and it was made permanent. But she could not afford to go on living at Cumberland House and left it empty from 1793 to 1800, when, tiring of paying interest on the £15,000 the Duke had raised on it, she conveyed her lease to the mortgagees, Messrs. Birch, Chambers and Hobbs, bankers, who sold it the following year to the Union Club. This did not prosper and the property was acquired by the Board of Ordnance. In the reign of King Edward VII it was demolished, and the Royal Automobile Club now stands on the site.

The Duchess, after leaving Cumberland House for good in January, 1793, went to live in Bath where she took a house in the North Parade. *The Times* for February 23 reported that there was talk of her remaining there for most of the time in future as she was treated 'with Royal attention'. At the Balls constantly frequented by her, 'the Minute Dancers, etc., bow and curtsey to her, as done at Court only to the Queen'.

Such deference must have delighted the widow, but she was not to enjoy it for long. That summer, *The Times* of June 1 contained the news that she had suffered a paralytic stroke whilst at Margate. She recovered, however, and went to recuperate at Tunbridge Wells.

There bad news reached her in the autumn. War had been declared by the National Convention in France on England that February and in June the Reign of Terror had begun. Temple Luttrell, Anne's brother, had daringly taken part in the ferrying across the Channel of aristos fleeing from certain death in Paris. On September 18, he was caught in Boulogne and taken to the capital where his captors exhibited him to the mob incorrectly as the brother of the King of England. Narrowly escaping the guillotine, he was confined in the Abbaye and Luxembourg prisons from October 24, 1793, to February 14, 1795. He died in Paris on January 14, 1803.

In the autumn of 1794, the Prince of Wales, feeling sorry for his aunt, offered her the use of the Royal Pavilion in Brighton for the winter. There, either she was indiscreet or some mischief-maker pretended she had made some derogatory remarks about his having broken with Mrs Fitzherbert (her close friend) to marry Princess Caroline, his cousin, in a desperate attempt to get Parliament to pay his debts over half a million pounds. This was reported to Carlton House in exaggerated form and he was offended.

When the Duchess heard about it, she immediately wrote to the Prince on December 20 from Brighton: 'I thought your Royal Highness had known me better, after an intimacy of fourteen years, than to believe it possible I should hold such a discourse as is imputed to me & which could only proceed from folly & malignity, the most atrocious & the most opposite to the whole tenure of my life as well as to those sentiments towards your Royal Highness, for the sincerity of which I appeal, Sir, to your penetration. I have nothing to ask of your Royal Highness but the continuance of that good opinion my conduct has never ceased to deserve. I am, Sir, neither the rival nor the enemy of any of the candidates for your Royal Highness's favor, but if it is their pleasure that your Royal Highness should no longer honour me with the same friendship you have hitherto profess'd, I shall quit England with less regret & with a fixed determination never to return.'[13]

The Prince replied on January 20, 1795, apologizing for not having answered her letter earlier due to pressures on his time. He assured her that nothing could be more painful to him than the reports which he had heard from all quarters in a manner which he could not feel conscious of ever having merited from her. But her letter had given him great satisfaction as he really always felt it very unlikely that a person like her, who for so many years had experienced his unremitted friendship, should suddenly and without any cause allow her opinion of him to be totally changed. 'I am truly happy on learning from General Garth that Brighton has been the means of affording you some amusement, & that you enjoy your health.'[14]

On April 8 the Prince was married to Caroline in the Chapel Royal, St James's, looking 'like death and full of confusion as if he wishes to hide himself' to quote Lord Malmesbury. The Duchess was hurt that she was not invited to be a guest at the wedding festivities, so on the 22nd she wrote to him that he must know from experience that no one had on all occasions shown more anxiety for his happiness than herself. 'I did hope to be one of the first to congratulate your Royal Highness on your marriage & to have an Audience of the Princess of Wales.' She regretted that so much time had elapsed since she had seen him. She was certain of the friendship that he had constantly professed for her and hoped he would not be displeased if she intruded upon his time to remind him of her 'respectful attachment'.[15]

The correspondence then appears to have ceased, and on September 29 *The Times* reported that the Duchess had sailed for Cuxhaven with the intention of spending the winter in Italy. She and her nephew remained friends, however, for the same paper states four years later that the Prince of Wales had again lent 'the Pavilion at Brighton for the winter to the Duchess of Cumberland who had arrived at Yarmouth from Cuxhaven on September 9'.[16]

The twilight of the Duchess's life was spent mostly abroad, the solitary and sad frequenter of Spa and similar resorts. When in London, she stayed at Little Campden House in Kensington. The last reference to her in the Royal Archives appears in a letter from the Duke of Clarence writing to the Prince of Wales from Bushby House in late May, 1808. He begins: 'In case you should not have heard from the Duchess of Cumberland I enclose a letter I received from her this morning. I will thank you to return it.'[17]

Seven months later, she died at Gorizia near Trieste on December 28.

By her will dated February 15, 1808, Anne left her nephew, the Prince of Wales, a miniature with her cypher, and two whole length portraits of the Duke of Cumberland and herself painted by Gainsborough. To 'my friend, Mrs Fitzherbert, a ring with the hair of the late Duke, set in diamonds' and to another friend, Mrs Selina Freemantle, 'a picture of the late Duke, set in diamonds, and the chain I wear with it and likewise my diamond necklace and my best diamond ring'.

The two portraits now hang at either end of the State Dining Room in Buckingham Palace. On the wall between them facing the windows extend in a row paintings of Frederick, Prince of Wales, George III, George IV, Queen Charlotte, and Augusta, Princess of Wales. The most striking of the six is that of the Duchess of Cumberland. It is an irony of fate that the former Mrs Horton, who, when alive was treated like an outcast by George III, should in death have her likeness within a few feet of him. She looks a truly regal figure in her robes of state. Over her imposing ruby velvet gown with its golden gauze underdress she wears a mantle of red velvet, lined with ermine. On a table beside her glistens a coronet. As H. Clifford Smith wrote in his *Buckingham Palace*: 'No reproduction can do justice to the artistic quality of this magnificent example of Gainsborough's art which depends for so much of its beauty on the subtleties of its rich and harmonious setting.'

Lady Elizabeth Luttrell had an unhappier end. The year before the Duke's death a contributor to *The Times* had called her 'the life of every gay circle where she mixes. She has great vivacity, wit and good humour, with a fortune that would richly gild the pill of matrimony. What her Ladyship's objections are to that state we cannot conceive, as there are many who confessedly wear her chains'.[18]

The reason for this Luttrell's remaining single was probably that she had only one passion in life—gambling. She played high and cheated much, and gave herself such airs that she was commonly called the Princess Elizabeth. When her sister left Cumberland House, she had to move from the west wing. They then parted company. Her luck started to desert her. She and a Mrs Sturt were convicted at Marlborough Street Office in March, 1797, on a charge of illegal gambling in the St James's house of Lady Buckingham (reported as sleeping with a blunderbuss and a pair of pistols at her side to protect her faro bank). The defendents, four in all, gave faro parties in each other's houses in rotation, and they were fined £50 each. Then, in November, Elizabeth was sued in the King's Bench for a debt of £7,000. There she found a hairdresser who owed £70, which she agreed to pay if he would marry her. Once he had done this, claiming immunity from imprisonment as her husband was now responsible for her debts, she immediately went overseas.[19]

According to Sir Robert Heron in his *Notes*, abroad 'she descended lower and lower until, being convicted of picking pockets at Augsburg, she was condemned to clean the streets, chained to a wheelbarrow. In that miserable situation she terminated her existence by poison.'[20]

CHAPTER NINETEEN

Olive, Princess of Cumberland

On April 3, 1772, there was born a girl who was to claim that she was the daughter of Henry Frederick, Duke of Cumberland, and Olive Wilmot whose father, the Reverend James Wilmot, D.D., Fellow of Trinity College, Oxford, had married them in private at eleven o'clock on the evening of March 4, 1767, in the Grosvenor Square house of Lord Archer, whose wife kept a notorious gambling establishment there where the gilded youth of the day were stripped of their gold.

The couple are further supposed to have lived together through all the bridegroom's many affairs until in October, 1771, when Olive was pregnant, the Duke deserted her and bigamously married Anne Horton. The abandoned wife then gave birth to a daughter, christened Olive after her mother. It was to be alleged that King George III, in order to shield his younger brother, persuaded the infant's great-uncle, Robert Wilmot, to have her rebaptized as his own daughter in substitution for the still-born baby to which his wife had given birth at the same time. The child's true mother then went to live in France, where she was said to have died of a broken heart on December 5, 1774.

Young Olive eventually married Thomas Serres, a gifted painter, under whom she had been studying. Thanks to his training, she so developed her talent that, after exhibiting in the Royal Academy, she was appointed landscape painter in 1805 to the future King George IV. But her marriage failed, and in 1804 she was legally separated and went to live with a Scotsman, a gravedigger's son, William Strange Petrie, who had given up his job as a clerk in Edinburgh to try and earn a living as a tracer of pedigrees. Leaving Scotland as a result of his having stolen a trunk of documents from Holyrood Palace, he came to London where he pretended to be the natural son of the Duke of Clarence (later William IV) and called himself Fitzclarence.[1] He then met Olive Serres and she went to live with him.

Abetted by her genealogist lover, Mrs Serres now began making startling claims. In her book, *The Princess of Cumberland's statement to the English Nation*, published in 1822, by which time both Dr James Wilmot and his brother, Robert, were dead, she asserted that George Greville, 2nd Earl of Warwick, once in love with her mother but supplanted in her affections by the Duke of Cumberland, had been present at the secret wedding together with the Earl of Chatham. Dr Wilmot had entrusted both men with the custody of documents proving the marriage; those with Chatham had passed on his death into the care of the Earl of Warwick. Then, in 1815, falling seriously ill and believing his days numbered, Warwick confided the facts to his friend, the Duke of Kent, George III's fourth son, thus revealing that Olive was the Duke's cousin and daughter of his uncle, the Duke of Cumberland.

The very next day, according to Mrs Serres, the two men called at her house in Seymour Place. The Duke of Kent said that Lord Warwick had certain important revelations to make concerning her origin, but that she must first swear to keep what she was told secret 'until they could regulate rights for her advantage'. This she did, and he then proceeded with his disclosures. The Duke had then taken her in his arms, saying: 'You will do credit, my dear cousin, to the royal family. I will protect you, Olive, with my heart's best blood and see you get restored to your royal rights.'

That the Duke of Kent regarded Olive Serres as a cousin was supported later by the affidavit of his confidential servant, Anthony Hillman, who declared that she used to visit the Duke and that he had often seen them together, 'when His Royal Highness always behaved towards her with the greatest respect and regard. I was very frequently employed by His Royal Highness to carry packets and letters from him to Mrs Serres, when he frequently said, "Hillman, take this to my cousin, Serres" ... I have frequently attended His Royal Highness on his visiting Mrs Serres. When her present Majesty [Queen Victoria] was born, I received from the Duke's steward, by order of the Duke, a packet containing a phial of some of the christening wine, and some of the cake, to take to Mrs Serres, which I took and I saw her open the packet containing the wine and cake.'

Robert Owen, regarding whose veracity there can be little doubt, wrote in his autobiography: 'His Royal Highness the Duke of Kent, introduced Mrs Serres to me as his cousin, and as legally entitled to the rank of Princess Olive of Cumberland. He was deeply interested in her cause, and in that of her only daughter and child, Lavinia. I see that he requests me in one of his letters at that date, to advance on his account to Mrs Serres £500.'

Contemporaries describe Olive Serres as good-looking with charm and a strong personality. *Farington's Diary* for May 2, 1813, records that Sir Thomas Lawrence the painter spoke very highly of her 'as being a woman possessed of extraordinary talents'. She wrote poems, plays, historical romances, articles on astrology, theological essays, memoirs, songs, even the libretto of an opera. What throws her royal pretensions into question was her close association with William Strange Petrie who after claiming to be the Duke of Clarence's natural son changed his tune in 1820 on the death of the Duke of Kent and alleged that the latter was his real father—and impudently called himself 'Fitz-Strathearn', one of the titles of Mrs Serres's supposed grandfather, the Duke of Cumberland. In her *Memoirs*, published in 1825, Miss C. E. Cary accuses Petrie of having forged documents to suggest that Queen Charlotte had tried to poison George IV's wife, Caroline, and she goes on to say that he could imitate any handwriting.

Mrs Serres must have known the falseness of her lover's claim to be the Duke of Kent's son and yet she dared to describe him as such in a letter to Lord Sidmouth, the Home Secretary, in December, 1821: 'View, my Lord, the sorrows of myself (the niece of your late Sovereign, King George the Third, and only offspring of his royal brother Henry Frederick, Duke of Cumberland)—behold me, faint and in agony and anguish, extended upon a solitary bed, with but one friend (the late beloved Duke of Kent's son) to administer consolation, from whose hands my medicines are taken.'

Following the death of George III and his son, the Duke of Kent, within a short while of each other in 1820, Olive petitioned the House of Commons on July 14 that year, claiming that she was the daughter of the Duke of Cumberland, whose secret marriage to her mother occurred in 1767 and whose later marriage to Anne Horton did not in any way affect the validity of the first. She pleaded that she was entitled to the Duke's property, and had in her possession a document bearing George III's sign manual in which he accepted her as his deceased brother's daughter. She asked the House to investigate her claims, but her petition was ignored.

Within a few days of the two royal funerals Olive wrote to the new King George IV requesting an audience so that she could show him the papers on which she based her case. She received no reply, but the Duke of Clarence (later William IV) and his younger brother, the Duke of Sussex, hearing about the matter, called on her, independently of each other, examined the documents in question and the former expressed his satisfaction as to their authenticity.

Thomas Creevey records in his *Diary* for January 29, 1821, that the Duke of Sussex, who was George III's fifth son, 'entertained us with stories of his cousin, Olivia of Cumberland, with whom, for fun's sake, as he says, he had various interviews, during which she has always pressed upon him, in support of her claims, her remarkable likeness to the Royal Family. Upon one occasion, being rather off her guard from temper or liquor, she snatched off her wig all at once and said, 'Why, did you ever in your life see such a likeness to yourself?" '

Creevey, who was inclined to be sceptical and disparaging, gives us this pen portrait of Olive Serres when they both attended the Lord Mayor's banquet the previous year: 'My attention was directed to a much more splendid object—the Princess Olivia of Cumberland. No one can have any doubts of the royalty of *her* image. She is the very image of our Royal Family. Her person is upon the model of the Princess Elizabeth, only at least three times her size. She wore the most brilliant rose-coloured satin gown you ever saw, with fancy shawls (more than one) flung in different forms over her shoulders, after the manner of the late Lady Hamilton. Then she had diamonds in profusion hung from every part of her head, but her nose, and the whole was covered with feathers that would have done credit to any hearse ... As we approached the great and splendid hall, the procession halted for nearly ten minutes, which we, in the rear could not comprehend. It turned out that the Princess Olivia of Cumberland had made her claim, as Princess of the Blood, to sit at the right hand of my Lord Mayor. The worthy magistrates, however, with great spirit, resisted these pretensions and, after much altercation, she was compelled to sit at another table.'

But, later, Creevey states that: 'On retiring after the banquet her train was borne by the ladies of eight Aldermen; and in the drawing-room refreshments were handed to her by the Lady Mayoress in person. She also visited in state Drury Lane Theatre, where she was received by the manager in full evening dress.'[2]

Not having received a reply from King George IV to her request for an audience, Olive's next move following her appearance at the Lord Mayor's Banquet was to petition the King in December, submitting twelve affidavits supporting her, among which were those of the Duke of Kent's former Equerry, Sir Frederick Wetherall, and the Earl of Warwick's former Agent and Executor, John Dickenson. This documentary evidence was submitted to the Crown's legal advisers on December 31, 1820, and on January 23, 1821, Olive's lawyer, Mr Henry Bell, was informed by Mr Hobson, an Under Secretary, that a decision on the petition of his client would be reached next day.

With the unpublished correspondence of Lord Liverpool, the then Prime Minister, in the Department of Manuscripts of the British Library, is an undated memorandum of about this time, marked on its back: 'Mr Dickenson respecting Mrs Serres and stating he has seen a certificate of a private marriage of the late King as Prince of Wales, 1759,' and which reads: 'Among the papers entrusted to the care of the late Earl of Warwick by Dr Wilmot is a very important document, unconnected with the Birth of Mrs Serres, and from the strictest investigation by Mr Dickenson and other persons, there does not appear the slightest ground to suspect a Forgery on her part. And as the Lawyers who have been consulted say they could gain any Estate or any sum of money from the certificate relative to Mrs Serres' birth and as the Clergy say the Certificates are perfectly satisfactory Mr Dickenson from such opinions has been induced to give credit to another Document of infinitely more Consequence, and has used all his Endeavours to prevent its being made publick.

'The Document alluded to is a Certificate of a private and legal marriage of the Late King when Prince of Wales in the year 1759 at which Mr Pitt and others were present and it was subsequently witnessed by Mr Pitt when created a Peer. The King had a son and a daughter by this wife. The son is living but the daughter died 2 years ago.

'The validity of this Certificate is strongly corroborated by Letter and other Circumstances which give an Air of more than probability to it.

'Mr Dickenson was shown this and other papers immediately after the late King's death and since that time he has been extremely anxious that the present King would be graciously pleased to allow Mrs Serres's pretensions to the Honor she aspires to to be examined by the proper authorities for in case her documents should be proved to be not authentic then the publication of this Certificate would not excite that Sensation so much to be dreaded from the present temper of the nation. Mr Dickenson has paid every attention in his power to Mrs

Serres from a conviction of the truth of her documents and has exerted all the Influence he possesses over her to prevent her publication of this Act of the late King's and he flatters himself that he has had it in his power to serve the King, the Royal Family and the Nation.'

The Certificate in question was in the form of a written declaration by Dr Wilmot, dated April 17, 1759, which went: 'This is to certify that the marriage of these parties, George, Prince of Wales, to Hannah Lightfoot, was duly solemnized this day, according to the rites and ceremonies of the Church of England at their residence at Peckham, by myself.' Appended to this were the signatures of 'George Guelph', 'Hannah Lightfoot', and of 'Witness of the marriage of these parties', 'William Pitt' and 'Anne Taylor'.

On the other side of this document was another Certificate, also signed by Dr Wilmot, that stated: 'The marriage of the underwritten parties was duly solemnized according to the rights and ceremonies of the Church of England at Thomas, Lord Archer's House, London, March the 4th, 1767, by myself.' The signatures, 'Henry Frederick' and 'Olive Wilmot' were added to this, followed by 'Present at the marriage of these parties, Brooke [the Earl of Warwick], J. Addez' and 'Attested before J. Dunning, Chatham.' Addez was the Rev. James Addez, D.D. Chatham was William Pitt the Elder, who had apparently witnessed George's marriage on the other side of the paper to Hannah Lightfoot, and who in 1767 had become Earl of Chatham. The Duke of Cumberland was a friend of his, and, it will be recalled, went to his assistance and prevented him from falling to to the ground following his apoplectic seizure at the end of his famous speech in the House of Lords on April 7, 1778.

It would seem that 'the strictest investigation by Mr Dickenson and other persons' cannot have revealed that, as stated in the Prologue, Hannah had married Isaac Axford in 1753 and that, as he was still alive in 1759, her alleged marriage then to George III, as Prince of Wales, would have no legality.

Mrs Serres maintained that the reason for Dr Wilmot's having recorded his daughter's marriage on the reverse of the other certificate was so that she might have the means of compelling the Royal Family to honour the promise made in another document dated 'Kew Palace, May 2, 1773' and signed 'George R' and witnessed by Chatham that stated: 'whereas it is our royal command that the birth of Olive, the Duke of Cumberland's daughter, is not to be made known to the nation during our reign; but from a sense of religious duty, we will that she be acknowledged by the royal family after our death, should she survive ourselves, in return for confidential services rendered ourselves by Dr Wilmot in the year 1759.' These 'confidential services' must refer to his alleged marriage of George to Hannah Lightfoot, Olive Serres claimed.

There is no further mention of the matter in Lord Liverpool's papers, but some time in late January, 1821, according to Mrs Ryvves,[3] Olive's daughter, Henry Bell, the lawyer, called on her mother and said in the hearing of several named witnesses, including Sir Gerard Noel, M.P., and John Dickenson, Warwick's executor, that King George IV 'had been graciously pleased to acknowledge her Highness in the Privy Council that day as Princess of Cumberland'. He accordingly prepared a statement in his own handwriting endorsed 'For Newspapers as to the acknowledgement of H.H.P. Olive,' and which read: 'We have authority to state that the claims of her Highness Olive, Princess of Cumberland, having been proved to the satisfaction of his Majesty, and that his Majesty has in consequence given direction that the same may be made known through the usual official channels. Our present limits will not allow to say more than that we understand a suitable provision, with all the usual privileges are to be accorded her Highness without the least delay.'

This visit proved the last Olive was to receive from her lawyer. On March 19, 1821, the Home Secretary, Lord Sidmouth, invited Mr Bell to call upon him between one and two p.m. next day. A fortnight later Mr Bell refused to see his client or write to her again, and gave her to understand that he would no longer act for her. He shortly afterwards moved from his modest home in John Street, Adelphi, to an imposing residence owned by the Crown at 19 Whitehall Place. Then, years later, Mrs Ryves[4] claimed that Bell's widow on her death bed told her doctor, a Thomas Hooper, that she wished to see Mrs Ryves. When this was arranged, she then revealed 'the reason why Mr Bell stopped so suddenly was his having been handsomely remunerated for his services ... It was the Duke of York, said the dying lady, who had prevented the Princess being put into possession of the means to maintain her rank, as he was personally afraid of the Princess coming forward with other papers touching herself and family, and therefore determined to prevent any assistance or attention being shown by his brother, the King, or the Ministry.' The widow then handed Mrs Ryves correspondence between Lord Sidmouth, the Home Secretary, and her late husband which, she claimed, proved that he had been bribed. The Duke of York, following the death of Princess Charlotte, was the next in line to the throne and had a direct interest in the matter.

Whatever doubts one may have regarding the veracity of Olive Wilmot Serres's statements, her daughter, Mrs Ryves, appears to have been honest and truthful. Nevertheless, it is difficult to believe that George IV himself would ever have officially acknowledged Olive as Princess of Cumberland. In his *Memoirs of George IV* Robert Huish, who was intimately associated with him, wrote: 'Almost the last act of the Duke of Kent was the perusal of a letter from the Prince Regent, to whom the Duke had given some offence for the credit which he gave to the claims of a certain lady, the *soi-disant* Princess Olive of Cumberland, to be admitted as one of the legitimates into the royal family. The Prince Regent took alarm at this introduction of a new member of the royal family, and he castigated his royal brother very severely for giving even the semblance of his sanction to so spurious a claim. The death of the Duke following almost immediately put an end to the dispute and also to the introduction of Mrs Serres to the distinguished honour of being a member of the royal family.'[5]

Mr Bell's, her own lawyer's desertion in the spring of 1821 did not depress Mrs Serres. Irrepressible as ever, she called on the Vicar of St Mary's, Islington's Parish Church, and consequently on September 6, at her own request, he rechristened her—'Olive, only daughter of Henry Frederick, Duke of Cumberland.'

Following this, 'Princess Olive' drove about London in a carriage with the royal arms painted on it and accompanied by servants in appropriate livery. But, living beyond her means, she was arrested for debt. This she stubbornly withstood, claiming immunity on account of her birth. When such a plea failed, she submitted a document that appeared to be an early will of George III, which she maintained had been among Dr Wilmot's papers brought to her by the Duke of Kent. It read: 'George R. St James's. In the case of our Royal Demise we give and bequeath to Olive, our brother of Cumberland's daughter, the sum of Fifteen Thousand pounds commanding our heir and successor to pay the same privately to our said Niece for her own use as a recompense for the misfortunes she may have known through the father. June 2nd, 1775. Witnesses—J. Dunning, Chatham, Warwick.' John Dunning was then Solicitor-General and Chancellor of the Duchy of Lancaster. He defended the Duke of Cumberland in the Grosvenor lawsuit.

When this was treated with derision, Olive tried to obtain legal permission to inspect George's official will. The *Gentleman's Magazine* for June 19, 1822, reports: 'The cause of Olive, Princess of Cumberland, respecting his late Majesty's will of £15,000 in her favour, was heard in the Prerogative Court, which was crowded to excess. At ten o'clock Sir John Nicoll took his seat, and shortly after, Dr Dodson and Dr Lushington (her Counsel) accompanied by General Desseux, *soi-disant* Captain Fitz-Strathearn and others ... A few minutes before one o'clock Olive, Princess of Cumberland, entered the Court and took her seat ...' It will be noted that Petrie alias Fitz-Strathearn had now appointed himself a Captain. The Court rejected the application, stating that it held no jurisdiction in such a case as the will of a Sovereign cannot be proved.

Olive Wilmot Serres failed in her campaign to be recognized as a Princess. Her last days were spent in pathetic poverty. She died on November 21, 1834, and is buried in St James's, Piccadilly, as 'Olive Cumberland'. The account in the *Daily Telegraph* of the interment states that it was conducted with 'pretension suited rather to the position she aspired to than to the one she had actually occupied. Several ladies and gentlemen moving in the best society attended the funeral; the coffin was composed of the costly materials usually appropriated to royalty, and bore an inscription setting forth the titles and honours to which the deceased had so long laid claims'.

Mary L. Pendered and Justinian Mallett, authors of *Princess or Pretender*, published in 1939, a well researched study of Olive Wilmot Serres, reached no definite conclusion except that she was 'almost certainly the daughter of the Duke of Cumberland and possibly a legitimate daughter' but that some of her supporting documents were undoubtedly forged, if not by herself 'then by various shady characters such as Petrie, alias Fitzclarence or Strathearn with whom she was associated'.

It may be that Olive was the daughter of the Duke of Cumberland and Anne Horton, who were married on October 2, 1771. As already mentioned, Horace Walpole wrote to his friend in Florence on November 7 that the Duchess was then pregnant. If this were so, then the child must have been conceived before the marriage. Now Olive was born on April 3, 1772.

As already mentioned in Chapter Thirteen, page 113, the *General Evening Post* reported on March 24: 'We are assured that Her Royal Highness of Cumberland is in a state of pregnancy' and also that 'the

Duke and Duchess of Cumberland set off for Windsor on Monday morning from their house in Pall Mall'. Then, four days later, the same paper informed its readers that 'on Wednesday night Lord North waited on the Duke of Cumberland at Cumberland House in Pall Mall, with whom he had a long conference'.

What brought the Duke back so soon to London and caused the Prime Minister to pay him so lengthy a visit? The records of the period do not tell us and we hear no more of the Duchess's pregnancy. Could it be that Olive was her child and was then sent away to be brought up by the Wilmots through pressure from the King, unwilling to recognize a descendant of the Luttrells as in line, however distant, to the throne? Could he have threatened to cut off the Cumberlands' allowance? Some support is lent to such a hypothesis by the fact that Olive's eldest daughter, born in 1797, was christened Lavinia Janetta Horton Serres, the third name being that of the Duchess of Cumberland before she married the Duke.

An obvious objection to such a theory is why, after defying the King by marrying without his permission, should the Cumberlands later comply with his request thus to dispose of their child? Or could it be that Cumberland had wed before marrying Anne Horton, making such a union a bigamous one?

It might be that Olive Wilmot Serres was told by the Earl of Warwick she was a daughter of the Duke, but that he did not tell her the whole story and died before he could, and that she with Petrie's assistance then proceeded to elaborate the story, adorning it with such fantastic features that it became impossible for the Royal Family to accept her as a relative, either legitimate or illegitimate.

Among the documents produced by Mrs Serres was a will allegedly made by the Duke, in which he left to 'Olive, my daughter, the supposed child of Mr Robert Wilmot, all my real and freehold estate after the demise of the King should I depart this life. Amen. Henry.' Witnesses to the signature were shown as 'J. Dunning, Robert Wilmot, and the Earl of Chatham.'

There were also various deeds, purporting to be in the Duke of Kent's handwriting and signed by him, that gave to 'my cousin, Olive, Princess of Cumberland one-third of my estate, land and mines, situate in Canada, North America' and also 'to my dearest coz ... four hundred pounds yearly during her life'. The last mentioned was actually paid by the Duke to her whilst he was alive, and the 'agreement' was an obvious attempt to persuade his executors to continue payment after his death. This further authorized her to receive ten thousand pounds 'of whatever person who may sell or dispose of my house, furniture and estate situate at Castlebar Hill' and bequeathed to her ten thousands pounds 'should I depart this life before my estate of Castlebar is disposed of'.

Another document concerned Olive's daughter, Lavinia, and in this Kent bound himself not only to pay her four hundred pounds yearly for life but stipulated that she should be 'the young lady companion' of his daughter, the future Queen Victoria, 'when that dear infant attains her fourth year'.

CHAPTER TWENTY

'A Claim to the Throne'

Olive Wilmot Serres's death in 1834 did not end the matter. Her daughter, Mrs Lavinia Ryves, devoted her life to trying to become recognized as Henry Frederick, Duke of Cumberland's lawful granddaughter, and in 1858 she published 'An Appeal for Royalty: a Letter to her Most Gracious Majesty Queen Victoria from Lavinia, Princess of Cumberland and Duchess of Lancaster.' This commenced: 'After patient endurance of most cruel wrongs through a period of thirty-eight years, during which I have been plunged from ... true friendship on the part of Your Majesty's late royal father to a state of entire neglect by all those persons to whom His Royal Highness expressed his solemn wishes—even on his death-bed—that I shall be protected: I am at length compelled to make this public appeal to Your Majesty's sense of justice ...

'My motives in doing this cannot be misunderstood, when it is remembered, that, walking in the footsteps of my late Royal and revered mother ... I have hitherto scrupulously guarded ... the great state secret, which so deeply affects the honour of the House of Brunswick and which the accident of birth threw into my keeping ...'

But now her patience had been exhausted as her son through poverty had been 'almost reduced to a skeleton' and she felt bound in justice to herself and 'the cause of historic truth, to place upon record in a manner more exact and perfect than has yet been done, the secret history of the First Marriage of King George III, and to show how that fatal act has reacted on his innocent royal niece, my revered mother, and has marked with misery and suffering the days of her daughter ...' Mrs Ryves then proceeded to relate once more her case in the pamphlet and also reproduced in it, for the first time, the alleged marriage certificate of George III and Hannah. Like her mother, she also styled herself 'Duchess of Lancaster'. She was at least sensible enough not to demand the arrears of its revenues since the Duke of Cumberland's death, which would have totalled over a million pounds, but she did claim £105,520 in respect of the other bequests she and her mother had not received.

But this 'Appeal' produced no results, so Lavinia decided to take the matter into the law courts and attempted to have her own legitimacy established under the Legitimacy Declaration Act of 1848.

There was considerable sympathy for Mrs Ryves. Like her mother, Olive, she was of regal appearance and had an undeniable resemblance to the Royal Family. Even a paper sympathetic to the Establishment like the *Daily Telegraph* commented in 1861: 'It is of course impossible to determine how far the daughter of Doctor Wilmot was deceived and betrayed by the Duke of Cumberland. That some connection existed between them is not denied. It is true that it was once distinctly intimated that Mrs Ryves should receive the countenance of the Throne provided she would renounce an assumption which might even, if accepted in the fullest sense, invalidate the succession right of the Queen herself to the Crown of England.'

In 1866 the trial opened in the Court of Probate and Divorce before Lord Chief Justice, Sir Alexander Cockburn, Lord Baron Pollock, and Judge Ordinary Sir James Wilde. The Crown was defended by a formidable team—Sir Roundell Palmer, the Attorney-General (six years later to reach the Woolsack as Lord Selbourne), Sir Robert Porrett Collier, the Solicitor-General, and Robert Phillimore, the Queen's Advocate. Mrs Ryves as plaintiff was represented by Dr J. Walter Smith and an outer barrister, Mr D. W. Thomas, who were of inferior legal calibre to the Crown's advocates. A strange feature of the case was that every day Mrs Ryves arrived at the Court in a royal carriage with footmen in livery. This had been lent her by the Duke of Cambridge, according to one writer. Edward VII, then Prince of Wales, attended the proceedings from start to finish as a spectator.

In his opening speech, Dr Smith related the story of the claimant's alleged ancestry, which was already well known to the public. When he came to the birth of Olive Wilmot Serres, supposed daughter of Olive Wilmot and the Duke of Cumberland, he said that Dr Wilmot agreed to conceal the child's true parentage at George III's request, providing there was a written record, certified by the King and witnesses, as to what had been done, so that at some future date after that monarch's death the girl at his express wish should be acknowledged by the royal family and restored to her correct station in life.

Dr Smith produced what he claimed was this record, (the statement dated Kew Palace, May 2, 1773, and apparently signed by 'George R', already quoted in the preceding chapter) which declared that the King so wished 'in return for confidential services' rendered by Dr Wilmot in 1759 when the latter had wed him to Hannah Lightfoot. Counsel next displayed what he contended was her certificate of marriage to the then Prince of Wales, and turning it over said that it had another signed by Wilmot on the back showing that he had married his own daughter to Henry Frederick, Duke of Cumberland on March 4, 1767. The father's motive in doing this, the barrister argued, was so that Olive might possess the documentary evidence to make the Royal Family recognize her. He stressed that the statement and the certificates had all been witnessed by the Earl of Chatham and had been kept by him till his death in 1778, when they had been passed into the Earl of Warwick's custody and then with other papers into that of the Duke of Kent, who had handed all to Olive Serres.

Dr Smith told the Court that the seventy documents which he would show them, containing among others forty-three signatures of Dr Wilmot, thirty-six of Lord Chatham, twelve of George III, and eighteen of the Duke of Kent, had repeatedly been brought to the notice of the ministers of the Crown.

Among these was one bearing signatures purporting to be those of the Wilmot brothers, the Earl of Chatham and John Dunning after the statement that 'Olive the daughter of Henry Frederick, Duke of Cumberland, and Olive, his wife, was born on April 3, 1772, at Warwick'.

'J. Wilmot' certified, too, that the girl was privately baptised 'by myself at my mother Mrs Sarah Wilmot's residence in the Parish of St Mary's, Warwick, three hours after the said infant's birth, by the name of Olive'.

Next Mrs Ryves's Counsel submitted for examination a document in which Dr James Wilmot and his brother Robert certified that the baby was rebaptized in order that she might pass as the latter's daughter and 'that such child of the Duke of Cumberland was entered in the register of St Nicholas, at Warwick, as Olive Wilmot only'. Certainly the rebaptism took place, for the registers contain the entry: 'April 15, 1772. Olive daughter of Robert and Anna Maria Wilmot.'

As evidence that this was done at the King's behest Dr Smith produced another paper initialled 'G.R.' and dated April 4, 1772, and addressed to Lord Chatham stating that 'it is our Royal Will that Olive our Niece be baptized Olive Wilmot to operate during our Royal pleasure'.

Then Counsel for the Plaintiff drew attention to a statement by J. Wilmot and J. Dunning and dated May 3, 1774, that read: 'In the face of Almighty God we, the undersigned, solemnly certify that His Majesty gave his Royal command that Olive, the legitimate daughter of Henry Frederick, Duke of Cumberland, by Olive, his first wife, should be rebaptised as the supposed child of Robert Wilmot, of Warwick to save her Royal father, who had committed an act of bigamy by marrying Anne Horton.'

The most astonishing and unconvincing exhibit was what was supposed to be Hannah Lightfoot's will made at Hampstead on July 7, 1768, in which she commends her two sons and her daughter 'to the kind protection of their Royal Father, my husband, His Majesty George III bequeathing whatever property I die possessed of to such dear offspring of my ill fated marriage. In case of the death of each of my children, I give and bequeath to Olive Wilmot, daughter of my best friend, Dr. Wilmot, whatever property I am entitled to or in possession of at the time of my death. Amen.' This was signed 'Hannah Regina' with 'J. Dunning' and 'W. Pitt' as witnesses.

As already stated in the Prologue, after marrying Isaac Axford in 1753, Hannah disappeared, then in 1759 he remarried which suggests that he had heard of her death. If this were certain, then a will dated 1768 must be a forgery.

The production of the Hannah Lightfoot documents in court was fatal. The Lord Chief Justice after inspecting them commented: 'The Court is, as I understand, asked solemnly to declare, on the strength of two certificates, coming I know not whence, written on two scraps of paper, that the marriage, the only marriage of George III which the world believes to have taken place, between His Majesty and Queen Charlotte, was an invalid marriage, and consequently that all the Sovereigns who have sat on the throne since his death, including Her present Majesty, were not entitled to sit on the throne ... I believe them to be gross and rank forgeries. The Court has no difficulty in coming to the conclusion, even assuming the signatures had that character of genuineness which they have not, that what is asserted in these documents has not the slightest foundation in fact.'

From this, it appears that the Lord Chief Justice, like the Prime

Minister, Lord Liverpool and his advisers in 1821 (see page 189), was unaware of Hannah Lightfoot's marriage to Isaac Axford on December 11, 1753, at the Mayfair Chapel in Curzon Street and recorded in the registers now part of those for St George's, Hanover Square (see page ix, Prologue). Such a marriage would have invalidated her alleged one to George III as Prince of Wales in 1759, so that he remained single in law and his marriage to Prince Charlotte in 1761 the only one to be recognized.

When Mrs Ryves was cross-examined, she said that in 1815 the Earl of Warwick brought her mother three files of papers, one of which he stated had been handed him by Dr Wilmot, the second by the Earl of Chatham, and the third which had always been in his care. Warwick opened the first two files and read aloud what was written on their contents in the presence of the Duke of Kent, her mother, Mrs Serres, and herself. After examining everything carefully, the Duke had declared that he was perfectly satisfied that the signatures of George III were genuine. The Duke had then acknowledged her mother as his cousin and entitled to be called Princess Olive, the only legitimate issue of the Duke of Cumberland's marriage, and said that in view of Warwick's precarious state of health he himself would take on the sole protection and guardianship of Mrs Serres and herself.

Regarding the third set of papers, Mrs Ryves said that they were labelled: 'To the care of the Earl of Warwick for Olive Serres, not to be acted upon until the Death of the King. J.W.' She went on that there was much discussion as to whether or not the package should be opened before the King died, but the Duke of Kent 'persisted in his desire to know its contents, and the seals were broken'. This was in late 1819, and one document, the plaintiff continued, read: 'Olive provided the royal family acknowledge you, keep secret all the papers which are connected with the King's first marriage; but should the family's desertion be manifested (should you outlive the King) then, and only then, make known all the state secrets which I have left in the Earl of Warwick's keeping for your knowledge. Such papers I bequeath to you for your sole and uncontrolled property to use and act upon as you deem fit, according to the expediency of things. Receive this as the sacred will of James Wilmot.' This was dated June, 1789, and was witnessed by 'Warwick'.

Mrs Ryves, although she was in her seventieth year, stood for hours in the witness box, clearly sustained by an almost fanatic belief in the justice of her cause. Although the finest legal talent in the country was massed against her in the service of the Crown, never once did she falter.

The foremost handwriting expert in the country, Mr Netherclift, testified that he had inspected the marriage certificates claimed to have been made out by Dr Wilmot and believed them to be authentic. When cross-examined, however, he admitted not having seen Wilmot's actual writing, but only tracings shown him by Mrs Ryves or her solicitor. As a result, Registers from Trinity College, Oxford, were brought forward and he was asked to compare the samples of the Doctor's penmanship they contained with the certificates. After doing so, he maintained his original opinion, adding that signatures of George III on the latter were also genuine. He was shown other documents signed by the King and after studying them kept firmly to his convictions despite the bullying of Sir Roundell Palmer, the Attorney-General, backed by the hostile Lord Chief Justice himself, who tried in every way to discredit his evidence. The only signature about which he expressed doubt was that of Dunning.

Palmer had skilfully ignored discussion of what the case was really about, whether or not the plaintiff was Cumberland's legitimate granddaughter, to concentrate instead on the alleged marriage of George III to Hannah Lightfoot. 'This is nothing less than a claim to the throne,' he insisted in his devastating speech to the jury. Who could possibly believe that, had such a union taken place, Hannah and her two children would have remained silent when the King married Queen Charlotte? And that Dr Wilmot would have continued to preach before the royal couple knowing that the King had committed bigamy?

Plaintiff's mother, Olive Serres, was 'a person of ill-regulated ambition'. As for the documents produced, there was every reason to believe that they were concocted by her as she was 'an artist and practised calligraphist who had gone through such a course of study as well prepared her for the publication of forged documents'. The internal evidence of the papers themselves proved that they were forgeries. If every expert that ever lived swore to their genuineness, they still could not possibly believe them to be genuine. They were all written on little scraps and slips of paper, such as no one would have used for recording transactions of such a kind and 'in every one of these pieces the watermark of date was wanting'.

Here Sir Roundell Palmer paused as the foreman of the jury indicated that he wished to speak. This was to announce that they were all of the opinion that the signatures on the documents were not authentic. The Lord Chief Justice at once commented: 'You share the opinion which my learned brothers and I entertained for a long time.'

Dr Smith in his reply said that his client's case had been prejudiced at the outset by the observation of the Attorney-General that it was a claim on the part of the plaintiff to the Throne. 'If there was any such claim, however, it was on behalf of Hannah Lightfoot's children, and the Lightfoot documents were so mixed up with the documents upon which I relied that I was obliged to give them in evidence.'

He continued: 'It is incredible that a forger should have fabricated such a mass of unnecessary documents. Their informality is a strong proof of their genuineness. A woman of the character of Mrs Serres, as described by the Attorney-General, would be incapable of having forged them ... Certainly the person who wrote the admitted letters of Olive Serres, so rambling, so warmly devoted, so weak and so unbusinesslike, could not possibly be a forger, who is always a person of cool command, of clear mind, and steady hand.'

The Lord Chief Justice summing up declared: 'Two or three of the documents appear to be such outrages upon all probability, that even if there had been strong evidence of the genuineness of the handwriting, no man of common sense could come to the conclusion that they were genuine.'

The jury immediately returned a verdict that they were not satisfied that the late Olive Serres was the legitimate daughter of Henry Frederick, Duke of Cumberland, or that he was married to Olive Wilmot on March 4, 1767. The Lord Chief Justice ordered all the documents produced to be seized. They have since been in the custody of the Crown, and permission to inspect them has always been refused.

Mrs Ryves was a determined old lady. She appealed to the House of Lords. Those who believed in her cause raised a fund through public subscriptions. As she could no longer afford much legal aid, she herself arrived to conduct her own case. Again she was unlucky. The Lords refused to listen to her on the technical grounds that no bill of exception had been entered and no motion for a new trial made.

Even after this blow, Mrs Ryves went on seeking some way of re-opening the case until, with her death, the curtain finally descended on litigation that, had she won, might have had far-reaching repercussions.

Pretenders are frequent phenomena, and however extravagant their claims, there always will remain, even after exposure, a feeling that there might be some truth hidden under the overlying inventions.

Sources

Abbreviation: RA = Royal Archives

PROLOGUE

1 John, Lord Hervey, *Some Materials Towards Memoirs of the Reign of King George III*, page 859
2 Ibid, page 842.
3 Ibid, page 885.
4 John Heneage Jesse, *Memoirs of the Life and Reign of King George III*, volume i, page 21.
5 Averyl Edwards, *Frederick Louis, Prince of Wales*, pages 445–46.

CHAPTER ONE

1 Horace Walpole, *Letters*, edited by Mrs Paget Toynbee, volume iv, page 267, letter 631, PS to George Montagu.
2 Lady Louisa Stuart's *Memoir*, printed in *The Letters and Journals of Lady Mary Coke*, edited by the Honourable J. A. Home, page lxxxv.
3 Horace Walpole, *Last Journals*, volume i, note to page 106.
4 A. Cecil Hampshire, *Royal Sailors*, page 16.
5 Ibid, page 17.
6 Horace Walpole, *Letters*, volume ii, page 209, letter 224.
7 Ibid, volume iv, page 182, letter 588, September 2, 1758, to Hon. Henry Seymour Conway.
8 Lady Louise Stuart's *Memoir*, page xcii.
9 Ibid, page lxxxviii.
10 Ibid, page lxxxiii.
11 Horace Walpole, *Memoirs of the Reign of King George III*, volume iii, pages 74–75.
12 RA 54288.
13 Historical Manuscripts Commission, *Carlisle MSS*, page 217, October 16, 1767.
14 Lady Louisa Stuart's *Memoir*, page xcii.
15 Ibid, page xciii.
16 *The Letters and Journals of Lady Mary Coke*, volume ii, page 138.
17 Alfred John Dunkin, *Archaelogical Mine*, volume iii, pages 3–18.
18 Mrs Anne Archer, *Memoirs*, volume iv, pages 232–33.

CHAPTER TWO

1 George Selwyn, *Correspondence*, volume i, page 334.
2 Lady Sarah Lennox, *Life and Letters*, edited by Lady Ilchester and Lord Stavordale, page 75.
3 *The Letters and Journals of Lady Mary Coke*, volume i, page 67, October 6, 1766.
4 Ibid, page 81, October 23, 1766.
5 Horace Walpole, *Letters*, volume iv, page 367, letter 1295, February 27, 1770.

CHAPTER THREE

1 Horace Walpole, *Letters*, volume ii, pages 156–57, letter 203, November 29, 1745, to Sir Horace Mann.
2 John Heneage Jesse, *Memoirs of the Life and Reign of King George III*, volume ii, page 2.
3 Horace Walpole, *Memoirs of the Reign of King George III*, volume iii, page 267.

4 Margaret L. Mare and W. H. Quarrell, *Lichtenberg's Visits to England as described in his letters and diaries*, page 78.
5 *The Letters and Journals of Lady Mary Coke*, volume ii, page 242.
6 Ibid, page 271.
7 Ibid, volume iii, page 82.
8 Mrs Anne Archer, *Memoirs*, volume i, page 169–75.

CHAPTER FOUR

1 Horace Walpole, *Letters*, volume vi, page 188, letter 1009, to the Earl of Hertford.
2 'Civilian', *Free thoughts ... occasioned by the late intrigues between the Duke of Cumberland and Henrietta, wife of Lord Grosvenor.*
3 Quoted by Percy Hetherington Fitzgerald in *The Royal Dukes*, page 9.
4 *The Letters and Journals of Lady Mary Coke*, volume i, page 27.
5 Ibid, page 98.
6 Ibid, page 100.
7 Ibid, page 116.
8 Ibid, page 120.
9 Ibid, volume ii, page 20.
10 Ibid, page 38.
11 Ibid, page 198.
12 Ibid, page 366.
13 Ibid, page 397.

CHAPTER FIVE

1 All the sworn statements quoted are given in the printed *Copies of the depositions of the witnesses examined in the Cause of Divorce between the Right Honourable Lord Grosvenor and the Right Honourable Lady Grosvenor, his wife* (London, 1771).
2 All the letters quoted are given in full in the printed *Trial of the D— of C—d for criminal conversation with Lady G—r. including the letters between his Royal Highness and her Ladyship* (London, 1770).
3 *The Letters and Journals of Lady Mary Coke*, volume iii, page 148.

CHAPTER SIX

1 *Whitehall Evening Post*, July 18, 1770.

CHAPTER SEVEN

1 *The Letters and Journals of Lady Mary Coke*, volume iii, pages 202–3.
2 Ibid., page 204.

CHAPTER EIGHT

1 *Town and Country Magazine*, March, 1770.
2 *Universal Magazine*, March, 1770.
3 *The Letters and Journals of Lady Mary Coke*, volume iii, page 244.
4 Ibid, page 245.
5 Ibid, page 250.
6 Mrs. Delany, *The Autobiography and Correspondence of*, volume i, page 292.

CHAPTER NINE

1 *The Letters and Journals of Lady Mary Coke*, volume iii, page 254.
2 Ibid, page 257.
3 Ibid, page 258, July 16, 1770.
4 John Heneage Jesse, *Memoirs of the Life and Reign of King George III*, volume ii, page 3.
5 RA 15900.

CHAPTER TEN

1 *The Craftsman* and the *Morning Chronicle* for August 17, 1771.

2 *The Letters and Journals of Lady Mary Coke*, volume iii, page 438.
3 *Morning Chronicle*, September 5, 1771.
4 *The Craftsman*, September 7, 1771.
5 *London Evening Post*, September 18, 1771.
6 *St James's Chronicle*, September 16, 1771.
7 *The Craftsman*, September 21, 1771.
8 *Lloyd's Evening Post*, September 21, 1771.
9 *The Craftsman*, September 28, 1771.

CHAPTER ELEVEN

1 Horace Walpole, *Letters*, volume viii, page 104, letter 1380, November 7, 1771, to Sir Horace Mann.
2 Horace Walpole, *Memoirs of the Reign of King George III*, volume iv, page 237.
3 *The Craftsman*, February 1, 1772.
4 *London Evening Post*, November 7, 1771.
5 RA 54427-8.
6 RA 15948-9.
7 RA 15934.
8 RA 15948-9.
9 *The Craftsman*, November 8, 1771.
10 *Annual Register*, November, 1771.
11 RA 54471.
12 *London Evening Post*, November 7, 1771.
13 Horace Walpole, *Letters*, volume viii, page 102, letter 1380.
14 Lady Louisa Stuart, *Memoir*, page xcv.
15 *The Letters and Journals of Lady Mary Coke*, volume iii, page 483.
16 RA 15944.
17 John Doran, *'Mann' and Manners at the Court of Florence*, volume ii, page 231.
18 RA 15938.
19 RA 54323-4.
20 RA 54329.
21 Mrs Delany, *Autobiography and Correspondence*, edited by Lady Llanover, volume i, page 363.
22 Horace Walpole, *Letters*, volume viii, page 113, letter 1384.
23 This pedigree in its original case covered with red morocco was on sale by a Mr E. Menken of 50, Great Russell-street, London, W.C.1, in 1909, according to Sir H. C. M. Lyte, *A History of Dunster and of the Families of Mohun and Luttrell*, pages 539/40.
24 *London Evening Post*, December 11, 1771.
25 *Morning Herald*, December 14, 1771.
26 *London Evening Post*, December 14, 1771.
27 *Morning Chronicle*, December 27, 1771.
28 *The Craftsman*, September 5, 1772.
29 *The Craftsman*, October 10, 1772.
30 *The Craftsman*, April 17, 1773.
31 *The Craftsman*, July 10, 1773.
32 *London Evening Post*, February 18, 1777.
33 *London Evening Post*, May 29, 1777.
34 *St James's Chronicle*, September 11, 1780.
35 *The Craftsman*, January 4, 1772.
36 *The Craftsman*, January 6, 1772.
37 Horace Walpole, *Letters*, volume viii, page 162, letter 1401.
38 *The Craftsman*, January 18, 1772.
39 *The Craftsman*, January 25, 1772.
40 *The Craftsman*, April 11, 1772.

CHAPTER TWELVE

1 Mrs Elizabeth Carter, *Letters*, volume iii, October 4, 1766.
2 Nors, *Court of Christian VII*, page 118.

3 Horace Walpole, *Letters*, volume vii, page 213, letter 1225, August 13, 1768.
4 Ibid, page 218, letter 1227, August 16, 1768.
5 Ibid, page 224, letter 1229, August 24, 1768.
6 Ibid, page 229, letter 1232, September 22, 1768.
7 Ibid, volume viii, page 151, letter 1397, March 5, 1772.
8 RA 15980.
9 RA 15992.
10 RA 16030.

CHAPTER THIRTEEN

1 Parliamentary History, volume 17, page 383.
2 Horace Walpole, *The Last Journals of*, volume i, page 44.
3 Ibid, page 24.
4 Ibid, page 30.
5 Sir John Fortescue, Correspondence of King George III, volume iii, letter 1025A.
6 *Parliamentary History*, volume 17, page 387.
7 Ibid, page 388.
8 Ibid, page 389.
9 Ibid, page 391.
10 Ibid, page 410.
11 Horace Walpole, *The Last Journals of*, volume i, page 66.
12 Ibid, page 44.
13 Horace Walpole, *Letters*, volume viii, page 171, letter 1409.
14 Horace Walpole, *The Last Journals of*, volume i, pages 100–101.
15 RA 54333.
16 Horace Walpole, *Letters*, volume viii, page 205, letter 1428.
17 Lady Louisa Stuart, *Memoir*, page xciv.
18 *The Letters and Journals of Lady Mary Coke*, volume iv, page 122.
19 *The Craftsman*, June 6, 1772.
20 Horace Walpole, *Letters*, volume viii, page 113, letter 1384, December 4, 1771.
21 *The Letters and Journals of Lady Mary Coke*, volume iv, pages 90-91.
22 Mrs Delany, *Autobiography and Correspondence*, volume i, page 465.
23 Historical Manuscripts Commission, *Dartmouth MSS*, volume iii, page 210.
24 *The Letters and Journals of Lady Mary Coke*, volume iv, page 149.
25 W. Harrison, *A History of London*, page 531.
26 Lady Louisa Stuart, *Memoirs*, pages xcvi–vii.
27 *The Letters and Journals of Lady Mary Coke*, volume iv, page 214.
28 Percy Hetherington Fitzgerald, *The Royal Dukes*, volume ii, page 204.
29 Ibid, page 195.
30 Ibid, page 205.

CHAPTER FOURTEEN

1 *Gentleman's Magazine*, 1773, page 464.
2 Horace Walpole, *Letters*, volume viii, page 342, letter 1493.
3 John Doran, '*Mann' and Manners at the Court of Florence*, page 252.
4 Ibid, page 253.
5 *The Letters and Journals of Lady Mary Coke*, volume iv, page 279.
6 Ibid, volume iv, page 289.
7 Ibid, volume iv, page 293.
8 John Doran, '*Mann' and Manners at the Court of Florence*, volume ii, pages 264-265.
9 Ibid, page 266.
10 Lady Louisa Stuart, *Memoir*, page xcvi.
11 *The Letters and Journals of Lady Mary Coke*, page 445.
12 Ibid, page 448.
13 Sir John Fortescue, *Correspondence of King George III*, volume iii, letter 1559.
14 Ibid, letter 1574.

15 Horace Walpole, *Letters*, volume ix, page 154, letter 1603.
16 Ibid, page 165, letter 1607.
17 *London Evening Post*, July 9, 1775.
18 Horace Walpole, *Letters*, volume ix, page 245.
19 Historical Manuscripts Commission. *Sackville MSS*, volume i, page 345.
20 This extract and the subsequent ones come from the unpublished *Letters to John Strange, British Resident at Venice, 1773–1777*, preserved in the Department of Manuscripts of the British Library.
21 Historical Manuscripts Commission. *Sackville MSS*, volume i, page 350.
22 Ibid, page 352.
23 Horace Walpole, *Letters*, supplementary volume iii, page 250, letter 156.
24 Horace Walpole, *Last Journals*, volume ii, page 415.
25 Sir John Fortescue, *Correspondence of King George III*, volume iii, letter 2087.

CHAPTER FIFTEEN

1 Horace Walpole, *Letters*, volume viii, page 153, letter 1603.
2 Robert Huish, *Life of George III*, pages 366–7.
3 Horace Walpole, *Letters*, volume x, page 133, letter 1807.
4 *London Evening Post*, May 20, 1777.
5 *Annual Register*, July, 1775.
6 John Stockdale, *Parliamentary Register* (for reports of debates, 1774-1786).
7 John Heneage Jesse, *Memoirs of the Life and Reign of King George III*, volume ii, page 211.
8 RA 54443.

CHAPTER SIXTEEN

1 *St James's Chronicle*, June 13, 1780.
2 RA 54354.
3 RA 41771.
4 RA 41772.
5 *St James's Chronicle*, June 20, 1780.
6 A. Aspinall, *Correspondence of George, Prince of Wales*, 1770–1812, volume i, page 32, note 5.
7 Ibid, page 31.
8 *St James's Chronicle*, August 15, 1780.
9 RA 54451.
10 RA 54452.
11 RA 54458.
12 RA 41780–1.
13 RA 54454–5.
14 Horace Walpole, *Letters*, volume xi, page 414, letter 2157.
15 Ibid, page 418, letter 2159.
16 *St James's Chronicle*, February 16, 1781.
17 *General Evening Post*, March 6, 1781.
18 RA 43408–9.
19 John Heneage Jesse, *King George III*, volume ii, pages 366–7.
20 Horace Walpole, *The Last Journals of*, volume ii, pages 480–1.
21 Ibid, page 457.
22 RA 43469.
23 Historical Manuscripts Commission. Carlisle MSS, page 575.
24 Ibid, page 582.
25 Sir John Fortescue, *Correspondence of King George III*, volume v, pages 217–221.

CHAPTER SEVENTEEN

1 Dr Awaiter, *Thoughts on Brighthelmston, concerning Sea-bathing and Drinking Sea-Water*, pages 18–19.
2 *The Gentleman's Magazine*, March 18, 1783.
3 Historical Manuscripts Commission. Carlisle MSS, page 381.
4 RA 54452.

5 RA 54460-1.
6 RA 54462.
7 RA 54463-4.
8 RA 54469-70.
9 RA 50237-8.
10 RA 54471-2.
11 RA 54473-4.
12 John Doran, *'Mann' and Manners at the Court of Florence*, page 417.
13 RA 41867-8.
14 RA 54476-7.
15 RA 54480-1.
16 RA 54482.
17 Sir Nathaniel Wraxall, *Memoirs of his own time*, volume iv, p. 319-22.
18 RA 54484-5.
19 RA 54382-3.
20 Percy Hetherington Fitzgerald, *The Royal Dukes*, volume ii, p. 205.
21 Lady Louisa Stuart, *The Letters of*, selected by R. Brimley Johnson, p. 88.
22 J. A. Erredge, *History of Brighthelmston*, p. 232.
23 Duke of Buckingham and Chandos, *Memoirs of the Courts and Cabinets of George III*, volume ii, p. 150.
24 Lady Jerningham, *The Letters of*, volume i, p. 34.

CHAPTER EIGHTEEN

1 RA 54488.
2 RA 54491-2.
3 A. Aspinall, *The Later Correspondence of George III*, volume i, page 624.
4 RA 54396.
5 A. Aspinall, *Correspondence of George, Prince of Wales, 1770-1812*, volume ii, page 92, note 1.
6 RA 44885.
7 RA 54495.
8 RA 41957-8.
9 A. Aspinall, *Correspondence of George, Prince of Wales, 1770-1812*, volume ii, pages 106-7, letter 536.
10 RA 54496-7.
11 RA 54499-500.
12 RA 43994-6.
13 RA 54504.
14 RA 42072-3.
15 A. Aspinall, *Correspondence of George, Prince of Wales, 1770-1812*, volume iii, page 57, letter 989.
16 *The Times*, October 31, 1799.
17 RA 44954-5.
18 *The Times*, November 29, 1789.
19 *The Farington Diary*, volume i, page 222.
20 Sir Robert Heron, *Notes*, page 293.

CHAPTER NINETEEN

1 *Notes and Queries*, 4th Series, volume ii, pages 451, 498.
2 *Correspondence and Diaries of Thomas Creevey*, edited by Sir Herbert Maxwell, pages 339-40.
3 From Mrs Ryves's letters sent to various newspapers after her case had been dismissed by the House of Lords, quoted in Mary L. Pendered and Justinian Mallett's *Princess or Pretender*, pages 182 and 277.
4 Mrs Ryves, *In the House of Lords. On Appeal ... Case and Appendix for the Appellant.* (Privately printed, 1867.)
5 Robert Huish, *Memoirs of George IV*, volume ii, page 277.

Select Bibliography

Adolphus, J., *History of the Reign of George III* (1840)
Almon, John, *Parliamentary Register*, debates 1774–80
Archer, Mrs Ann, *Memoirs* (1792)
Aspinall, A., *The Later Correspondence of George III* (5 vols., 1962–70)
Correspondence of George, Prince of Wales, 1770–1812 (8 vols, 1963–71)
Ayling, Stanley, *George III* (1972)
Bishop, J. G., *A Peep into the Past: Brighton in the Olden Time* (1892)
Boulton, Wm. B., *Thomas Gainsborough* (1905)
Brougham, Henry, *Statesmen in the Times of George III* (1839)
Buckingham and Chandos, Duke of, *Memoirs of the Courts and Cabinets of George III* (2 vols, 1855)
Brooke, John, *King George III* (Constable, 1972)
Cary, Miss C. E., *Memoirs* (1825)
Coke, Lady Mary, *The Letters and Journals of* (1889–96)
'Civilian', *Free thoughts ... occasioned by the late intrigue between the Duke of Cumberland and Henrietta, wife of Lord Grosvenor* (1771)
Cumberland, Henry Frederick, Duke of, *The genuine copies of letters which passed between the Duke of Cumberland and the Lady Grosvenor* (1770)
A Full and Complete History of His R—l H— the D— of C—d and Lady G—r, The Fair Adultress (1770)
The Trial of the D— of C—d for criminal conversation with Lady G—r, including the letters between his Royal Highness and her Ladyship (1770)
A Circumstantial Narrative of a late Remarkable Trial (1770)
Delany, Mrs, *The Autobiography and Correspondence of* (1862) Ed. Lady Llanover, (London, 1862, 3 vols)
Erredge, J. A., *History of Brighthelmstone* (1862)
Farington, Joseph, *The Farington Diary* (8 vols., 1922)
Fitzgerald, Percy Hetherington, *Life of George IV* (1881)
The Royal Dukes (1882)
Fortescue, Sir John, *Correspondence of King George III* (6 vols., 1927–8)
Fulford, Roger, *George the Fourth* (1949)
George, M. Dorothy, *Catalogue of Personal & Political Prints in the British Museum* (1935–54)
Gore, John, *Life and Times of Creevey* (1937)
Gerard, Francis, *Some Irish Beauties* (1895)
Grosvenor, Richard, *Copies of the depositions of the witnesses examined in the Cause of Divorce between the Right Honourable Lord Grosvenor and the Right Honourable Lady Grosvenor, his wife* (1771)
Harwood, T. E., *Windsor, Old and New* (1929)
Heron, Sir Robert, *Notes* (1850)
Hobhouse, Christopher, *Fox* (Constables and Murray, 1947)
Huish, Robert, *The Public and Private Life of George III* (1821)
Jerningham, Lady, *The Jerningham Letters* (2 vols., 1896)
Jesse, John Heneage, *Memoirs of the Life and Reign of King George III* (1867)
Junius, *The Letters of* (1802)
Lyte, Sir H. C. M., *A History of Dunster and of the Families of Mohun and Luttrell* (1909)
Maxwell, Sir Herbert, *The Creevey Papers, edited by* (Murray, 1903)
Macauley, Elizabeth Wright, *The Wrongs of Her Royal Highness the Princess Olive of Cumberland* (1833)
Melville, Lewis, *Brighton* (1909)

Merrifield, Mrs, *Brighton, Past and Present* (1857)
Musgrave, Clifford, *Brighton* (Faber, 1970)
Papendiek, Charlotte, *Court and Private Life in the Time of Queen Charlotte* (Bentley, 1887)
Pendered, Mary L. and Justinian Mallett, *Princess or Pretender* (Hurst and Blackett, 1939)
Pigott, Charles, *The Jockey Club* (1792)
The Female Jockey Club (1794)
Plumb, J. H., *The First Four Georges* (Batsford, 1968)
Russell, Lord John, *Memorials and Correspondence of Charles James Fox* (1853)
Serres, Olive Wilmot, *Documents to prove Mrs Olive Serres to be the Legitimate daughter of Henry Frederick, Duke of Cumberland* (Printed by A. Searle, 160 Tottenham Court Road, London, 1820)
The Princess of Cumberland's Statement to the English Nation, including Certificates and Confirmations of the Princess Olive's Royal Parents' Marriage and her Birth (Printed for her by Retford and Robins, 36, London Road, Southwark, 1822)
The Princess of Cumberland to the English Nation (1829)
The First Part of the Authenticated proofs of the Legitimacy of Her Royal Highness Olive, Princess of Cumberland. (Printed for her by W. Lake, 60 Old Street, London, 1830)
Ryves, Mrs Lavinia Janetta Horton Ryves, *In the House of Lords, On Appeal from Her Majesty's Court for Divorce and Matrimonial Causes, Between Lavinia Janetta Horton Ryves, Appellant, and Her Majesty's Attorney General and William Henry Ryves, Respondents. Case and Appendix for the Appellant, Lavinia Janetta Horton Ryves, 12 Murray Street, Camden Square, London, N.W.1, 1867*
Sedgwick, Romney, *Letters from George III to Lord Bute, 1756–1766.*
Stockdale, John, *Parliamentary Register* (for reports of debates, 1774–1780)
Stuart, Lady Louisa, *Memoir, printed in 'The Letters and Journals of Lady Mary Coke, edited by the Honourable J. A. Home* (1889–96)
Thomas, Wm. J., *Hannah Lightfoot* (1867)
Waldegrave, Earl, *Memoirs* (1821)
Walpole, Horace, *The Works of* (London, 1798–1825)
Memoirs of the Reign of King George the Third (1845)
The Letters of (Oxford, 1903–25)
The Last Journals of, from 1771–1783 (London, 1859)
Wilkins, W. H., *Queen of Tears* (Longmans, 1904)
Wraxall, Sir Nathaniel, *Historical and Posthumous Memoirs of his Own Time* (1772–1784) Ed. H. B. Wheatley. (London, 1884)

THE HOUSE OF HANOVER

Ernest Augustus, Elector of Hanover

King George I = Sophia Dorothea of Zell

King George II = Caroline of Anspach

Frederick Lewis, Prince of Wales 1707–1751 = Augusta of Saxe Gotha 1719–1772

William Augustus, Duke of Cumberland 1721–1765

Amelia d. 1786

Louisa = Frederick V King of Denmark

1 other son, 3 daughters

King George III 1738–1820 = Charlotte of Mecklenburg-Strelitz

Edward Augustus, Duke of York 1739–1767

William Henry, Duke of Gloucester 1743–1805 = Maria, Dowager Countess Waldegrave 1736–1807

William Duke of Gloucester 1776–1834

Sophia Matilda 1773–1844

Henry Frederick, Duke of Cumberland 1745–1790 = Anne Horton

Augusta = Duke of Brunswick

Caroline Matilda 1750–1765 = King Christian VII of Denmark 1749–1808

1 other son, 2 other daughters

King George IV 1762–1830 = Caroline 1768–1821

Frederick Duke of York 1763–1827 = Frederica of Prussia

William, Duke of Clarence King William IV 1765–1837

Edward Duke of Kent 1767–1820 = Mary Louisa Victoria of Saxe Coburg Saalfeld

Queen Victoria

Ernest Duke of Cumberland King of Hanover 1771–1851

Augustus Duke of Sussex 1773–1843

Adolphus Duke of Cambridge 1774–1850

2 other sons
6 other daughters

Index

Aalborg, 107
Abingdon Races, 142
Abbaye, 181
Abraham, Nathaniel, 47
Adair, Robert, 92, 132, 133
Adam, Robert, 119
Addez, J., 190
Adelphi, 191
Admiral of the Blue Squadron of the Fleet, 12, 143
Admiral of the White, 170
Admiralty, 33
Aix-la-Chappelle, 164
Albemarle Street, 167
Algernon, Lord, 79
Almack's, 13, 24-26, 38, 152
Almon, John, 113
Alnwick, 66, 78, 80
Altona, 102, 103
Amelia, Princess, 3, 15, 16, 22, 23, 64, 92, 116, 118, 128, 148
America, 85, 142, 165, 194
American Rebellion, 136
Amherst, Lord, 145
Ancaster, Duchess of, 167
Anderton, John, 43, 49, 51
Anne, Queen, 12, 22
Annual Boat Race, 156
Annual Register, 7, 13, 14, 124
Apsley, Lord, 72, 121, 122
Archer, Lady, 177
Archer, Lord, 185, 190
Archer, Mrs Anne, 7, 17, 18, 21, 22
Ardennes, 138
Argyll, John Duke of, 3
Arlington Street, 89
Ascot, 13, 117, 142
Audience Chamber, 146
Augusta, Princess Dowager, vii–ix, 1, 102, 107
Augusta, Princess of Wales, 3, 138, 182, 183
Augsburg, 134, 184
Aurora, 138
Austria, 76
Austria, Empress of, 126
Avignon, 160
Awaiter, Dr 155
Axford, Isaac, ix, 190, 199, 200

Bal d'Amour, 97
Barnes, 65, 82, 95, 96
Barrington, Lady, 24
Basle, 125
Bateman, Lord, 21
Bath, 181
Baumgarten, 149, 176
Bayley, Mr, 74, 76, 82
Bayler, Mrs, 75–78, 81-83, 92, 95, 142
Beauclerk, Lady Catherine, 24
Bedford, Duke of, 168, 177
Belgrave, Lady Elizabeth, 99
Belgrave, Viscount see Grosvenor, Lord
Bell, Henry, 189, 191
Belton, Robert, 51
Bennet, Edward, 24, 42, 51, 58
Berkeley Street, 98
Berlin, 180
Berwick, 79, 80
Bescannon, Duchess of, 163
Bettesworth, Dr, 72
Billington, Mrs, 118
Birch, Chambers and Hobbs, 180
Birch, Hannah, 32, 40, 44
Blackfriar's Bridge, 139, 156
Blackheath, 99, 152
Blackstone, Sir William, 62
Blane, George Dr, 164, 170, 171
Blane, Gilbert, 172
Blenkett, J, 94
Bloomsbury Square, 61
Boisgermain, Mrs, 60, 71
Bologna, 132
Bolton, Arabella, 85
Bolton, Duke of, 117
Bond Street, 20, 52
Bourbons, 142
Bourne, John, 31, 58
Bow Street, 69
Boulogne, 181

Index

Brettingham, Mathew, 118
Bridgeman, Charles, 22
British Envoy, The, 92
British Library's Department of Manuscripts, 78, 189
Brooke, John, 55, 58, 118
Brook's Club, 151
Braithwaite, Captain John, 163
Brighthelmstone, 154, 158
Brighton, 155-159, 164, 167, 174, 181, 182
Brunswick, Heriditary Prince of, 138
Brussels, 141, 176
Bryan, Mr, 132
Buckingham, Duke of, 169
Buckingham House, 120, 150
Buckingham, Lady, 184
Buckingham Palace, 183
Bull Coventry, 41
Bunbury, Lady Sarah, 9
Burgoyne, General, 142
Burke, Edmund, 53
Burke's Peerage, 18
Burton, John, 58
Bushby House, 182
Bute, Lady, 159
Bute, Lord, viii
Buxton, Mr, 71, 72

Calais, 89, 124, 159, 177
Caligula, 104
Calne, 56
Camarthen, Lord, 64
Cambridge, 103, 166
Cambridge, Duke of, 197
Camden, Lord, 72, 112
Canterbury, Archbishop of, 121
Carhampton, 85
Carhampton, Lord, 165, 179
Carlisle, Earl of, 158
Carlisle, 5th Earl of, 151
Carlisle House, 13
Carlisle, Lord, 5, 14
Carlton House, 95, 159, 165
Caroline Matilda, Queen of Denmark, vii, 8, 102-105, 107-109
Caroline, Princess, 130, 181, 182
Caroline, Queen, vii, viii, 22, 187
Carpenter, Lady Almeria, 165, 177
Carter, Mrs, 102
Cary, Miss C. E., 187
Castlebar Hill, 195
Castle Howard, 151
Castlemaine, Lady (Barbara Villiers), 13, 14
Catholic Relief Bill, 144
Cavendish Square, 19, 23, 26, 31, 44, 128, 148
Cecil, Lord David, 32
Celle, Duke of, 108, 109
Chapel Royal, St James's, 102, 148, 182
Charles, Prince of Wales, 139
Charles I, King, 11
Charles II, King, viii, 11, 13, 14, 112
Charlotte, Princess, 192, 200
Charlotte, Queen, 14, 55, 100, 107, 108, 128, 145, 146, 166, 183, 199, 201
Chatham, Earl of, 190, 192, 198-200
Chatham, Lord, 141, 194
Chelmsford, 67
Chelsea, 157
Chester, 20, 41, 43, 49, 50, 57, 70, 71
Chesterfield, Lord, 152
Chillingham Castle, 66
Cholmondley, Lord, 96, 99, 151
Christ Church, Oxford, 85
Christian VIII, King of Denmark, 8, 102, 103
Christiansborg Palace, 107
Christies, 176
Chronicle see *St James's Chronicle*
Church of England, 190
Citizen, The, x
Clarence, Duke of (William IV), 146, 170, 171, 173, 177, 182, 185, 187, 188
Clemens, Mrs Maria, 9
Cliveden, 11
Cockburn, Sir Alexander, 197
Coke, Lady Mary, 3, 6, 9, 15, 16, 19, 24, 25, 38, 52-55, 64, 76, 92, 116-118, 120, 125, 126, 128
Coke, Viscount, 3
Colleton, Mrs Frances, 152
Collier, Sir Robert Porrett, 197
Connaught, William Earl of, see Gloucester, Duke of
Cornely's, Mrs, 10, 13, 25, 96, 97, 100
Consistory Court, 72
Copenhagen, 8, 108
Corps Diplomatique, 177
Cosway, 86, 117
Council of Regency, 5
Court of Probate and Divorce, 197
Court Miscellany, 146
Covent Garden, 97, 118
Coventry, 41, 57
Cowper, Countess, 35
Cranbourne Lodge, 128
Craftsman, The, 66, 72, 76, 82, 83, 101, 113, 125-128
Craven Hill, 70
Creevey, Thomas, 188
Croft, Sir Herbert, 67
Croper, Mr, 31, 36
Crown of England, 197
Cumberland, 157
Cumberland, Duchess of, 91, 100, 113, 116, 120, 124-129, 138, 139, 141, 142, 144, 146, 148, 154, 156-164, 167, 169-171, 178-183, 194
Cumberland Fleet Society, 138, 156, 157
Cumberland, Henry Frederick Duke of, x, 1, 6,

10-19, 24-28, 30-38, 40-44, 47-52, 54-56, 59, 61, 62, 64, 65, 74-83, 86-96, 99, 110-120, 123-129, 131, 136-165, 167-180, 185-187, 192-194, 196-202
Cumberland House, 27, 37, 94, 113, 118, 120, 124, 128, 145, 147, 148, 150-152, 157-159, 165, 171, 175, 176, 178-181, 182, 194
Cumberland Lodge, 13
Cumberland Packet, 177
Cumberland, Princess Oliva (Olivia), 192-194, 196, 200
Cumberland, William Augustus Duke of ('Butcher'), 11, 13, 23
Curzon Street, 200
Cuxhaven, 182

Daily Telegraph, 193, 197
Dartmouth, Earl of, 117
Davies, Mary, 20
Davis, Poll, 91
Deaken, Colonel, 81, 124
de Crillon, Duke, 160
Dee, Miss, 166
de Hochepied, Baron see Porter, General
Delany, Mrs, 55, 93, 117
de Lamballe, Princess, 168
de la Salle, Marquis, 161
Delaval, Sir Francis, 4, 78
Delaval, Sir John Hussey, 78-80
de la Warr, Earl, x
de Maysebourg-Zuschen, Leonore, viii
Denmark, 102, 106-109
Dennison, Thomas, 38, 42, 43, 51, 52
Deptford, 82
Derby, 20
Devonshire, Duke of, 151
Devonshire, Elizabeth Duchess of
Dewes, Miss, 55
de Wurmar, Baron, 125
Dickenson, John, 189, 191
Doctor's Commons, 67, 71
D'Onhoff, (Dunhoff) Camilla Elizabeth Countess, 18, 19, 26-28, 31, 36, 38, 44, 58, 66, 78
Don Joseph, 142
Dormer Collection, 162
Dorset, Duke of, x, 145
Dover, 85, 124
Downing Street, 175
Drury Lane, 98, 141, 188
Dublin, 84
Dublin, Countess of, 125
Dublin, Earl of, 125
Duke's Lodge, 96
Duke Street, St James's, 69, 70, 98
Dunning, John, 56, 59, 60, 122, 190, 192, 194, 199, 201
Durham, 9, 56

Eagle, 139, 140, 157
Earl's Court, 99
East India Company, 160
Eaton, 20, 39, 41-47, 49, 50, 58, 71
Eccleston, 41, 42
Edgecumbe, Lord, 145
Edinburgh, 185
Edinburgh, William Duke of see Gloucester, William Duke of
Edward III, King, 112
Edward IV, King, 10
Edward VII, King, 180, 197
Edward, Prince Duke of York, 1, 2, 4
Elephant see von Kielmansegge
Elizabeth, Queen, 3
Elliott, Anne, 15, 16
Elmes, Elizabeth, 68
Epsom, 68, 69
Ernest, King of Hanover, 12
Erredge, 158
Essex, 1
Essex, Countess of, 3
Eton, 84
Exeter, Bishop of, 122

Falcon, Chester, 41, 70
Farington's Diary, 187
Fenoulet, Lady, 89
Ferrara, 132
Ferrers, Countess of, 163
Fisher, Kitty, 1, 2
Finch, Lady Charlotte, 9
Fitzclarence, 185, 193
Fitzherbert, Mrs Maria, 113-115, 121, 129, 135, 148, 160-163, 166, 167, 169, 171, 177, 181
Fitzpatrick, Colonel, 141
Flanders, 71
Florence, 8, 76, 89, 92, 104, 114, 125, 127, 132, 148, 152, 163, 193
Flowers, 127
Fly, 138
Folkestone, Lord, 112
Foote, Samuel, 4, 61, 78
Fordyce, Lady Mary, 90
Fort Belvedere, 13
Fortescue Papers, 94
Foulkes, Captain, 29, 39, 47, 49
Four Crosses, Wolverhampton, 41
Fox, Charles James, 110-112, 136, 149, 151, 160, 168
France, 89, 125, 142, 181
Francis, Sir Philip, viii
Frederiksberg, 103
Frederick V, King of Denmark, 102
Frederick, Prince (son of George III), 5, 11, 102
Frederick, Sir Thomas, 69
Freeholder's Magazine, The, 74
Freemasons, 157, 168

French Revolution, 178
Fulham, 118

Gainsborough, 86, 117, 183
Gale, Mr, 98
Galloway, Lord, 167
Garter King of Arms, 173
Garth, Colonel, 124
Garth, General George, 172, 174, 175, 178, 182
General Evening Post, 77, 82, 92, 113, 193
Geneva, 166
Gentleman's Magazine, 99, 171, 173, 193
George I, King, viii, ix
George II, King, vii–ix, 22, 23, 110
George III, King, viii–x, 1, 4, 8, 9, 12, 13, 53–56, 61, 66, 86, 88, 89, 100, 102, 107–114, 118, 120, 122, 123, 127, 130, 132, 133, 135, 142, 145–150, 152, 153, 157, 160, 164, 166–169, 171–175, 178, 183, 185, 187, 189, 190, 194, 196–201
George IV, King (see also Prince of Wales, Prince Regent, 'Prinny'), 7, 75, 113, 118, 136, 141, 146, 148–152, 154, 156, 158–162, 164, 165, 167–173, 175, 177, 180–185, 187, 188
George VI, 101
George VI's Letter Patent, 101
Germain, Lord George, 129
Germany, 76, 93, 109
Gibbons, Edward, 72, 121
Gibraltar, 31, 75
Giddings, Robert, 31, 40–43, 47, 49, 50, 52, 60
Gilby, Sarah, 51, 59
Gloucester, Bishop of, 110
Gloucester, Maria, Duthossof (Dowager Countess of Waldergrave), 8, 114, 116, 119, 127, 129, 131, 132, 134, 146, 148, 163, 166
Gloucester House, 120, 128, 1235, 148
Gloucester, William Henry Duke of, P1, 5, 6, 8–10, 14, 65, 75, 76, 90, 92, 93, 107, 113–115, 119–122, 127–135, 143, 144, 148, 163, 165–167, 169, 171, 172
Gordon, Lord George, 144
Gordon Riots, 144
Grafton, 82
Grafton, Henry Fitzroy Duke of, 14, 53, 85, 150
Gray, Mr, 176
Great Seal of the Realm, 101
Green, 176
Greenfield, Mr, 129
Greenwich, 6
Greenwich, Lady, 52, 65, 92
Greville, 23
Greville, George, 186
Griffiths, William, 42
Grosvenor, Lady Henrietta, 17, 19, 20, 24–33, 35–54, 57–60, 64–69, 72, 73, 76, 82, 95–99
Grosvenor, Lord Richard, Baron Grosvenor, later Earl Grosvenor of Eaton, 20–25, 29, 32, 35, 36, 38–40, 42–47, 50, 52–58, 60, 61, 66–72, 97, 99, 112, 152
Grosvenor Square, 32, 37, 39, 44, 185
Grosvenor, Thomas, 44–46
Groves, Rev. William, 6
Gunnersby, 16, 23, 64
Gwynne, Charlotte see Tipping, Alice

Hackwood, 16
Hales, Sir Edward, 82, 142
Halkin, 42, 45, 47
Hall, Mr, 76
Hamilton, Emma, 162, 188
Hamilton, Mary, 145
Hamilton, Sir William, 162
Hampstead, 199
Handel, 176
Hanover, viii, 4, 136, 149
Hanoverians, viii
Hanover Square, 23, 66
Harcourt, Lady, 166
Harcourt, Lord, 137
Harley, see Oxford, Countess of
Harley Street, 23
Harvey, General, 134
Harwich, 102
Hawkins, Charles, 172
Haymarket, 4, 30, 62, 98
Haydn, 176
Hayes, 142
Hayes, Mrs Charlotte, 69, 70, 98
Hayward, Miss Clara, 98
Henderson, Mr, 141
Henry VII's Chapel, 5, 172
Henry VIII, King, 100
Herbert, Hon. Nicholas, 113
Hereford, 82
Heron, Sir Robert, 184
Hertford, Lord, 94, 135
Hertford Street, 83, 87, 123
Hervey, Lord, vii
Hill, Mrs, 35, 37, 39
Hillman, Anthony, 186
Hobson, 189
Hodges, Mrs, 117, 128
Holland, Lord, 23
Holtke see von Holtke
Holyrood Palace, 185
Home, Countess of, 80
Hope, Lady Anne, 167
Hopetown, Lady, 167
Horton, Mrs Anne, 75–77, 83, 84, 86–89, 91, 92, 94, 95, 100, 101, 113, 116–118, 121, 123, 127, 138, 162, 175–178, 183, 185, 187, 193, 194, 199
Horton, Christopher, 86
House of Commons, 88, 110, 141, 144, 187
House of Lords, 93, 96, 111, 121, 136, 142, 147, 172, 200

Hove, 155
How, Mary, 60, 71, 72
Howard, Sir George, 145
Howard, Henrietta, viii
Howe, Lord, 1, 136, 145
Hunt, 65
Hurd, Bishop, ix
Huish, Robert, ix, 149
Hyde, Justice, 177
Hyde Park, 22, 145

India Bill, 160
Ingram, Elizabeth, 14
Ireland, 84, 85
Irnham, Lord, 85, 90, 91, 92
Italy, 76, 92, 113, 125

James I, King, 84
James II, King, 84
Jebb, Dr Richard, 92, 132-134
Jennings, Captain, 131, 133
Jermyn Street, 60
Jerningham, Lady, 169
Jersey, Countess of, 177
Jesse, John Heneage, 12, 88, 150, 151
Jockey Club, 99, 178
Johnson, Betty, 69
Johnson, Dr, 176
Johnson, Thomas, 93
Jones, Barbara, 41
Jones, John, 59
Jones, Polly, 16-18, 69
Juliana Maria, Dowager Queen of Denmark, 103, 107
'Junius', 90

Keith, Sir Robert Murray, 107, 108
Kensington, 182
Kensington Gardens, 1, 22, 38
Kensington Palace, 39
Kent, Duke of, 6, 186, 187, 189, 192, 194, 195, 198, 200
Keppel, Admiral, 145
Kerich, 125
Kew, ix, 146, 190, 198
King's Bench, Court of, 55, 64-66, 184
King's Fisher, 139
King's Head, Epsom, 69
King Priam, 142
King's Place, 17, 37, 98
King's Street, Soho, 69
Kitchingham, Captain, 140, 157
Knole, x
Knightsbridge, 20
Knights of the Bath, 117
Knights of the Garter, 75
Konigsmark, 108

Lake, Lt-Colonel Gerard, 149
Lambeth, 138
Lambeth Marsh, 20
Lancaster, Duchess of, 196
Langford, Mrs, 59
Lawes, Sir Nicholas, 85
Lawrence, Thomas, 187
Lee, Dr George, 122
Legge, Hon. William, 117
Leghorn, 92, 163
Le Grand, Edward, 152, 153
Le Havre, 2
Leicester Fields, 67, 68
Leicester Fields Hotel, 67
Leicester House, vii, ix, 8, 102
Legitimacy Declaration Act, 197
Leopold I, Emperor, 99
Letters & Journals of Lady Mary Coke, The, 3
Levoz, 138
Lewes, 154, 158
Lewes Advertiser, 167
Lewes Journal, 168
Lightfoot, Hannah, ix, x, 86, 190, 191, 196, 198-202
Ligonier, Lady, 89, 97
Lille, 176
Lisbon, 75
Lisle, Mrs, 71, 72
Little Isaac, 142
Liverpool, Lord, 189, 191, 200
Lloyds Coffee House, 86
London, Bishop of, 123
London Evening Post, 32, 55, 57, 81, 82, 125, 130, 138, 140-142
Lord Chamberlain, 100
Lords of the Treasury, 180
Louis XV, King, 125
Louis XVI, King, 131
Luttrell, Anne see Horton, Anne
Luttrell, Elizabeth, 87, 89, 117, 119, 120, 124, 128, 129, 141, 160, 163, 165, 172, 174-176, 178, 183, 188
Luttrell, Col. Henry Lawes, 85-87, 89-91
Luttrell, James, 85, 124, 141, 152, 153
Luttrell, Captain John Temple, 85, 139, 141, 181
Luttrell, Simon, 84, 85, 91
Luttrell, Temple Simon, 85
Luxembourg, 181
Lymington, 171

Macleod, Lady Emily, 6

Mallett, Justinian, 193
Manchester, Duke of, 159, 160, 168
Mann, Sir Horace, 8, 89, 92, 93, 103, 104, 108, 114, 125-127, 130, 131, 148, 152, 163
Mansfield, Lord, 55, 56, 60, 61, 62, 66, 91, 110, 127
Mansion House, 13

Marble Arch, 20
Marford Hill, 43, 47, 57, 59
Margate, 181
Marine Pavilion, 163
Marlborough Street Office, 183
Marseilles, 5, 163
Mason, Rev. William, 100
Martindale, Henry, 64
Mayfair Chapel, 200
'Maypole' see von Schulenbourg
Mecklenburgh, Princess of, 91
Mediterranean, 12, 143
Melbourne, Lady, 177
Melbourne, Lord, 177
Mexborough, Lady, 4
Middlesex, 86, 91, 103
Middlesex Advertiser, 90
Middlesex Journal, 76, 156
Milan, 163
Minorca, 75
Mitchell, Mrs, 17, 18
Molesworth, Mrs, 70
Monaco, Prince of, 5
Montagu, George, 103
Montreal, 5
'Morgan, Squire' see Cumberland, Duke of
Morning Chronicle, 76, 156
Morning Herald, The, 94, 157
Morrison, Colonel, 5
Mountbatten, Earl, 139
Mowbray Herald Extraordinary, 94
Mullman, Mrs, 60
Museum, Sir John Soane's, 119
Murray see Mansfield, Lord
Musgrave, Sir William, 5

Naples, 163
National Convention, 181
Newgate, 81, 92
Nesbitt, 91
Netherclift, 201
Newcastle, 78-81
Newmarket, 36, 39, 44, 49, 70, 72
Newton, Elizabeth see Elmes, Elizabeth
Newton, Captain, 142
Nocturnal Revels, 97, 98
Noel, Sir Gerard, 191
Norfolk, Duchess of, 15, 54
Norfolk, Duke of, 168
North, Lord, 65, 85, 110, 111, 113, 116, 129, 135, 143, 153, 168
North Parade, 181
Northcote, James, 121
Northumberland, Duke of, 78, 79, 145
Northumberland House, 22
Notting Hill, 54
Noutka Sound, 170

O'Kelly, Count Dennis, 98
Old Palace-yard, 172
Olivia, Princess of Cumberland, 186, 188, 190
Opera, 135, 159, 163
Oriel College, Oxford, 6
Osnabruck, Bishop of see Edward, Prince, Duke of York
Oxford, 20, 85, 185, 201
Oxford, Bishop of, 110
Oxford, Countess of, 32
Oxford Road, 100
Oxford Street, 20, 66
Owen, Robert, 186

Padua, 131
Pall Mall, 4, 9, 29, 30, 37, 57, 65, 75, 94, 97, 113, 119, 131, 150, 168, 171, 177, 194
Palmer, Sir Roundell, 197, 201
Pantheon, 13, 100
Paris, 124, 159, 160, 161, 181
Parliament, 130, 181
Parma, Arch-Duchess of, 126
Peckham, x
Pelham, Dr, 155
Pembroke, Countess of, 169
Pendered, Mary L, 193
Pennell, 172
Percy, Dr Thomas, 78-80
Perdita, 141
Petrie, William Strange, 185, 187, 193
Phillimore, Robert, 197
Phillips, Mrs, 98
Phipps, Captain, 110
Piccadilly, 3, 37, 68
Pigott, Charles, 20, 140, 178
Pigot, Lord, 145
Pitt the Elder, 20, 190
Pitt the Younger, 85, 97, 174, 175, 178, 190, 199
Pleydell, Captain, 131-135
Plymouth, 171
Poland, 62
Poland, Stanislaus Poniatowski, King of, 18, 19
Political Register, 113
Pollock, Lord Baron, 197
Pomfret, Lady, 9
Pompey, 142
Pope, The, 93, 127, 176
Port, Mrs, 117
Porter, General, 99
Portland Roads, 33, 34
Portsmouth, 2, 6, 75, 171
Potsdam, 67
Prendergast, Mrs, 96, 97
Prince Regent see George IV
Prior, Mathew, 33, 34
Privy Council, 111, 145
Provost, General, 124, 126, 127
Prussia, King of, 176

Public Advertiser, 138
Putney Bridge, 138, 139, 157

Quakers, ix
Quebec Street, 66
Queensberry, Duke of, 145
Queensberry, Marquis of, 168
Queen's Birthday, 178
Queen's House, 146, 152, 159

Rainsford, Colonel, 122, 129
'*Ramillies*', 2
Ramus, 133
Ranelagh, 13, 25, 27, 86
Ranzau-Ascheberg, Count, 105, 106
Ray, Martha, 14
Reda, Mrs Mary, 29-32, 35, 58, 66, 67
Red Lion, Whitchurch, 41, 59
Redoute, 138
Reign of Terror, 181
Reynolds, Sir Joshua, x, 20, 86, 102, 117, 121
Richardson, Jane, 41
Richmond, Duchess of, 3, 168, 177
Richmond, Duke of, 111, 136, 142, 168, 177
Richmond Lodge, 88
Rochfort, Lord, 129
Roberts, Mr, 138
Roberts, Elizabeth, 67, 68
Robinson, Mary, 137, 141, 149
Robinson, Robert, 67
Robinson, Thomas, 59
Rockingham, Marquis of, 112
Rodney, 2, 136
Roeskilde, 102
Roman Catholic, 4
Rome, 93, 131, 163
Romney, 86, 117, 121, 162
Rotterdam, 102
Royal Academy, 185
Royal Albion Hotel, 154
Royal Archives, 32, 134
Royal Automobile Club, 180
Royal Family, 198
Royalist, 139
Royal Marriage Act, 10, 19, 113, 116, 162
Royal Marriage Bill, 110
Royal Masonic Institute, 157
Royal Pavilion, 181
Royal Thames Yacht Club, 138, 139
Russell, Richard, 154-156
Rutland, Duchess of, 177
Rutland, Duke of, 137
Rupert, Prince, 12
Ryves, Mrs Lavinia (see also Serres), x, 191, 192, 196, 197, 200, 202

Sackville, Lord George, 131, 133
Salisbury, Marquess of, 171
Saracen's Head, Towcester, 40, 58, 59
Sandwich, Earl of, 14
Saratoga, 142
Saumgarten, 150
Savile, Sir George, 144
Scarborrow, Mr, 37, 48
Schwellenberg, Madame, 91
Sea-Horse, 139
Seaton, 78, 80, 81
Selbourne, Lord, 197
Selwyn, George, 5, 9, 24, 158
Senior Service, 1
Serres, Lavinia Janetta Horton, 194, 195
Serres, Mrs Olive (see also Wilmot, Olive), x, 113, 186-198, 200-202
Serres, Thomas, 185
Seven Years War, 85
Seymour Place, 186
Sheldon, Anne see Archer, Mrs Anne
Sheridan, Mr, 137
Sidmouth, Lord, 187, 191
Skinner, 60, 61
Smith, H Clifford, 183
Smith, Dr, 202
Smith, Dr J Walter, 197, 198
Smith, Mary, 60
Smith's Gardens, 139
Society of Friends, ix
Sprat, Jack, 39, 44, 66
Soho, 16, 69
Soho Square, 10
Solent, 139
Sophia Charlotte, Princess of Mechlenburgh-Strelitz, viii
Sophia Matilda, Princess, 135, 166, 167, 177
Southampton, 74, 117, 127
Spa, 138, 140, 141, 163, 164, 176, 182
Spain, 62, 170
Spencer, Mary, 59
Spithead, 33
St Albans, 40, 50-52, 57, 59, 95
St Albans, Duke of, 177
St Anne's, 155
St James's, ix, 19, 24, 27, 37, 45, 50, 55, 64, 69, 75, 82, 94, 96, 100, 102, 104, 116, 119, 140, 147, 184, 193
St George's Chapel, Windsor, 75, 116, 117, 167
St George's Day, 169
St George's, Hanover Square, ix, 23, 66
St James's Chronicle, 75, 136, 137, 156
St James's Palace, 100
St Malo, 2
St Martins in the Fields, 89
St Mary's, Warwick, 198
St Nicholas, Warwick, 139
St Omer, 124
St Paul's, 169
St Peter's, 127

Stables, Mr, 68
Stephens, John, 45, 51, 59
Steine, 156
Storer, Anthony, 151
Stevens, Mathew, 39, 40, 45–49, 51, 52, 59, 70
Stevens, Rev. William, 87, 123
Stockbridge, 85, 99
Strafford, Lady Anne, 3, 24, 25, 38, 52, 54, 64, 76, 117, 118, 125, 126, 128
Strafford, Lord, 24, 25, 55, 103
Strand, 90
Strange, John, 132, 134
Strasbourg, 125, 160, 161
Strathearn, 193
Strawberry Hill, 94
Struensee, John, 104–107
Stuart, Prince Charles Edward, 6
Stubbs, 20
Stuart, Lady Louisa, 3, 6, 12, 85, 86, 90, 116, 119, 120, 136, 159, 167
Stuart, Mrs, 183
Suffolk, Earl of, 2
Sulphur, 142
Sunninghill, 17, 87
Sussex Advertiser, 158
Sussex, Duke of, 188
Sutherland, Captain, 89
Sutton, Elizabeth, 27–29, 58
Swann, John, 41, 43, 47
Switzerland, 127
Swellenburgh, Madame, see Schwellenberg, Madame

Tankerville, Charles Earl of, 18, 66, 178
Tartar, 142
Tavistock Street, 37
Taylor, Anne, 190
Taylor, Rev. Mr, 58
Taylor, Thomas, 157
Temple, 74, 157
Temple, Lord, 142
Teodoli Palace, 131
Thames, 78, 156
Thomas, D. W., 197
Thurlow, Chancellor, 112
Thynne, Mr, 152
Times, The, 168, 176, 177, 182, 183
Tipping, Alice, 69–71
Toll House, Marford Hill, 43, 44, 47, 59
Toms, Edward, 44–47, 49
Towcester, 40, 57–59
Town and Country Magazine, 6, 7, 12, 15, 16, 18, 19, 24, 66, 74, 86, 95
Townshend, Mrs, 21
Treaty of Westphalia, 4
Trevor, Bishop of Durham, 56
Tremilly, Mrs, 60
Trent, 132
Trieste, 116
Trinity College, Oxford, 185, 201
Trinity House, 81
Tunbridge Wells, 29, 181
Turin, 163
Turk, 168
Turner, Captain, 99
Turner, Sir Gregory Page, 99
Tuscany, Grand Duke of, 76
'Twitcher, Jeremy' see Sandwich Earl of
Tyrconnel, Earl of, 165

Upper Ossory, Countess of, 94, 124, 137

Valiant, 170, 173
Vanburgh, Sir John, 78
Vauxhall, 13, 18, 25, 138, 140, 157
Venice, 15, 131, 135
Venus, 12, 31, 32, 75
Vemberght, Mary see Reda, Mrs
Vernon, Caroline ('Carry'), 25, 27, 33, 35, 37, 39, 45, 46, 48, 50, 64
Vernon, Lady Harriot, 3, 22, 24, 25, 48, 53–55, 64
Vernon, Henry, 22, 71
Vernon, Henrietta, 22, 23, 54, 58
Vernon, William, 26
Verona, 132
Vienna, 76, 92, 126
Vice-Admiral of the Blue, 2
Victoria, Queen, 6, 12, 186, 195, 196
Vigars, 49
Villiers, Barbara see Castlemain, Countess of
von Gramm, Madame, 103
von Holtke, Count, 8, 103, 104
von Kielmansegge, Charlotte Sophia, viii
von Platen, Countess, viii
von Schulenbourg, Ermengarde Melusine, Duchess of Kendal, viii

Waldegrave, Maria Dowager Countess, 9, 76, 93, 114, 115, 122
Waldegrave, Earl, 8
Wales, Princess of see Augusta, Princess of Wales
Wales, Frederick Prince of, vii, 8
Walmoden, Madame, Countess of Yarmouth, viii
Walpole, Sir Edward, 9, 131, 134
Walpole, Horace, 3, 5, 8, 9, 10, 12, 22, 78, 84, 85, 87, 89, 90, 92, 94, 100, 103, 104, 108, 114, 115, 117, 118, 124, 125, 127, 130, 131, 134, 136, 137, 144, 148, 150, 152, 163, 193
Walpole, Hon. Thomas, 148
Walthamstow, 35
Wapping, ix
Warsaw, 18
Warwick, 2nd Earl of, 186, 189–192, 194, 198, 200
Waters Mrs, 60
Wedderburn, Alexander, 56–60
West, Benjamin, ix, 20, 36

West End, 94
Westminster Abbey, 116, 139, 172
Westminster Bridge, 17, 138
Westminster Hall, 39, 55, 61, 71
Wetherall, Sir Frederick, 189
Weymouth, 33, 34, 166, 170
Whigs, 135, 136
Whitehall Evening Post, 65
Whitehall Place, 191
White Hart, St Albans, 40, 50, 51, 59
Whitehawk Down, 158
Wilde, Sir James, 197
Wilkes, John, 56, 86, 89
William Frederick, Prince, 8, 9, 131, 135, 165, 167, 177
William IV (see also Clarence, Duke of), 170, 173, 185
Wilmot, Ann, 69
Wilmot, Dr Robert, 185, 186, 189-192, 194, 197-201
Wilmot, Olive (see also Serres, Olive), x, 185, 197-199, 202
Wilmot, Rev. James, 185, 186, 198, 199
Wilmot, Sarah, 198
Wilton, 113
Windsor, 14, 32, 75, 76, 87, 93, 94, 96, 113, 116, 122, 127, 128, 130, 142, 146, 150, 167, 171
Windsor, Duchess of, 94, 100, 101
Windsor Forest, 147
Windsor Great Park, 9, 13, 146
Windsor Lodge, 99, 126, 140, 149, 171, 175, 178
Withers, Philip, 169
Wokingham, 17
Wolcot, Sir John, 178
Wolverhampton, 41
Woodville, Elizabeth, 10
Wraxall, Sir Nathaniel, ix, 8, 90, 164-166
Wyatt, James, 100

Yarmouth, 182
Yarmouth, Countess of see Walmolden, Madame
Yates, Mrs, 137
Yeoman of the Guard, 173
York, 21, 44, 104
York, Dowager Duchess of, 125, 177
York, Edward Duke of, 6, 7, 12, 191, 192
York, Frederick Duke of, 149, 151, 166, 171, 173, 176, 177, 180

Zamperini, Signorina Anna, 15, 19